Chambers

Dictionary of
Modern Quotations

Chambers

Dictionary of
Modern
Quotations

Edited by
Nigel Rees

Chambers

Published 1993 by W & R Chambers Ltd
43–45 Annandale Street, Edinburgh EH7 4AZ

© Nigel Rees 1993

British Library Cataloguing in Publication Data
A catalogue record for this book is available from the British Library.

ISBN 0 550 21030 X

Typeset by Buccleuch Printers Ltd, Hawick
Printed in England by Clays Ltd, St Ives plc

CONTENTS

INTRODUCTION

A dictionary of quotations can help you find the source of a saying or it can guide you towards a saying which might help you illustrate a theme. Put another way, one approach for the dictionary compiler is to examine quotations that *actually do get quoted* and the other is for him to suggest what he thinks *ought to be quoted*.

In compiling *Chambers Dictionary of Modern Quotations* I have, for the most part, concerned myself with the first approach – tracing the sources of well-known phrases and sayings that actually do get quoted or alluded to.

A quotation is anything written or spoken which another person chooses to repeat. I have limited my choice, however, to phrases and sayings that I have heard being quoted by someone other than myself and usually on more than one occasion.

Seventeen years spent devising the BBC radio programme "*Quote … Unquote*" have given me a pretty good idea of what people do quote and what puzzles them about modern quotations in particular. As a result of requests I have received from listeners, viewers, librarians and journalists, I have built up a store of information which I hope will lead to more accurate attribution than is sometimes the case in such books.

Oddly, the more modern the quotation, the greater likelihood there seems to be of some dispute arising over its source or correct form. Classical quotations may be said to have settled in to their niches securely. In an age when there is more communication than ever before, it is paradoxically often more difficult to check what exactly was said last week than what was said a century ago. I have been fortunate in having access to sound recordings of many 20th-century speeches, film sound-tracks and so on, and I hope, as a result, that I am able to give more accurate versions of some quotations than is usually the case.

On the other hand, I am aware that I may have created as many new misattributions as I have corrected old ones. I would be pleased to hear from readers who think they have superior knowledge. If previous form is anything to go by, I do not anticipate any reluctance on their part to put me right. When this book first appeared in another form as *A Dictionary of Twentieth Century Quotations* (Fontana Paperbacks, 1987) I was particularly glad to receive the constructive criticisms of: William Garner; Arthur Illes; M.R. Lewis; and especially Donald Hickling. In revising it, I have been helped on specific points by the BBC Radio Research Library, London; the

London Bureau of the *New York Times*; and the British Library Newspaper Library, Colindale.

There are many ways in which to lay out a dictionary of quotations. I have avoided grouping the sayings into subject or theme categories, as this can make it difficult to check a known quotation and is of only minor usefulness anyway. The chief aim has been to make it easy for the reader to locate the quotation he or she is interested in. By using the key-word index, this should present no problem, never mind where I have chosen to place a quotation within the book—at times somewhat arbitrarily.

On the whole, I have attributed sayings to individuals, listed in alphabetical order. But how to deal with lines from films, shows, TV programmes and advertising copy? Should I put them under the scriptwriter's name, the actor's name, or the show's name?

I have chosen to put such quotes—often the product of group creative effort—under the show's name (e. g. Bogart's sayings from *Casablanca*), though where the origination is quite clearly the responsibility of a named writer or particular entertainer, I have, in some cases, been inconsistent and put the quotation under these names.

So, the quotations are listed under author (or show) in alphabetical order or sorted into a number of specialist categories, viz:

ANONYMOUS SAYINGS
BOOK TITLES
CATCHPHRASES
EPITAPHS
FILM TITLES
INSCRIPTIONS
PLAY TITLES
PROVERBS
SLOGANS
SONG TITLES
TELEGRAMS AND CABLES
TELEVISION PROGRAMME TITLES

I have tried to keep cross-referencing to a minimum and have chosen to mark many quotations merely 'attrib' or 'untraced' rather than give a less than useful secondary source.

Both the dictionary and the index are in 'letter by letter order'—ie in alphabetical order, not of complete words but of letter order within a sentence (ignoring word breaks, hyphens and spaces). Within individual entries, the order of quotations is approximately chronological except where it is stated to be alphabetical.

What is to be done about common misquotations? Should they be left out? My feeling is that the usefulness of this kind of dictionary is increased if common misquotations are included. However, such misquotations (or frequently confused renderings) are marked by a special symbol □ and accompanied by a note on how the confusion has arisen.

There is a tendency in modern dictionaries of quotations, quite rightly, to include popular song lyrics. The question here is, where to stop? I have tried to limit myself to lines which have been quoted in other contexts and have not simply become familiar through frequent performance.

Where possible, I have tried to give some indication of when a line was first written or spoken. This is an almost impossible task when dealing with informally-uttered remarks. With lines from books and shows, the date is usually that of first publication or performance.

The concern of this book is towards 20th-century quotations in the English language (British and American versions) after an arbitrary starting point of 1900. For those writers like Shaw and Kipling whose work straddled the turn of the century, I have chosen only those quotations which appear to have originated in the twentieth.

As to why it is necessary at all, I can only admit to my own frustration (and obsessiveness) when trying to confirm a saying that has drifted into my ken and which I cannot find in a considerable library of other such dictionaries. Realizing that it is not sufficient simply to record the first appearance of a saying, I feel there is a need in a dictionary of this kind to monitor how phrases have been borrowed and modified over the years. I also take care to distinguish between the true creators and those who have merely popularized the coinages of others.

Another reason for the book is the splendid vagueness that people have in the use of quotations—misquoting, misattributing, mangling—nicely illustrated I feel by what was said by the widow of a man who had died during the D-Day 1944 landings in Normandy. Paying a visit to the battlefield 40 years later, she was asked by a television interviewer why she had made the journey. She replied, 'As they said in the Bible, or in the paper, part of a foreign field is forever England'.

As they said in the Bible, or in the paper ...

Ah well, that narrows it down a bit.

Should she be reading this, I think she will find the answer to her problem on page 49.

Nigel Rees
London, 1993

ACE, Goodman
US writer (1899–1982)

1   TV . . . is our latest medium—we call it a medium because nothing's well done.

   Letter (1954) to Groucho Marx included in *The Groucho Letters*
   See also **KOVACS 192:2.**

ACHESON, Dean
US Democratic politician (1893–1971)

2   Great Britain . . . has lost an Empire and not yet found a role. The attempt to play a separate power role—that is, a role apart from Europe, a role based on a 'special relationship' with the United States, a role based on being the head of a 'Commonwealth' . . . this role is about to be played out . . . Her Majesty's Government is now attempting, wisely in my opinion, to re-enter Europe.

   Speech, Military Academy, West Point, 5 December 1962

ACKERLEY, J. R.
British writer (1896–1967)

3   I was born in 1896, and my parents were married in 1919.

   My Father and Myself (1968)
   Opening words.

ADAMSON, Harold
US songwriter (1906–80)

4   Comin' in on a wing and a prayer.

   Title of song (1943)
   Reputedly based on words said by a pilot coming in to land with a badly-damaged plane. Title of 1944 US film: *Wing and a Prayer.*

ADLER, Polly
US madam (1900–62)

5   A House is Not a Home.

   Title of memoirs (1954)

AGA KHAN III
Muslim leader (1877–1957)

6   *Defending his taste for alcohol:*
   I'm so holy that when I touch wine, it turns into water.

   Attrib by John Colville, *Footprints in Time*

AGATE, James
British drama critic (1877–1947)

1   A professional is a man who can do his job when he doesn't feel like it. An amateur is a man who can't do his job when he does feel like it.

Attrib

AGNEW, Spiro T.
US Republican Vice President (1918–   )

2   I agree with you that the name of Spiro Agnew is not a household name. I certainly hope that it will become one within the next couple of months.

Interview with Mike Wallace of ABC TV, on becoming Vice-Presidential candidate, 8/9 August 1968

3   To some extent, if you've seen one city slum you've seen them all.

Speech, Detroit, 18 October 1968

4   *On media pundits:*
A spirit of national masochism prevails, encouraged by an effete corps of impudent snobs who characterize themselves as intellectuals.

Speech, New Orleans, 19 October 1969

5   *On media pundits:*
In the United States today we have more than our share of the nattering nabobs of negativism. They have formed their own 4-H Club—the 'hopeless, hysterical hypochondriacs of history'.

Speech, San Diego, 11 September 1970
Speech written by William Safire

AKINS, Zoë
US playwright (1886–1958)

6   *The Greeks Had a Word for It.*

Title of play (1929)
Akins told Burton Stevenson that in dialogue cut from her play the word was for a type of woman. One character thinks that 'tart' is meant but another corrects this and says 'free soul' is more to the point.

ALBEE, Edward
US playwright (1928–   )

7   I'll tell you what game we'll play. We're done with Humiliate the Host . . . and we don't want to play Hump the Hostess . . . We'll play a round of Get the Guests.

Who's Afraid of Virginia Woolf? (1962)
See also **PLAY TITLES 256:2.**

ALDEN, Robert
US theologian (1937–   )

1   There is not enough darkness in all the world to put out the light of even one small candle.

Attrib

ALGIERS
US film 1938

2   □ Come with me to the Casbah.

Supposedly said by Charles Boyer to Hedy Lamarr, but not in the film.

ALGREN, Nelson
US novelist and short story writer (1909–81)

3   Never eat at a place called Mom's. Never play cards with a man called Doc. Never go to bed with a woman whose troubles are greater than your own.

A Walk on the Wild Side (1956)

ALI, Muhammad (formerly Cassius Clay)
US heavyweight boxing champion (1942–   )

4   I am the greatest.

His slogan from *c*1962

5   Float like a butterfly, sting like a bee.

Motto from *c*1964
Devised by an aide, Drew 'Bundini' Brown.

6   *Announcing his retirement:*
I want to get out with my greatness intact.

Quoted in the *Observer*, 4 July 1974

7   You don't want no pie in the sky when you die,
You want something here on the ground while you're still around.

Quoted in 1978
See also **HILL 162:2.**

ALL ABOUT EVE
US film 1950. Script by Joseph L. Mankiewicz. With Bette Davis as Eve.

8   *Eve:* Fasten your seatbelts. It's going to be a bumpy night.

Soundtrack

ALLEN, Fred
US comedian (1894–1956)

1 Hollywood—a place where people from Iowa mistake themselves for movie stars.
   Attrib

2 Hanging is too good for a man who makes puns. He should be drawn and quoted.
   Attrib

ALLEN, Woody
US film actor, writer and director (1937–   )

3 Sex between a man and a woman can be wonderful—provided you get between the right man and the right woman.
   Attrib

4 Not only is there no God, but try getting a plumber on weekends.
   'My Philosophy', *Getting Even* (1975)

5 *Woman:* You are the greatest lover I have ever known.
   Allen: Well, I practise a lot when I'm on my own.
   Love and Death (1975)

6 *On sex:*
   Fun? That was the most fun I've ever had without laughing.
   Annie Hall (1977)
   Written with Marshall Brickman. Also attrib to Humphrey Bogart in the form: 'It was the most fun I ever had without laughing.'

7 Don't knock masturbation, it's sex with someone you love.
   ibid

8 It's not that I'm afraid to die, I just don't want to be there when it happens.
   'Death (A Play)', *Without Feathers* (1978)

ALLSOP, Kenneth
British writer and broadcaster (1920–73)

9 In work the greatest satisfaction lies—the satisfaction of stretching yourself, using your abilities and making them expand, and knowing that you have accomplished something that could have been done only by you using your unique apparatus. This is really the centre of life, and those who never orientate themselves in this direction are missing more than they ever know.
   Letters to His Daughter (1974)

ALTRINCHAM, Lord (later disclaimed peerage and known as John Grigg)
British writer (1924–)

1   *On Queen Elizabeth II's style of public speaking:*
Frankly a pain in the neck.

National and English Review, August 1958

2   The personality conveyed by the utterances which are put into her mouth is that of a priggish schoolgirl, captain of the hockey team, a prefect, and a recent candidate for confirmation. It is not thus that she will be able to come into her own as an independent and distinctive character.

ibid

AMERY, L. S.
British Conservative MP (1873–1955)

3   *To the acting Opposition leader, Arthur Greenwood:*
☐ Speak for England, Arthur!

Speech, House of Commons, 2 September 1939
(interjection not recorded in *Hansard*)
On the eve of war, Prime Minister Neville Chamberlain had held out the prospect of a further Munich-type peace conference and had not announced any ultimatum to Germany. Amery, in his own account, omits the 'Arthur'. Robert Boothby said (1964) that he (Boothby) shouted: '*You* speak for Britain'.

4   *To Neville Chamberlain:*
This is what Cromwell said to the Long Parliament when he thought it was no longer fit to conduct the affairs of the nation: 'You have sat too long here for any good you have been doing. Depart, I say, and let us have done with you. In the name of God, go!'

Speech, House of Commons, 7 May 1940
Quoting Oliver Cromwell's words when dismissing the Rump of the Long Parliament, 1653.

AMIN, Idi
Ugandan soldier and President (1925–)

5   *Public message to Lord Snowdon, on the break-up of his marriage to Princess Margaret:*
Your experience will be a lesson to all of us men to be careful not to marry ladies in very high positions.

Quoted in A. Barrow, *International Gossip* (1983)

AMIS, Kingsley (later Sir Kingsley)
British novelist, poet and critic (1922–)

1   Bowen's Beer Makes You Drunk.

  I Like It Here (1958)
  'Barnet Bowen' suggests this is the only type of beer slogan that will
  really appeal.

2   *On 'the delusion that there are thousands of young people who are capable of*
  benefiting from university training but have somehow failed to find their
  way there':
  I wish I could have a little tape-and-loudspeaker arrangement sewn
  into the binding of this magazine, to be triggered off by the light
  reflected from the reader's eyes on to this part of the page, and set
  to bawl out at several bels: MORE WILL MEAN WORSE.

  Article in *Encounter*, July 1960

ANDERSON, Robert
US playwright (1917–)

3   Tea and Sympathy.

  Title of play (1953)

ANDERTON, Sir James
British policeman (1932–)

4   *As Chief Constable of Greater Manchester, on 'those most at risk from*
  AIDS':
  Everywhere I go I see increasing evidence of people swirling
  around in a human cesspit of their own making.

  Speech, Prestwick, 11 December 1986

5   God works in mysterious ways. Given my love of God and my belief
  in God and in Jesus Christ, I have to accept that I may well be used
  by God in this way [as a prophet].

  Radio interview, 18 January 1987

6   Corporal punishment should be administered so that they actually
  beg for mercy. They should be punished until they repent of their
  sins. I'd thrash some criminals myself, most surely. I could punish
  people quite easily.

  Interview, *Woman's Own*, December 1987

ANDREWS, Elizabeth
Royal chambermaid

7   *On finding an intruder in Queen Elizabeth II's bedroom:*
  Bloody hell, Ma'am, what's he doing here?

  Quoted in *Daily Mail*, July 1982

ANIMAL CRACKERS

US film 1930. Script by Morrie Ryskind, from musical by himself and George S. Kaufman. With Groucho Marx.

1   *Groucho:* One morning I shot an elephant in my pyjamas. How he got in my pyjamas I'll never know.

Soundtrack

ANKA, Paul

US singer and songwriter (1941–   )

2   And now the end is near
And so I face the final curtain,
My friend, I'll say it clear,
I'll state my case of which I'm certain.
I've lived a life that's full, I've travelled each and evr'y high-way
And more, much more than this, I did it my way.

Song, 'My Way' (1969)
Based on a French composition, *'Comme d'habitude'.*

ANNA CHRISTIE

US film 1930. Script by Frances Marion, from the play by Eugene O'Neill. With Greta Garbo as Anna Christie.

3   *Anna (to barman):* Gimme a viskey. Ginger ale on the side. And don't be stingy, baby.

Soundtrack

4   Garbo Talks!

Promotional slogan

ANNAN REPORT ON BROADCASTING

British official inquiry

5   The BBC does itself untold harm by its excessive sensitivity. At the first breath of criticism the Corporation adopts a posture of a hedgehog at bay.

Report of the Committee on the Future of Broadcasting (1977)

ANNE, HRH the Princess (later the Princess Royal)

British Royal (1950–   )

6   *To the press, a few days before her engagement to Captain Mark Phillips:*
There is no romance between us. He is here solely to exercise the horses.

Attrib remark, 1973

1   *On her first encounter with a horse:*
    One was presented with a small, hairy individual and, out of
    general curiosity, one climbed on.

    Princess Anne and Mark Phillips Talking Horses with Genevieve Murphy
    (1976)

2   When I appear in public, people expect me to neigh, grind my
    teeth, paw the ground and swish my tail.

    Attrib

3   *On pregnancy:*
    It's a very boring time. I am not particularly maternal—it's an
    occupational hazard of being a wife.

    TV interview, quoted in the *Daily Express*, 14 April 1981

4   *To press photographers at Badminton horse trials:*
    Why don't you naff off!

    Reported in the *Daily Mirror*, 17 April 1982

ANNENBERG, Walter
US publisher and diplomat (1908–   )

5   *To Queen Elizabeth II, when she asked him about his accommodation as
    Ambassador to the Court of St James:*
    We're in the Embassy residence, subject, of course, to some of the
    discomfiture as a result of a need for, uh, elements of
    refurbishment and rehabilitation.

    TV film, *Royal Family* (1969)

ANONYMOUS SAYINGS
(in approximate chronological order)

6   It pays to advertise.

    Already current by *c*1912 when Cole Porter used it as the title of an
    early song, and probably an 'American proverb' dating from the 1870s.

7   [There were] Russians with snow on their boots.

    In September 1914, there was an unfounded rumour that a million
    Russian troops had landed at Aberdeen and passed through England
    on their way to the Western Front.

8   Fifty million Frenchmen can't be wrong.

    Ironic expression which probably originated with US servicemen in
    France during the First World War. Used in song lyric (1927).

9   My eyes are dim
    I cannot see
    I have not brought my specs with me.

    From trad. song, 'In the Quartermaster's Stores'.

1   What a wonderful bird the frog are!
    When he walk, he fly almost;
    When he sing, he cry almost.
    He ain't got no tail hardly, either.
    He sit on what he ain't got almost.

    Quoted in a letter to *The Times* (20 May 1935) but already over twenty
    years old by then.

2   Der spring is sprung
    Der grass is riz
    I wonder where dem boidies is?

    Der little boids is on the wing,
    Ain't dat absoid?
    Der little wings is on der boid!

    American (Bronx, New York), quoted in *Verse and Worse* (1952).

3   Never work with animals or children.

    Show business maxim.

4   All of you young people [are from] a lost generation *(une génération
    perdue)*.

    French garage owner to an apprentice who had made a shoddy repair
    to Gertrude Stein's car after the First World War.

5   I went to New Zealand but it was closed.

    Joke current from the 1920s.

6   I know two things about the horse
    And one of them is rather coarse.

    Anonymous rhyme.

7   Don't tell my mother I'm in politics—she thinks I play the piano in
    a whorehouse.

    American saying from the Depression.

8   The duty of a newspaper is to comfort the afflicted and afflict the
    comfortable.

    Saying, probably of American origin, current by 1930s. Also included
    in the film *Inherit the Wind* (1960).

9   The son-in-law also rises.

    Hollywood observation when Louis B. Mayer promoted his daughter's
    husband (David O. Selznick), *c*1933.
    Alluding to **HEMINGWAY 159:5.**

10 Can't act, can't sing, slightly bald. Can dance a little.

    Hollywood executive, allegedly, on Fred Astaire's first screen test.

1 He died as he lived—at sea.

On Ramsay MacDonald who died during a cruise (1937).

2 Box-office poison.

Verdict of the US Independent Motion Picture Theatre Proprietors on Katharine Hepburn, 1938. However, in the same year, the *Independent Film Journal* also put Mae West, Greta Garbo, Joan Crawford, Marlene Dietrich and Fred Astaire in the same category.

3 Hark the herald angels sing
Mrs Simpson's pinched our king.

Quoted by Clement Attlee in letter dated 26 December 1938.

4 Overpaid, overfed, oversexed and over here.

Second World War observation about American GIs in Europe.

5 Go to hell, Babe Ruth—American, you die.

Battle cry of Japanese soldiers first heard in the Pacific, 1942.

6 Hitler
Has only got one ball!
Goering
Has two, but very small!
Himmler
Has something similar,
But poor old Goebbels
Has no balls at all!

Second World War song (to the tune of 'Colonel Bogey').

7 You're phoney. Everything about you is phoney. Even your hair—which looks false—is real.

American diplomat to Brendan Bracken during the Second World War.

8 *Describing what it was like to be in a battle:*
Oh, my dear fellow, the noise . . . and the people!

Variously attributed, especially to a certain Captain Strahan at the Battle of Bastogne (1944), but probably dates from Dunkirk (1940).

9 Inspiration is the act of drawing up a chair to the writing desk.

Anonymous saying.

10 Carnation milk is the best in the land;
Here I sit with a can in my hand—
No tits to pull, no hay to pitch,
You just punch a hole in the son of a bitch.

Anonymous rhyme.

1   If anything can go wrong, it will.

'Murphy's Law'—most probably dating from the 1940s in the US. It has been suggested that Capt. E. Murphy of the California Northrop aviation firm may have formulated it.

2   Oh no, thank you, I only smoke on special occasions.

Labour minister when asked if he would like a cigar, while dining with King George VI.

3   Quite so. But I have not been on a ship for fifteen years and they still call me 'Admiral'.

Italian admiral when Eva Peron complained that she had been called a 'whore' on a visit to northern Italy.

4   The audience came out whistling the set.

Critic on Irving Berlin's *Miss Liberty* (1949).

5   Would you buy a used car from this man?

Joke about Richard M. Nixon, current from *c*1952.

6   The best contraceptive is a glass of cold water: not before or after, but instead.

Delegate at International Planned Parenthood Federation Conference.

7   Has anyone here been raped and speaks English?

BBC television reporter to Belgian civilians waiting to escape the war in the Congo (1960).

8   Death is nature's way of telling you to slow down.

Joke current in the US by 1960.

9   Those who say they give the public what it wants begin by underestimating public taste, and end by debauching it.

Quoted by the Committee on Broadcasting, 1960 (UK) in 'the Pilkington Report'.

10 Hooray, hooray,
    The first of May,
    Outdoor sex
    Begins today.

Rhyme, current at Oxford University, 1964, though probably much older.

11 *The Times* is a tribal noticeboard.

A candidate for the editorship of the paper's Woman's Page in the 1960s—said to have been Suzanne Puddefoot.

1   Because you're in Chatham.

Heckler's reply when Harold Wilson asked rhetorically,'Why do I emphasize the importance of the Royal Navy?' (1964).

2   To save the town, it became necessary to destroy it.

American officer on the town of Ben Tre, Vietnam, during Tet offensive, according to AP dispatch, 8 February 1968.

3   Beautiful girls, walk a little slower when you walk by me.

Graffito seen in New York City by Gordon Jenkins (b1910) who included the line in his song 'This Is All I Ask' (1960s).

4   Anyone who isn't confused here doesn't really understand what's going on.

Belfast citizen, 1970. Also attributed to Ed Murrow about Vietnam.

5   The Troubles are the elephant in your drawing-room.

Ulster saying, quoted in *The Guardian*, 26 June 1988.

6   Oh dear, what a pity. Nannies are so hard to come by these days.

Aristocratic old lady, to police officer inquiring into the murder of Lord Lucan's nanny, 1974.

7   *Of Gerald R. Ford in 1974:*
A year ago he was unknown throughout America, now he's unknown throughout the world.

8   Ah well, they say it's not as bad as they say it is.

Irish woman, on the situation in Ulster, 1970s.

9   We get nothing and we can't go home because you can't eat sun.

Black Liverpudlian (on unemployment and immigration), 1976.

10   [Alberto] Juantorena opens wide his legs and shows his class.

British commentator at 1976 Montreal Olympics. This has been wrongly ascribed to David Coleman; it was probably said by Ron Pickering.

11   I know why the sun never sets on the British Empire: God wouldn't trust an Englishman in the dark.

Ascribed to 'Duncan Spaeth' in N. McPhee's *Book of Insults* (1978).

12   This must be the first time a rat has come to the aid of a sinking ship.

BBC spokesman on puppet Roland Rat's success at TV-am, 1983.

13   The longest suicide note ever penned in history.

Labour Shadow Cabinet member (thought to be Gerald Kaufman) on the party's election manifesto, 1983.

1 He didn't love God, he just fancied him.
   On W. H. Auden.

2 Capitalism is the exploitation of man by man. Communism is the complete opposite.
   Described by Laurence J. Peter as a 'Polish proverb.'

THE APARTMENT
US film 1960. Script by Billy Wilder and I. A. L. Diamond. With Shirley Maclaine as Miss Kubelik and Jack Lemmon as C. C. Baxter.

3 *Miss Kubelik:* Why can't I ever fall in love with somebody nice like you?
   C. C. Baxter: Yeah, well, that's the way it crumbles, cookie-wise.
   Soundtrack

THE ARCHERS
UK radio series (BBC) since 1951.

4 An everyday story of country folk.
   Introductory announcement

5 Oooo arr, me ol' pal, me ol' beauty.
   Stock phrase of 'Walter Gabriel' (played by Chriss Gittins, *d*1988)

ARENDT, Hannah
German-born US philosopher (1906–75)

6 The fearsome, word-and-thought-defying banality of evil.
   Eichmann in Jerusalem: A Report on the Banality of Evil (1963)

ARENS, Richard
US lawyer (1913–69)

7 Are . you now or have you ever been a member of a godless conspiracy controlled by a foreign power?
   Quoted in P. Lewis, *The Fifties*
   His version of the more usual question, 'Are you now or have you ever been a member of the Communist Party?', put to those appearing at hearings of the House of Representatives Committee on UnAmerican Activities (1947–*c*1957), especially by J. Parnell Thomas.

ARE YOU BEING SERVED?
UK TV comedy series (BBC) from 1974. Script by David Croft and Jeremy Lloyd. With John Inman as Mr Humphries.

8 *Mr Humphries:* I'm free!
   Catchphrase

ARKELL, Reginald
British poet (1882–1959)

1   There is a lady, sweet and kind
    As any lady you will find.
    I've known her nearly all my life;
    She is, in fact, my present wife.

    In daylight, she is kind to all,
    But, as the evening shadows fall,
    With jam-pot, salt and sugar-tongs
    She starts to right her garden's wrongs.

    'The Lady with the Lamp', *Green Fingers* (1934)

    'There is a lady sweet and kind' is also the first line of a poem
    attributed to Thomas Ford (*d*1648).

ARMSTRONG, Neil
US astronaut (1930–   )

2   *On lunar touch-down of space module, Apollo XI mission:*
    Tranquillity Base here—the Eagle has landed.

    TV coverage, 20 July 1969

3   *On becoming the first man to step on the surface of the moon:*
    That's one small step for [a] man, one giant leap for mankind.

    ibid

    The 'a' was not audible, spoiling the sense. On his return from the
    moon, Armstrong attempted to correct the inaccuracy—with little
    success.

ARMSTRONG, Sir Robert (later Lord Armstrong)
British civil servant (1927–   )

4   *When asked about a letter he had written intended to convey a misleading
    impression:*
    As one person said, it is perhaps being economical with the truth
    . . . It is not very original, I'm afraid.

    During cross-examination in the Supreme Court of New South Wales,
    18 November 1986

    Indeed, any number of people had used the phrase before him,
    including Edmund Burke, Mark Twain and Samuel Pepys.

ARNO, Peter
US cartoonist (1904–68)

5   *Caption to cartoon of technician walking away from crashed plane:*
    Well, back to the old drawing-board.

    New Yorker, early 1940s

    Helped popularize, even if it did not originate, the phrase 'Back to the
    drawing-board'.

1 *Caption to cartoon of man flirting with a woman:*
   Tell me about yourself—your struggles, your dreams, your
   telephone number.

   Untraced

ASKEY, Arthur
British entertainer (1900–82)

2 Ay thang yew! ('I thank you!')

   Catchphrase

3 Big-hearted Arthur, that's me.

   Catchphrase

4 Doesn't it make you want to spit?

   Catchphrase

5 Hello, playmates!

   Catchphrase

6 Here and now, before your very eyes.

   Catchphrase

ASQUITH, H. H. (later 1st Earl of Oxford and Asquith)
British Liberal Prime Minister (1852–1928)

7 *To a persistent inquirer about the Parliament Act Procedure Bill:*
   You had better wait and see.

   Speech, House of Commons, 4 April 1910
   This was the fourth occasion on which he had said 'Wait and see.'

8 *At the Westminster Abbey funeral of Bonar Law, 5 November 1923:*
   It is fitting that we should have buried the Unknown Prime
   Minister by the side of the Unknown Soldier.

   Attrib

ASQUITH, Margot (later Countess of Oxford and Asquith)
Wife of H. H. Asquith (1864–1945)

9 *On Lord Kitchener (1914):*
   If Kitchener is not a great man, he is, at least, a great poster.

   Quoted in Sir P. Magnus, *Kitchener: Portrait of an Imperialist*
   In Lady Asquith's *Memories* (1933) she ascribes the view to her
   daughter, Elizabeth.

10 *On David Lloyd George:*
   He can't see a belt without hitting below it.

   Quoted by Baroness Asquith in TV programme *As I Remember*,
   30 April 1967

1   *On her husband:*
    His modesty amounts to deformity.
    ibid

2   *On a politician:*
    He always has his arm round your waist and his eye on the clock.
    ibid

3   *On a US General:*
    An imitation rough diamond.
    ibid

4   *On Lady Desborough:*
    She's as strong as an ox. She'll be turned into Bovril when she dies.
    ibid

5   *On the same friend:*
    She tells enough white lies to ice a wedding cake.
    ibid

6   *On F. E. Smith:*
    He's very clever, but sometimes his brains go to his head.
    ibid

7   *On Lord Dawson of Penn:*
    The King told me he would never have died if it had not been for that fool Dawson of Penn.
    Quoted in K. Rose, *George V*

8   *On Sir Stafford Cripps:*
    He has a brilliant mind until he makes it up.
    Quoted in *The Wit of the Asquiths*

9   *To Jean Harlow who had asked whether the 't' was pronounced in 'Margot':*
    □ No. The 't' is silent—as in 'Harlow'.
    A more likely perpetrator was Margot Grahame (1911–82), an actress who went from England to Hollywood in the 1930s and had brief success.

ASTOR, Nancy, Viscountess
American-born British MP (1879–1964)

10 I married beneath me. All women do.
    Speech, Oldham, 1951

1   *On the young Shirley Williams:*
    You'll never get on in politics, my dear, with *that* hair.
    Attrib
    Confirmed by the remark's recipient (1982).

2   *To her son, on her death-bed:*
    Jakie, is it my birthday or am I dying?
    Quoted in J. Grigg, *Nancy Astor: Portrait of a Pioneer*
    He replied: 'A bit of both, Mum.' Her last word was 'Waldorf' (the name of her husband.)

ATTLEE, Clement (later 1st Earl Attlee)
British Labour Prime Minister (1883–1967)

3   *In a letter to Harold Laski, Chairman of the Labour Party NEC, 20 August 1945:*
    You have no right whatever to speak on behalf of the Government. Foreign Affairs are in the capable hands of Ernest Bevin. His task is quite sufficiently difficult without the embarrassment of irresponsible statements of the kind which you are making . . . *a period of silence on your part would be welcome.*
    Quoted in *British Political Facts 1900–75*

4   *Of himself:*
    Few thought he was even a starter
    There were many who thought themselves smarter
    But he ended PM, CH and OM
    An Earl and a Knight of the Garter.
    Lines written on 8 April 1956, quoted in K. Harris, *Attlee*

AUDEN, W. H.
British-born poet (1907–73)

5   Private faces in public places
    Are wiser and nicer
    Than public faces in private places.
    'Marginalia' (1932)

6   August for the people and their favourite islands.
    'Birthday Poem' (1935)

7   This is the Night Mail crossing the Border
    Bringing the cheque and the postal order.
    'Night Mail' (1935)
    Commentary for Post Office documentary film.

8   Look, stranger, at this island now.
    'Look, Stranger' (1936)
    Another version is ' . . . on this island'.

1   Mad Ireland hurt you into poetry.
    Now Ireland has her madness and her weather still,
    For poetry makes nothing happen.
    'In Memory of W. B. Yeats' (1939)

2   In the deserts of the heart
    Let the healing fountain start,
    In the prison of his days
    Teach the free man how to praise.
    ibid

3   There is no such thing as the State
    And no one exists alone;
    Hunger allows no choice
    To the citizen or the police;
    We must love one another or die.
    'September 1, 1939'
    Auden tried to suppress the last line. A 1955 anthology has: 'We must
    love one another *and* die.'

4   Lay your sleeping head, my love,
    Human on my faithless arm.
    'Lullaby' (1940)

5   To the man-in-the-street, who, I'm sorry to say
    Is a keen observer of life,
    The word Intellectual suggests straight away
    A man who's untrue to his wife.
    'Note on Intellectuals' (1947)

6   Most people enjoy the sight of their own handwriting as they enjoy
    the smell of their own farts.
    'Writing', *The Dyer's Hand* (1962)
    See also **PROVERBS 263:4.**

7   When I find myself in the company of scientists, I feel like a shabby
    curate who has strayed by mistake into a drawing-room full of
    dukes.
    'The Poet and the City', in ibid

8   *To reporter:*
    Your cameraman might enjoy himself, because my face looks like a
    wedding cake left out in the rain.
    Quoted in H. Carpenter, *W. H. Auden*
    In *Maurice Bowra: a celebration* (1974), Noel Annan quotes Bowra as
    having once referred to the work of E. M. Forster as a 'wedding cake
    left out in the rain'.

1   A professor is one who talks in someone else's sleep.

   Quoted in *The Treasury of Humorous Quotations*

AUSTIN, Warren R.
US diplomat (1877–1962)

2   *In a debate on the Middle East:*
   [Jews and Arabs should settle their differences] like good
   Christians.

   Attrib

AWDRY, Revd W.
British author (1911–   )

3   After pushing [trucks] about here for a few weeks you'll know
   almost as much about them as Edward. Then you'll be a really
   Useful Engine.

   Thomas the Tank Engine (1946)

4   We are nationalised now, but the same engines still work the
   Region. I am glad, too, to tell you that the Fat Director, who
   understands our friends' ways, is still in charge, but is now the Fat
   Controller.

   Introduction, *James the Red Engine* (1948)

AXELROD, George
US screenwriter (1922–   )

5   The Seven Year Itch.

   Title of play (filmed 1955)
   Axelrod commented (1979): 'There was a phrase which referred to a
   somewhat unpleasant disease [but] nobody had used it in a [marital-]
   sexual context before. I do believe that I invented it in that sense.'

BADEN-POWELL, Robert (later Lord Baden-Powell)
British soldier and founder of the Boy Scouts (1857–1941)

1   Be Prepared . . . the meaning of the motto is that a scout must prepare himself by previous thinking out and practising how to act on any accident or emergency so that he is never taken by surprise; he knows exactly what to do when anything unexpected happens.

   Scouting for Boys (1908)
   Motto of the Scout movement.

2   On my honour I promise that I will do my best . . . to do my duty to God and the King . . . to help other people at all times . . . to obey the Scout Law.

   'Scout's oath' in ibid

3   A Scout smiles and whistles under all circumstances.

   Part of 'The Scout Law' in ibid

4   *On masturbation:*
   It is called in our schools 'beastliness', and this is about the best name for it . . . should it become a habit it quickly destroys both health and spirits; he becomes feeble in body and mind, and often ends in a lunatic asylum.

   ibid

5   Dyb-dyb-dyb.

   Shout used by Wolf Cubs
   Meaning 'Do your best'.

BAER, Arthur
US columnist and writer (1897?–1969)

6   Alimony is like buying oats for a dead horse.

   Attrib

BAGNOLD, Enid
British playwright (1889–1981)

7   The great and terrible step was taken. What else could you expect from a girl so expectant? 'Sex,' said Frank Harris, 'is the gateway to life.' So I went through the gateway in an upper room in the Café Royal.

   Enid Bagnold's Autobiography (1969)

BAIRNSFATHER, Bruce
British cartoonist (1888–1959)

1   Well, if you knows of a better 'ole, go to it.

   Caption to cartoon in *Fragments from France* (1915)
   Said by 'Ol' Bill', up to his waist in mud on the Somme. A film (US
   1926), based on the character, was called *The Better 'Ole.*

BAKER, Howard
US Republican politician (1925–   )

2   What did the President know, and when did he know it?

   Senate Watergate Committee hearings, 1973

BAKER, Hylda
British entertainer (1908–86)

3   *Of her silent foil, 'Cynthia':*
   She knows, you know!

   Catchphrase, from 1950s onwards .

BALDWIN, James
US novelist (1924–87)

4   If we do not now dare everything, the fulfilment of that prophecy,
   re-created from the Bible in song by a slave, is upon us: *God gave
   Noah the rainbow sign, No more water, the fire next time!*

   The Fire Next Time (1963)

BALDWIN, Stanley (later 1st Earl Baldwin of Bewdley)
British Conservative Prime Minister (1867–1947)

5   *Of the House of Commons in 1918:*
   They are a lot of hard-faced men . . . who look as if they had done
   well out of the war.

   Quoted in J. M. Keynes, *Economic Consequences of Peace*
   Baldwin is assumed to have been the 'Conservative politician' Keynes
   quoted.

6   *Attacking the press lords during a by-election campaign:*
   The papers conducted by Lord Rothermere and Lord Beaverbrook
   are not newspapers in the ordinary acceptance of the term. They
   are engines of propaganda, for the constantly changing policies,
   desires, personal wishes, personal likes and dislikes of two men . . .
   What the proprietorship of these papers is aiming at is power, and
   power without responsibility—the prerogative of the harlot
   throughout the ages.

   Speech, London, 18 March 1931
   His cousin, Rudyard Kipling, was the originator of this remark. Harold
   Macmillan recalled that his father-in-law, the Duke of Devonshire,
   exclaimed at this point, 'Good God, that's done it, he's lost us the tarts'
   vote.'

1   The bomber will always get through.
     Speech, House of Commons, 10 November 1932

2   *On becoming Prime Minister in 1933:*
     I met Curzon in Downing Street, from whom I got the sort of
     greeting a corpse would give to an undertaker.
     Attrib

3   There is a wind of nationalism and freedom blowing round the
     world, and blowing as strongly in Asia as elsewhere.
     Speech, London, 4 December 1934

4   *On the Abyssinia crisis:*
     □ I shall be but a short time tonight. I have seldom spoken with
     greater regret, for my lips are sealed.
     Speech, House of Commons, 10 December 1935
     Actually, he said 'my lips are not yet unsealed.'

5   I put before the whole House my own view with appalling frankness
     . . . supposing I had gone to the country and said . . . that we must
     rearm, does anybody think that this pacific democracy would have
     rallied to that cry at that moment? I cannot think of anything that
     would have made the loss of the election from my point of view
     more certain.
     Speech, House of Commons, 12 November 1936

6   *On his resignation:*
     Once I leave, I leave. I am not going to speak to the man on the
     bridge, and I am not going to spit on the deck.
     Statement to the Cabinet, 28 May 1937, later released to the press
     On his inauguration as Rector of Edinburgh University in 1925,
     Baldwin had expressed a view of the limitations on the freedom of a
     former Prime Minister in similar terms: 'A sailor does not spit on the
     deck, thereby strengthening his control and saving unnecessary work
     for someone else; nor does he speak to the man at the wheel, thereby
     leaving him to devote his whole time to his task and increasing the
     probability of the ship arriving at or near her destination.'

7   You will find in politics that you are much exposed to the
     attribution of false motive. Never complain and never explain.
     To Harold Nicolson, 21 July 1943, quoting Disraeli

BALFOUR, Arthur (later 1st Earl of Balfour)
British Conservative Prime Minister (1848–1930)

8   *To Frank Harris who had claimed that Christianity and journalism were
     the two main curses of civilization:*
     Christianity, yes, but why journalism?
     Quoted in M. Asquith, *Autobiography*

1 *As Foreign Secretary, to Lord Rothschild:*
His Majesty's Government looks with favour upon the establishment in Palestine of a national home for the Jewish people.
Letter, 2 November 1917
The 'Balfour Declaration.'

2 Nothing matters very much and very few things matter at all.
Attrib

BALL, Bobby
British comedian (1944–)

3 *To partner, Tommy Cannon:*
Rock on, Tommy!
Catchphrase, from 1970s onwards

BANKHEAD, Tallulah
US actress (1903–68)

4 *On the play **Aglavaine and Selysette** by Maurice Maeterlinck:*
There's less in this than meets the eye.
Remark, 3 January 1922

5 *On being greeted by a former admirer after many years:*
I thought I told you to wait in the car.
Attrib

6 *To admirer:*
I'll come and make love to you at five o'clock. If I'm late start without me.
Quoted in E. Morgan, *Somerset Maugham*

7 *Putting a donation in Salvation Army officer's tambourine:*
Don't bother to thank me. I know what a perfectly ghastly season it's been for you Spanish dancers.
Attrib

8 Cocaine habit-forming? Of course not. I ought to know. I've been using it for years.
Tallulah (1952)

9 *On herself:*
I'm as pure as driven slush.
Quoted in the *Observer*, 24 February 1957
See also **DIETZ 100:7.**

BARKER, Eric
British comic actor (1912–90)

1   Steady, Barker!

Catchphrase, from the 1940s

2   Carry on smokin'!

Stock phrase in BBC radio *Merry Go Round*, 1940s

BARNES, Clive
British-born theatre and ballet critic (1927–   )

3   *On Oh, Calcutta! (1969):*
This is the kind of show that gives pornography a dirty name.

Review in *New York Times*, 18 June 1969.

BARNES, Peter
British playwright (1931–   )

4   I know I am God because when I pray to him I find I'm talking to myself.

The Ruling Class (1968)

BARRIE, J. M. (later Sir James)
British playwright (1860–1937)

5   *Entry in notebook, as a student:*
Greatest horror—dream I am married—wake up shrieking.

Quoted in H. Carpenter, *Secret Gardens* (1985)

6   Every time a child says 'I don't believe in fairies,' there's a little fairy somewhere that falls down dead.
Peter Pan (1904)

7   To die will be an awfully big adventure.

ibid

8   Do you believe in fairies? Say quick that you believe. If you believe, clap your hands!

ibid

9   Second to the right, and straight on till morning

ibid

10   *Last words of 'Captain Hook':*
Floreat Etona!

ibid

Motto of Eton College. In *Peter Pan and Wendy*, the novel (1911), he merely says, 'Bad form!'

1   There are few more impressive sights in the world than a Scotsman on the make.

What Every Woman Knows (1908)

2   I know I'm not clever but I'm always right.

ibid

3   Every man who is high up likes to feel that he has done it himself; and the wife smiles, and lets it go at that. It's our only joke. Every woman knows that.

ibid

4   Never ascribe to an opponent motives meaner than your own.

Rectorial Address, St Andrews, 3 May 1922

5   *To H. G. Wells:*
It is all very well to be able to write books, but can you waggle your ears?

Quoted in J. A. Hamerton, *Barrie: The Story of a Genius*

BARRYMORE, John
US actor (1882–1942)

6   *Throwing a sea-bass to a noisily-coughing audience:*
Busy yourselves with *this*, you damned walruses, while the rest of us proceed with the libretto.

Quoted in B. Cerf, *Try and Stop Me*

7   *In visitors' book at theatrical digs, he wrote:*
'Quoth the Raven . . . '

Attrib

BARTON, Bruce
US advertising executive and Republican politician (1886–1967)

8   [Jesus] picked up twelve men from the bottom ranks of business and forged them into an organization that conquered the world.

The Man Nobody Knows: A discovery of the real Jesus (1924)

BARUCH, Bernard
US financier and Presidential adviser (1870–1965)

9   Let us not be deceived—we are today in the midst of a cold war.

Speech, South Carolina, 16 April 1947
The phrase was suggested to him by his speechwriter Herbert Bayard Swope who had been using it privately since 1940.

BATCHELOR, Horace
British businessman (1898–1977)

1   *For details of Infra-Draw method of winning football pools:*
Send now to Horace Batchelor, Dept 1, Keynsham—spelt
K-E-Y-N-S-H-A-M, Keynsham, Bristol.

Radio advertisements, from 1950s onwards
Usually spoken by another voice.

BATEMAN, H. M.
British cartoonist (1887–1970)

2   The Man Who . . . [committed some solecism or other]

Caption of cartoons in the 1920/30s
e.g.: 'The Man Who Missed the Ball on the First Tee at St Andrews',
'The Man Who Lit His Cigar Before the Royal Toast', 'The Girl Who
Ordered a Glass of Milk at the Café Royal', and, 'The Man Who Asked
for "A Double Scotch" in the Grand Pump Room at Bath'.

BATES, H. E.
British novelist and short story writer (1905–74)

3   Perfick wevver.

The Darling Buds of May (Chap.1) (1958)
Pa Larkin's use of 'perfick' extends through all the novels about the
Larkin family.

BAUM, L. Frank
US author (1856–1919)

4   The Wonderful Wizard of Oz.

Title of book (1900)

5   The Wicked Witch of the West.

Character in ibid

6   The road to the City of Emeralds is paved with yellow brick.

In ibid
See also **HARBURG 153:7.**

BAX, Sir Arnold
British composer (1883–1953)

7   *Quoting an anonymous Scotsman:*
You should make a point of trying every experience once,
excepting incest and folk-dancing.

Farewell, My Youth (1943)

1   *Of Arnold Bennett:*
[He] once remarked that his earliest recognition of his own middle age came at a certain appalling moment when he realized for the first time that the policeman at the corner was a mere youth.

ibid
This realization has also been attributed to Sir Seymour Hicks (1871–1949) in connection with old age.

BAYLIS, Lilian
British theatre manager and producer (1874–1937)

2   O God, send me some good actors—cheap.

Quoted in *The Guardian*, 1 March 1976

3   *On a less than adequate performance in **King Lear**:*
Quite a sweet little Goneril, don't you think?

ibid

'BEACHCOMBER' (J. B. Morton)
British humorist (1893–1979)

4   Hush, hush
Nobody cares!
Christopher Robin
Has
 Fallen
  Down-
   Stairs.

'Now We are Sick', *By the Way* (1931)

5   The man with the false nose had gone to that bourne from which no hollingsworth returns.

Gallimaufry (1936).
Alluding to Shakespeare: *Hamlet* (III.i.79)—'the undiscover'd country, from whose bourn/No traveller returns'. B & H was a noted London department store.

6   Erratum. In my article on the Price of Milk, 'Horses' should have read 'Cows' throughout.

The Best of Beachcomber (1963)

7   Justice must not only be seen to be done but has to be seen to be believed.

Attrib

8   Wagner is the Puccini of music.

Attrib

BEATTY, Sir David (later 1st Earl Beatty)
British admiral (1871–1936)

1   *To his Flag Captain, Ernle Chatfield, at the Battle of Jutland, 31 May 1916:*
There seems to be something wrong with our bloody ships today.
Quoted in *The Oxford Dictionary of Quotations* (1953)
Chatfield discounted any other wording.

BEAVERBROOK, Lord (Maxwell Aitken)
Canadian-born politician and newspaper proprietor (1879–1964)

2   I am the cat that walks alone.
Saying, quoted in A. J. P. Taylor, *Beaverbrook*
See **KIPLING 189:6.**

3   *To Winston Churchill, of Edward VIII during the Abdication crisis:*
Our cock won't fight.
Quoted in F. Donaldson, *Edward VIII*

4   *As Minister of Aircraft Production:*
Let me say that the credit belongs to the boys in the back rooms. It isn't the man who sits in the limelight like me who should have the praise. It is not the men who sit in prominent places. It is the men in the back rooms.
Radio broadcast, 19 March 1941
His inspiration for this phrase was Marlene Dietrich singing 'The Boys in the Back Room' in the film *Destry Rides Again* (1939).
See **LOESSER 205:3.**

5   *Advice to Tom Driberg in 1942:*
The British electors will not vote for a man who doesn't wear a hat.
Quoted in A. Watkins, *Brief Lives* (1982)

6   *Frequent inquiry at his newspaper office:*
Who's in charge of the clattering train?
Quoting an anonymous poem from *Punch* (1890).

7   *To Godfrey Winn:*
Go out and speak for the inarticulate and the submerged.
Quoted in E. Morgan, *Somerset Maugham*

8   *When asked why Winn was paid more than the rest of the staff:*
Because he shakes hands with people's hearts.
ibid

1   *On Earl Haig:*
    With the publication of his Private Papers in 1952, he committed
    suicide twenty-five years after his death.

    Men and Power (1956)

2   *On David Lloyd George:*
    He did not care which direction the car was travelling, so long as he
    was in the driver's seat.

    The Decline and Fall of Lloyd George (1963)
    See also **DAILY EXPRESS 93:4.**

BECKETT, Samuel

Irish playwright (1906–89)

3   Nothing happens, nobody comes, nobody goes, it's awful!

    Waiting for Godot (1954)

4   *Vladimir:* That passed the time.
    Estragon: It would have passed in any case.
    Vladimir: Yes, but not so rapidly.

    ibid

5   *Estragon:* Let's go.
    Vladimir: We can't.
    Estragon: Why not?
    Vladimir: We're waiting for Godot.

    ibid

BEECHAM, Sir Thomas

British orchestral conductor (1879–1961)

6   *To Utica Welles:*
    I don't like your Christian name. I'd like to change it.

    Attrib remark
    She replied, 'You can't, but you can change my surname.' And so they
    were married (1903).

7   *To a man called 'Ball':*
    Ball . . . how very singular.

    Quoted in N. Cardus, *Sir Thomas Beecham*

8   *On Elgar's A Flat Symphony:*
    The musical equivalent of the towers of St Pancras station—neo-
    Gothic, you know.

    ibid

1   There are two golden rules for an orchestra: start together and finish together. The public doesn't give a damn what goes on in between.

Quoted in H. Atkins & A. Newman, *Beecham Stories*

2   *On Beethoven's 7th Symphony:*
What can you do with it?—it's like a lot of yaks jumping about.

ibid

3   *On Herbert von Karajan:*
[He's a kind] of musical Malcolm Sargent.

ibid

BEERBOHM, Sir Max
British writer (1872–1956)

4   'I don't,' she added, 'know anything about music, really. But I know what I like.'

Zuleika Dobson (1911)

5   *On Pinero's eyebrows:*
[Like] the skins of some small mammal just not large enough to be used as mats.

Quoted in C. Hassall, *Edward Marsh*

6   *On being told that Maud Cunard was 'absolutely wonderful, she never changes':*
I am sorry to hear that.

Quoted in D. Fielding, *Emerald and Nancy* (1968)
See also **GIRAUDOUX 138:3.**

BEHAN, Brendan
Irish playwright (1923–64)

7   O, Death where is thy sting-a-ling-a-ling,
O, grave, thy victoree?
The Bells of Hell go ting-a-ling-a-ling
For you but not for me.

The Hostage (1958)
Adopting a song popular in the British Army 1914-18.

8   I was . . . court-martialled in my absence, sentenced to death in my absence. So I said, right, you can shoot me in my absence.

ibid (1962 version)

9   I saw a notice which said 'Drink Canada Dry' and I've just started.

Attrib
See also **PROVERBS 262:5.**

BELL, Daniel
US sociologist (1919–)

1   The Coming of Post-Industrial Society.
    Title of book (1973)

BELL, H. E.
British university administrator (1925–)

2   Parents are the very last people who ought to be allowed to have children.
    Speech at University of Reading, March 1977
    Compare **SHAW 289:3.**

BELLOC, Hilaire
British writer (1870–1953)

3   The chief defect of Henry King
    Was chewing little bits of string.
    'Henry King', *Cautionary Tales* (1907)

4   They answered, as they took their fees,
    'There is no cure for this disease.'
    ibid

5   And always keep a hold of Nurse
    For fear of finding something worse.
    'Jim' in ibid

6   My language fails
    Go out and govern New South Wales.
    'Lord Lundy' in ibid

7   From quiet homes and first beginning,
        Out to the undiscovered ends,
    There's nothing worth the wear of winning,
        But laughter and the love of friends.
    Verses (1910), 'Dedicatory Ode'

8   When I am dead, I hope it may be said:
    'His sins were scarlet, but his books were read.'
    Sonnets and Verse (1923), 'On His Books'

BELLOW, Saul
US novelist (1915–)

9   All a writer has to do to get a woman is to say he's a writer. It's an aphrodisiac.
    Attrib

BENCHLEY, Robert
US humorist (1889–1945)

1 I must get out of these wet clothes and into a dry martini.

   Line delivered in film *The Major and the Minor* (1942)

   Sometimes attributed to Alexander Woollcott, this line may actually
   have originated with Benchley's press agent or with his friend Charles
   Butterworth.

2 *Capsule criticism of long-running play* **Abie's Irish Rose** *(1922–7):*
   See Hebrews 13:8.

   Attrib

   The text reads: 'Jesus Christ the same yesterday, and today, and for
   ever.'

3 *Suggested epitaph for actress:*
   She sleeps alone at last.

   Attrib

4 *Telegram to the* **New Yorker** *on arriving in Venice:*
   STREETS FULL OF WATER. PLEASE ADVISE.

   Attrib

BENDA, Julien
French writer and philosopher (1867–1956)

5 *La trahison des clercs* ('The intellectuals' betrayal').

   Title of book (1927)

   The phrase denotes a compromise of intellectual integrity by writers,
   artists and thinkers.

BENN, Tony (formerly Viscount Stansgate)
British Labour politician (1925–   )

6 I am on the right wing of the middle of the road and with a strong
   radical bias.

   Remark, from the 1950s

7 *When Minister of Technology:*
   Broadcasting is really too important to be left to the broadcasters
   and somehow we must find some new way of using radio and
   television to allow us to talk to each other.

   Speech, Bristol, 18 October 1968.

   Compare **CLEMENCEAU 80:3** *and* **DE GAULLE 97:6.**

BENNETT, Alan
British playwright (1934–   )

1   Life, you know, is rather like opening a tin of sardines. We're all of us looking for the key.

'Take a pew', *Beyond the Fringe* (1961)

2   They are rolling up the maps all over Europe. We shall not see them lit again in our lifetime.

Forty Years On (1969)
Alluding to William Pitt the Younger *and to* **GREY 146:1**.

3   All women dress like their mothers, that is their tragedy. No man ever does. That is his.

ibid
Alluding to Oscar Wilde, 'All women become like their mothers . . .'

4   *On Sidney and Beatrice Webb:*
Two of the nicest people if ever there was one.

ibid
Not in the published script.

5   Why is it always the intelligent people who are socialists?

ibid

6   When a society has to resort to the lavatory for its humour, the writing is on the wall.

ibid

7   Sapper, Buchan, Dornford Yates, practitioners in that school of Snobbery with Violence that runs like a thread of good-class tweed through twentieth-century literature.

ibid
An obituary in *The Times* for Colin Watson (21 January 1983) credited him with the origination of the phrase 'snobbery with violence'. His book of that title did not appear, however, until 1971.

8   *In Bulldog Drummond parody:*
A divorced woman on the throne of the House of Windsor would be a pretty big feather in the cap of that bunch of rootless intellectuals, alien Jews and international pederasts who call themselves the Labour Party.

ibid

9   *Of Arianna Stassinopoulos, Greek-born writer:*
So boring you fall asleep halfway through her name.

Quoted in the *Observer*, 18 September 1983

1 You only have to survive in England and all is forgiven you . . . if you can eat a boiled egg at ninety in England they think you deserve a Nobel Prize.

On ITV, *South Bank Show*, 1984

2 *On being asked by Ian McKellen if he was homosexual:*
[That's] a little like asking a man crawling across the Sahara whether he would prefer Perrier or Malvern Water.

Attrib

BENNETT, Arnold
British writer (1867–1931)

3 Mrs Laye . . . told a good thing of a very old man on his dying bed giving advice to a youngster: 'I've had a long life, and it's been a merry one. Take my advice. Make love to every pretty woman you meet. And remember, if you get 5 per cent on your outlay it's a good return.'

Diary entry for 24 May 1904

4 'What great cause is he identified with?' 'He's identified . . . with the great cause of cheering us all up.'

The Card (1911)

5 Journalists say a thing that they know isn't true, in the hope that if they keep on saying it long enough it *will* be true.

The Title (1918)

6 Mr Lloyd George spoke for a hundred and seventeen minutes, in which period he was detected only once in the use of an argument.

'After the March Offensive', *Things That Have Interested Me* (1921–5)
See also **BAX 27:1.**

BENNY, Jack
US comedian (1894–1974)

7 *In reply to a robber demanding 'Your money or your life!':*
I'm thinking it over.

Remark
His basic joke, from the 1930s onwards.

BENSON, A. C.

British writer (1862–1925)

1   Land of Hope and Glory, Mother of the Free,
     How shall we extol thee, who are born of thee?
     Wider still and wider shall thy bounds be set;
     God who made thee mighty, make thee mightier yet.

     Coronation Ode (1902)

     Sung to music, originally known as the 'Pomp and Circumstance
     March No. 1', by Sir Edward Elgar.

BENSON, E. F.

British novelist (1867–1940)

2   Au reservoir!

     Passim in his 'Lucia' novels of the 1930s
     A reasonably common catchphrase of the period.

BENTLEY, E. C.

British writer (1875–1956)

3   Sir Christopher Wren
     Said, 'I am going to dine with some men.
     If anybody calls
     Say I am designing St Paul's.'

     Biography for Beginners (1905)
     An example of a 'clerihew', the short biographical verse form he
     invented.

BENTLEY, Nicolas

British cartoonist and writer (1907–78)

4   *Of Henry Campbell-Bannerman:*
     He is remembered chiefly as the man about whom all is forgotten.

     An Edwardian Album (1974)

5   His was the sort of career that made the Recording Angel think
     seriously about taking up shorthand.

     Attrib

6   No news is good news; no journalists is even better.

     Attrib

7   One should not exaggerate the importance of trifles. Life, for
     instance, is much too short to be taken seriously.

     Attrib

BENTSEN, Lloyd
US Republican Senator (1921–)

1 *To Dan Quayle who had evoked the name of John F. Kennedy:*
I served with Jack Kennedy. I knew Jack Kennedy. Jack Kennedy was a friend of mine. Senator, you're no Jack Kennedy.

Vice-Presidential TV debate, presidential election, 6 October 1988

BERLIN, Irving
US composer and lyricist (1888–1989)

2 A Pretty Girl is Like a Melody.

Title of song in *Ziegfeld Follies* (1919)

3 The song is ended
But the melody lingers on.

'The Song is Ended' (1927)

4 We joined the Navy to see the world,
And what did we see? We saw the sea.

'We Saw the Sea', *Follow the Fleet* (1936)

5 I'm dreaming of a white Christmas.

'White Christmas', *Holiday Inn* (1942)

6 Got no cheque books got no banks
Still I'd like to express my thanks—
I got the sun in the mornin' and the moon at night.

'I Got the Sun in the Mornin'', *Annie Get Your Gun* (1946)

7 There's No Business Like Show Business.

Title of song in ibid
Later the title of a musical film (1954).

8 Doin' What Comes Natur'lly.

Title of song in ibid

9 Anything You Can Do, I Can Do Better.

Title of song in ibid

10 The Hostess with Mostes' on the Ball.

Title of song, *Call me Madam* (1950)

BERNARD, Jeffrey
British journalist (1932–)

11 When people say, 'You're breaking my heart,' they do in fact usually mean that you're breaking their genitals.

In the *Spectator*, 31 May 1986

1   □ Jeffrey Bernard is unwell.

Occasional editorial explanation for the non-appearance of his pieces in the *Spectator*. Used as the title of a London stage show (1989) based on his writings.

BERNE, Eric
US psychologist and writer (1910–70)

2   Games People Play.

Title of book (1964)

BERNERS, Lord
British writer and composer (1883–1950)

3   *On T. E. Lawrence:*
     He's always backing into the limelight.

Attrib
Winston Churchill said the same thing.

BERRA, Yogi
US baseball player (1925–   )

4   The game isn't over till it's over.

Attrib

BERRY, Chuck
US singer/songwriter (1931–   )

5   Roll Over, Beethoven.

Title of song (1956)

BETJEMAN, Sir John
British Poet Laureate (1906–84)

6   Broad of Church and broad of mind,
     Broad before and broad behind,
     A keen ecclesiologist,
     A rather dirty Wykehamist.

'The Wykehamist' (1932)

7   Ghastly Good Taste, or, a depressing story of the Rise and Fall of English Architecture.

Title of book (1933)

8   Spirits of well-shot woodcock, partridge, snipe
     Flutter and bear him up the Norfolk sky.

'Death of King George V' (1937)

1   Come, friendly bombs, and fall on Slough.
     It isn't fit for humans now.
     'Slough' (1937)

2   Miss J. Hunter Dunn, Miss J. Hunter Dunn
     Furnish'd and burnish'd by Aldershot sun.
     'A Subaltern's Love-song' (1945)

3   Phone for the fish knives, Norman,
     As Cook is a little unnerved.
     'How to Get on in Society' (1954)

4   *When asked if he had any regrets:*
     Yes, I haven't had enough sex.
     Time With Betjeman, BBC TV, February 1983

5   [A man] not mentioned much nowadays.
     Saying, quoted in the *Observer*, 29 May 1988

BEVAN, Aneurin
Welsh Labour politician (1897–1960)

6   Listening to a speech by [Neville] Chamberlain is like paying a visit
     to Woolworths; everything in its place and nothing over sixpence.
     In *Tribune* (1937)

7   *Of J. B. Priestley:*
     Playing on a fuddled fiddle, somewhere in the muddled middle.
     Attrib 1940s

8   *Recalling the inter-war Depression:*
     That is why no amount of cajolery, and no attempts at ethical or
     social seduction, can eradicate from my heart a deep and burning
     hatred for the Tory Party that inflicted those experiences on me. So
     far as I am concerned they are lower than vermin.
     Speech, Manchester, 4 July 1948

9   In Place of Fear.
     Title of book about disarmament (1952)

10   We know what happens to people who stay in the middle of the
     road. They get run over.
     Quoted in the *Observer*, 9 December 1953

1   I know that the right kind of political leader for the Labour Party is a desiccated calculating machine.

Speech at meeting during Labour Party Conference, 29 September 1954
Taken as referring to Hugh Gaitskell, though Bevan denied this.

2   *Wishing to address the Prime Minister (Harold Macmillan) rather than the Foreign Secretary (Selwyn Lloyd) in a post-Suez debate:*
I am not going to spend any time whatsoever in attacking the Foreign Secretary. Quite honestly I am beginning to feel extremely sorry for him. If we complain about the tune, there is no reason to attack the monkey when the organ grinder is present.

Speech, House of Commons, 16 May 1957
Also attrib. to Churchill during the Second World War—replying to a query from the British Ambassador as to whether he should raise a question with Mussolini or Count Ciano, his Foreign Minister.

3   *Speaking against a motion proposing unilateral disarmament:*
If you carry this resolution . . . you will send a Foreign Secretary—whoever he may be—naked into the conference chamber.

Speech, Labour Party Conference, 3 October 1957

4   And you call that statesmanship. I call it an emotional spasm.

ibid

5   Socialism in the context of modern society [means] the conquest of the commanding heights of the economy.

Speech, two-day Labour Conference, November 1959
Recalling an earlier use by him of the phrase. Possibly originated by Lenin.

6   I read the newspaper avidly. It is my one form of continuous fiction.

Quoted in the *Observer*, 3 April 1960

BEVIN, Ernest
British Labour politician (1881–1951)

7   *On being told that another Labourite was 'his own worst enemy':*
Not while I'm alive, he ain't.

Quoted in M. Foot, *Aneurin Bevin 1945–60*
Reputedly levelled at Aneurin Bevan, Herbert Morrison, Emanuel Shinwell and others.

1   *On Foreign Affairs:*
    My policy is to be able to take a ticket at Victoria Station and go
    anywhere I damn well please.

    In the *Spectator*, 20 April 1951
    Francis Williams in his biography of Bevin (1952) has this version said
    to a diplomat about the most important objective of his foreign policy:
    'Just to be able to go down to Victoria station and take a ticket to where
    the hell I like without a passport.'

2   *On the cliché-ridden content of a speech by another politician (possibly*
    Anthony Eden):
    It was clitch after clitch after clitch.

    Attrib

BEYOND OUR KEN

UK radio comedy series (BBC), from 1954. Script by Eric Merriman. With
Kenneth Horne and Kenneth Williams.

3   *'Arthur Fallowfield' (Williams):*
    I think the answer lies in the soil.

    Catchphrase

4   *'Fallowfield':*
    I'm looking for someone to love.

    Catchphrase

5   *Old man (Williams), when asked how long he had been doing anything:*
    Thirty-five years!

    Catchphrase

BINYON, Laurence
British poet (1869–1943)

6   They shall grow not old, as we that are left grow old:
    Age shall not weary them, nor the years condemn.
    At the going down of the sun and in the morning
    We will remember them.

    'For the Fallen', printed in *The Times*, 21 September 1914
    Frequently misquoted as 'They shall not grow old . . . '

7   Now is the time for the burning of the leaves.

    'The Burning of the Leaves' (1942)

BIRCH, Nigel (later Lord Rhyl)
British Conservative MP (1906–81)

8   *On the resignation of Labour Chancellor Hugh Dalton:*
    My God! They've shot our fox!

    Remark, 13 November 1947

1   *On Harold Macmillan's sacking of Selwyn Lloyd:*
    For the second time the Prime Minister has got rid of a Chancellor
    of the Exchequer who tried to get expenditure under control.
    Once is more than enough.
    Letter, *The Times*, 14 July 1962

2   *On Harold Macmillan during the Profumo scandal:*
    I myself feel that the time will come very soon when my Right Hon.
    friend ought to make way for a much younger colleague . . .   I
    certainly will not quote at him the savage words of Cromwell, but
    perhaps some of the words of Browning might be appropriate in
    his poem on 'The Lost Leader', in which he wrote:
    'Let him never come back to us!
    There would be doubt, hesitation and pain.
    Forced praise on our part—the glimmer of twilight,
    Never glad confident morning again!'
    Speech, House of Commons, 17 June 1963

BIRT, John
British broadcasting executive (1944–   )

3   There is a bias in television journalism. It is not against any
    particular party or point of view—it is a bias against *understanding*.
    Article in *The Times*, 28 February 1975
    This launched a series of articles written jointly with Peter Jay.

BLAKE, Eubie
US jazz musician (1883–1983)

4   If I'd known I was gonna live this long, I'd have taken better care of
    myself.
    Quoted in the *Observer*, 13 February 1983
    Five days after marking his centennial, he died.

BLANCH, Lesley
British writer (1907–   )

5   The Wilder Shores of Love.
    Title of biographical study (1954)

BLEASDALE, Alan
British playwright (1946–   )

6   *Stock phrase of unemployed character, 'Yosser Hughes':*
    Gi' us a job [or gissa job], I could do that.
    TV play, *The Boys from the Blackstuff* (1982)

BLUNT, Alfred
British Bishop (1879–1957)

1   *On King Edward VIII:*
     The benefit of the King's Coronation depends under God upon . . .
     the faith, prayer and self-dedication of the King himself . . . We
     hope that he is aware of this need. Some of us wish that he gave
     more positive signs of such awareness.

     Address to diocesan conference, 1 December 1936
     With these words the Bishop unwittingly triggered off press comment
     on the Abdication crisis.

BLYTHE, Ronald
British writer (1922–)

2   As for the British churchman, he goes to church as he goes to the
     bathroom, with the minimum of fuss and no explanation if he can
     help it.

     The Age of Illusion (1963)

BOESKY, Ivan
US financier (1938–)

3   Greed is all right. Greed is healthy. You can be greedy and still feel
     good about yourself.

     Quoted in C. Churchill, *Serious Money* (1987)
     Compare **WALL STREET 338:2.**

BOGART, Humphrey
US film actor (1899–1957)

4   □ Tennis, anyone?

     Wrongly said to have been the sole line in his first play. An ABC TV
     programme, broadcast 9 May 1974, using old film, contained a denial
     by Bogart.
     See also **CASABLANCA 60:3, 5–10.**

BOLITHO, William
British writer (1890–1930)

5   The shortest way out of Manchester is notoriously a bottle of
     Gordon's gin.

     'Caliogstro and Seraphina', *Twelve Against the Gods*

BONHAM-CARTER, Lady Violet (later Baroness Asquith)
British Liberal political figure (1887–1969)

6   *Last words:*
     I feel amphibious.

     Quoted in the *Observer* Magazine, 24 January 1988

BOOK TITLES
(and where they come from)

1 All the President's Men (Bob Woodward and Carl Bernstein)

Alluding to the line 'All the king's horses/And all the king's men,/Couldn't put Humpty together again' from the nursery rhyme 'Humpty Dumpty' but also to the book and film about Huey Long, *All the King's Men*, and to a saying of Henry Kissinger's at the time of the 1970 Cambodia invasion: 'We are [all] the President's men and we must behave accordingly.'

2 Boldness Be My Friend (Richard Pape)

From Shakespeare, *Cymbeline*.

3 Breakfast of Champions (Kurt Vonnegut)

From the slogan for Wheaties, the US breakfast cereal.

4 A Bridge Too Far (Cornelius Ryan)

From a remark made by Lieut. General Sir Frederick Browning to Field Marshal Montgomery about the airborne landings in the Netherlands (1944) to capture eleven bridges needed for the invasion of Germany: 'But, sir, we may be going a bridge too far.'

5 Bury My Heart at Wounded Knee (Dee Brown)

From Stephen Vincent Benét, 'American Names' (1927).

6 A Confederacy of Dunces (John Kennedy Toole)

From Jonathan Swift's *Thoughts on Various Subjects* (1706): 'Many a true genius appears in the world—you may know him by this sign, that the dunces are all in confederacy against him.'

7 A Dance To the Music of Time (Anthony Powell)

From the title given to a painting by Nicolas Poussin in the Wallace Collection, London.

8 Diamonds are Forever (Ian Fleming)

Alluding to the slogan 'A Diamond is Forever' for De Beers Consolidated Mines (since 1939).

9 Do You Sincerely Want To Be Rich? (Charles Raw, *et al*)

Question posed to his salesmen, during training, by Bernie Cornfeld (1928–   ) who made his name and fortune selling investment plans.

10 Eating People is Wrong (Malcolm Bradbury)

From the song 'The Reluctant Cannibal' by Michael Flanders and Donald Swann.

11 Fun in a Chinese Laundry (Josef Von Sternberg)

From the title of an early Edison film.

1   God Protect Me From My Friends (Gavin Maxwell)

'I can look after my enemies, but God protect me from my friends' is a proverb common to many languages.

2   God Is An Englishman (R. F. Delderfield)

Apparently an original coinage, but reflecting a traditional point of view.

3   Gone With the Wind (Margaret Mitchell)

From Ernest Dowson's poem *Non Sum Qualis Eram* (1896): 'I have forgot much, Cynara! Gone with the wind . . . '

4   The Heart Is A Lonely Hunter (Carson McCullers)

From William Sharp's 'The Lonely Hunter'—'My heart is a lonely hunter that hunts on a lonely hill.'

5   The Houses in Between (Howard Spring)

From the music-hall song popularized by Gus Elen. Lyrics by Edgar Bateman. Music by George Le Brunn.

6   I Never Promised You A Rose Garden ('Hannah Green'/Joanne Greenberg)

The phrase appears to be original to this book (1964). A song 'Rose Garden' by Joe South incorporated it in 1968 and a film with it as the title followed in 1977.

7   Look Homeward, Angel! (Thomas Wolfe)

From 'Lycidas' by John Milton.

8   Love Is A Many-Splendored Thing (Han Suyin)

Alluding to Francis Thompson, 'The Kingdom of God': ''Tis ye, 'tis your estranged faces,/That miss the many-splendoured thing.'

9   The Moon and Sixpence (Somerset Maugham)

From a review in the *Times Literary Supplement* of *Of Human Bondage* which said the main character, 'Like so many young men, was so busy yearning for the moon that he never saw the sixpence at his feet.'

10 The Moon's A Balloon (David Niven)

From e.e. cummings, '& N &': 'Who knows if the moon's a balloon, coming out of a keen city in the sky—filled with pretty people?'

11 The Night Has a Thousand Eyes (Cornell Woolrich)

From the title of a poetic work by Francis Bourdillon (1878). Also used as a song title.

12 None But the Lonely Heart (Richard Llewellyn)

Adapted from an English title of Tchaikovsky's song 'None But the Weary Heart' (original words by Goethe.)

1 **Nostalgia Isn't What It Used To Be** (Simone Signoret)

From a graffito.

2 **Of Human Bondage** (Somerset Maugham)

From the title of one of the books in Spinoza's *Ethics* (1677).

3 **A Postillion Struck by Lightning** (Dirk Bogarde)

This is said to be a line from a nineteenth-century phrase book, but is possibly apocryphal.

4 **Random Harvest** (James Hilton)

From an error in a German official report which claimed that a town called 'Random' had been attacked, following a British official report that 'Bombs fell at Random'.

5 **Real Men Don't Eat Quiche** (Bruce Feirstein)

Original to the book but used earlier as the title of an article in *Playboy* (1962).

6 **The Shock of the New** (Robert Hughes)

From the title of Ian Dunlop's 1972 book on 'seven historic exhibitions of modern art'.

7 **Somebody Up There Likes Me** (Rocky Graziano)

Apparently coined for the 1956 autobiography of a world heavyweight boxing champion (and the subsequent film).

8 **Tender is the Night** (F. Scott Fitzgerald)

From the 'Ode to a Nightingale' by John Keats—'Already with thee! tender is the night.'

9 **To Serve Them All My Days** (R. F. Delderfield)

Not a quotation, although it contains echoes of 'And to serve him truly all the days of my life' from the Catechism in the *Book of Common Prayer* and 'Serve him all my days' from the Sunday school hymn 'I Must Like a Christian . . . '

10 **Tread Softly for You Tread on My Jokes** (Malcolm Muggeridge)

Alluding to 'Tread softly because you tread on my dreams' from 'He Wishes for the Cloths of Heaven' (1899) by W. B. Yeats.

11 **When the Kissing Had to Stop** (Constantine FitzGibbon)

From Robert Browning, 'A Toccata at Galuppi's': 'What of soul was left, I wonder, when the kissing had to stop.'

12 **Whistle Down the Wind** (Mary Hayley Bell)

Not intended as a quotation, but echoing Shakespeare, *Othello*: 'I'd whistle her off and let her down the wind' (a hawking metaphor). Also a nautical expression.

BORGES, Jorge Luis
Argentinian novelist (1899–1986)

1   *On the war with Britain over the Falklands, 1982:*
    The Falklands thing was a fight between two bald men over a comb.

    Quoted in *Time*, 14 February 1983
    Incorporating an old Russian saying.

BOSSIDY, John Collins
US oculist (1860–1928)

2   And this is good old Boston,
    The home of the bean and the cod,
    Where the Lowells talk only to Cabots,
    And the Cabots talk only to God.

    Toast at Harvard dinner (1910)

BOTHAM, Ian
British cricketer (1955–   )

3   *On Pakistan:*
    The sort of place everyone should send his mother-in-law for a
    month, all expenses paid.

    BBC Radio 2 interview, March 1984.

BOTTOMLEY, Horatio
British journalist (1860–1933)

4   *When sewing mail-bags in prison and being greeted by a visitor with the
    words, 'Ah, Bottomley, sewing?':*
    No, reaping.

    Attrib

5   If it's in *John Bull*, it is so.

    Saying

BOUGHTON, Rutland
British composer (1878–1960)

6   □ They laugh and are glad . . . are terrible!
    The Immortal Hour (1914)
    The text was by 'Fiona Macleod' (William Sharp).

BOWRA, Sir Maurice
British academic (1898–1971)

7   I am a man more dined against than dining.
    Attrib in J. Betjeman, *Summoned by Bells*

1   *On the wedding of a well-known literary pair in 1956:*
Splendid couple—I should know—slept with both of them.

Attrib

See also **AUDEN 18:8.**

BRADBURY, Malcolm
British novelist (1932–   )

2   The History Man.

Title of novel (1975)

BRADLEY, Omar
US General (1893–1981)

3   *On Gen. MacArthur's proposal to carry the Korean war into China:*
The wrong war, at the wrong place, at the wrong time, and with the wrong enemy.

Senate inquiry, May 1951

BRAINE, John
British novelist (1922–86)

4   Room at the Top.

Title of novel (1957)
Braine re-popularized this phrase. In reply to advice not to become a lawyer because it was an overcrowded profession, Daniel Webster (1782–1852) had replied, 'There is always room at the top.'

BRANDEIS, Louis D.
US jurist (1856–1941)

5   Publicity is justly commended as a remedy for social and industrial diseases. Sunlight is said to be the best of disinfectants; electric light the most efficient policeman.

In *Harper's Weekly*, 20 December 1913

BRANDO, Marlon
US film actor (1924–   )

6   □ An actor's a guy who, if you ain't talking about him, ain't listening.

Quoted in the *Observer*, January 1956
In fact, Brando appears to have been quoting George Glass (1910–84).

BRECHT, Bertholt
German playwright (1898–1956)

7   Mack the Knife. (transl. of 'Mackie Messer')

The Threepenny Opera (1928)

1   Alienation effect ('Verfremsdungseffect').

Concept, first promoted 1937
Theory of drama in which audience has to be reminded that it is
watching a play and nothing real.

BRESSLAW, Bernard
British actor (1933–)

2   Hello, it's me, Twinkletoes.

Catchphrase from radio series, *Educating Archie*, in the 1950s

3   I only arsked!

Catchphrase from TV series, *The Army Game* (1957–62)

BREZHNEV, Leonid
Soviet politician (1906–82)

4   *To President Carter at the signing of the SALT 2 arms limitation treaty:*
God will not forgive us if we fail.

Remark, Vienna, June 1979

5   The trouble with free elections is, you never know who is going to
win.

Attrib

THE BRIDGES AT TOKO-RI
US film 1954. Based on the novel by James Michener. With William Holden.

6   *Holden, as admiral, seeing men off on a mission from which they will not
return in the Korean war:*
Where do we get such men?

Soundtrack
Adapted by Ronald Reagan in 1984 as 'Where do we find such men?'

BRIDSON, D. G.
British radio producer (1910–80)

7   *On disc jockeys:*
The wriggling ponces of the spoken word.

Attrib

BRIEN, Alan
British journalist (1925–)

8   Violence is the repartee of the illiterate.

Article in *Punch*, 7 February 1973

BRITTAIN, Ronald
British Regimental Sergeant-Major (?1899–1981)

1   *Although he denied ever saying it, he was associated with:*
You 'orrible little man!

Attrib in his obituary, *The Times*, 12 January 1981

2   Wake up there!

ibid

'BRITTON, Colonel' (Douglas Ritchie)
British propagandist (1905–67)

3   *To resistance workers in occupied Europe:*
You wear no uniforms and your weapons differ from ours—but they
are not less deadly. The fact that you wear no uniforms is your
strength. The Nazi official and the German soldier don't know you.
But they fear you . . . The night is your friend. The 'V' is your sign.

Radio broadcast, summer of 1941

BROOKE, Rupert
British poet (1887–1915)

4   Unkempt about those hedges blows
An unofficial English rose.

'The Old Vicarage, Grantchester' (1912)

5   For Cambridge people rarely smile,
Being urban, squat, and packed with guile.

ibid

6   Stands the Church clock at ten to three?
And is there honey still for tea?

ibid

7   Now, God be thanked who has matched us with His hour,
And caught our youth, and wakened us from sleeping.
'Peace' (1914)

8   If I should die, think only this of me:
That there's some corner of a foreign field
That is for ever England.
'The Soldier' (1914)

9   A pulse in the eternal mind, no less
Gives somewhere back the thoughts by England given.
Her sights and sounds; dreams happy as her day;
And laughter, learnt of friends; and gentleness,
In hearts at peace, under an English heaven.

ibid

1 These I have loved.
'The Great Lover' (1914)

2 The cool kindliness of sheets, that soon
Smooth away trouble; and the rough male kiss of blankets.
ibid

3 *On Cathleen Nesbitt, the actress:*
Incredibly, inordinately, devastatingly, immortally, calamitously, he hearteningly, adorably beautiful.
Quoted in C. Hassall, *Rupert Brooke*
In a letter to her, responding to criticism that he was 'in love with words'.

BROOKNER, Anita
British novelist (1928–)

4 *On the tortoise and hare myth:*
In real life, of course, it is the hare who wins. Every time. Look around you. And in any case it is my contention that Aesop was writing for the tortoise market . . . Hares have no time to read. They are too busy winning the game.
Hôtel du Lac (1984)

5 I am forty-six, and have been for some years past.
Letter to *The Times*, 1985

BROWN, George (later Lord George-Brown)
British Labour politician (1914–85)

6 *When drunk, to the Apostolic Delegate:*
Lovely creature in scarlet, dance with me!
Attrib

7 Most British statesman have either drunk too much or womanised too much. I never fell into the second category.
Quoted in the *Observer*, 11 November 1974

BROWN, Helen Gurley
US journalist (1922–)

8 Sex and the Single Girl.
Title of book (1962)

9 Good girls go to heaven, bad girls go everywhere.
Promotional line for *Cosmopolitan* magazine
when she relaunched it in 1965.

BROWN, James
US singer/songwriter (1934–)

1 Say It Loud, 'I'm Black and I'm Proud.'
Title of song (1968)

BROWN, Jerry
US Democratic politician (1938–)

2 *Announcing his candidacy for the Democratic nomination:*
We carry in our hearts the true country and that can't be stolen. We follow in the spirit of our ancestors and that cannot be broken.
Speech, 21 October 1991
Quoting the song 'The Dead Heart' (1988), by the Australian rock group Midnight Oil, which has rather 'we follow in the steps of our ancestry . . . '

BROWN, John Mason
US critic (1900–69)

3 *On Tallulah Bankhead as Shakespeare's Cleopatra (in 1937):*
Tallulah Bankhead barged down the Nile last night and sank. As the Serpent of the Nile she proves to be no more dangerous than a garter snake.
Quoted in *Current Biography* (1941)

4 Some television programmes are so much chewing-gum for the eyes.
Interview, 28 July 1955
Quoting a friend of his young son.

BROWNE, Coral
Australian-born actress (1913–91)

5 *To companion when an enormous phallus was revealed as the centrepiece of the National Theatre production of* **Oedipus** *(1968):*
Nobody we know, dear.
Attrib

6 *To a gay actor looking for a part in* **King Lear:**
How about 'A Camp, near Dover'?
Attrib

7 *To Hollywood writer who had criticized the writing of Alan Bennett:*
Listen, dear, you couldn't write fuck on a dusty venetian blind.
Attrib in *Sunday Times Magazine*, 18 November 1984

8 *To friend who spotted her emerging from Brompton Oratory:*
Don't talk to me, dear, I'm in a state of fucking grace.
Attrib

BRUCE, Lenny
US satirist (1923–66)

1   *Leaping out of a second-floor window:*
I'm Super-jew!

Quoted in the *Observer*, 21 August 1966
He only sustained a broken leg.

BUCHAN, John (later Lord Tweedsmuir)
British politician and writer (1875–1940)

2   An atheist is a man who has no invisible means of support.

Attrib

BUCKLE, Richard
British ballet critic (1916–   )

3   *On the Beatles:*
John Lennon, Paul McCartney and George Harrison are the greatest composers since Beethoven, with Paul McCartney way out in front.

Review in the *Sunday Times*, 29 December 1963

BULMER-THOMAS, Ivor
British Labour, then Conservative, MP (1905–   )

4   *On Harold Wilson:*
If ever he went to school without any boots it was because he was too big for them.

Speech, Conservative Party Conference, 12 October 1949
See **WILSON 348:6.** Often wrongly attributed to Harold Macmillan.

BUNUEL, Luis
Spanish film director (1900–83)

5   I am still an atheist, thank God.

In *Le Monde*, 16 December 1959

BURNETT, W. R.
US author (1899–1982)

6   The Asphalt Jungle.

Title of novel (1949)
OED2 finds the phrase in use by 1920, however.

BURNS, George
US comedian (1896–   )

1   *Exchange with wife (Gracie Allen):*
    Burns: Say goodnight, Gracie.
    Allen: Goodnight, Gracie.

   Customary ending of TV series, *The Burns and Allen Show*, 1950s

2   Too bad that all the people who know how to run the country are busy driving taxicabs and cutting hair.

   Attrib remark, by 1977

3   The secret of acting is sincerity. If you can fake that, you've got it made.

   Attrib remark, by 1986

BURNS, John
British Labour politician (1858–1943)

4   I have seen the Mississippi. That is muddy water. I have seen the St Lawrence. That is crystal water. But the Thames is liquid history.

   Quoted in *Daily Mail*, 25 January 1943

BUSH, George
US Republican President (1924–   )

5   Voodoo economics.

   Remark, 1980

6   In deep doodoo.

   Remark, pre-1988
   Meaning, 'in the shit'.

7   My opponent won't rule out raising taxes, but I will. And the Congress will push me to raise taxes, and I'll say no, and they'll push again. And I'll say to them, *read my lips*, no new taxes.

   Speech accepting his party's presidential nomination, New Orleans,
   18 August 1988

8   I will keep America moving forward . . . for a better America, for an endless enduring dream and *a thousand points of light.*

   ibid
   The phrase, much used in his 1988 election campaign, referred to
   examples of individual endeavour and voluntary charity efforts.

1   America is never wholly herself unless she is engaged in high moral purpose. We as a people have such a purpose today. It is to make kinder the face of the nation and gentler the face of the world.

Inaugural speech, 20 January 1989
The 'kinder . . . gentler' theme had also occurred in the previously-quoted speech and during the campaign.

BUTLER, R. A. (later Lord Butler)
British Conservative politician (1902–82)

2   *On Sir Anthony Eden, who had been described as the offspring of a mad baronet and a beautiful woman:*
That's Anthony for you—half mad baronet, half beautiful woman.

Attrib

3   *On Sir Anthony Eden:*
☐ The best Prime Minister we have.

Press Association report, December 1955
At the time of attacks on Eden's performance as Prime Minister, Butler was boarding an aircraft when a reporter asked him, 'Mr Butler, would you say that this is the best Prime Minister we have?' Butler's 'hurried assent' was converted into the above statement. In due course, Butler himself became known as 'the best Prime Minister we *never* had'.

4   I think the Prime Minister has to be a butcher, and know the joints. That is perhaps where I have not been quite competent enough in knowing the ways that you cut up a carcass.

Interviewed on BBC Television, June 1966
Cf. Gladstone: 'The first essential for a Prime Minister is to be a good butcher.'

5   ☐ Politics is the art of the possible.

Butler's memoirs *The Art of the Possible* (1971) caused him to be credited with the origination of this phrase. However, in the preface to the paperback edition he pointed out that it had previously been attributed to Bismarck, Cavour, Pindar and Camus, among others.

BUTLER, Samuel
British writer (1835–1902)

6   *Last words:*
Have you brought the cheque book, Alfred?

Quoted in P. Henderson, *Samuel Butler: The Incarnate Bachelor*
To Alfred Cathie, his servant and friend.

BUTZ, Earl
US politician (1909–   )

1   *On the Pope's attitude to birth control:*
  He no play-a da game. He no make-a da rules!
  Remark, 1974
  A joke of the time. He lost his job as President Ford's Secretary of
  Agriculture after making a similar racist remark.

BYGRAVES, Max
British entertainer (1922–   )

2   Big 'ead.
  Catchphrase from BBC radio series, *Educating Archie*, 1950s

3   A good idea, son!
  Catchphrase in ibid

4   I've arrived and, to prove it, I'm here.
  Catchphrase in ibid

5   □ I wanna tell you a story.
  Catchphrase supplied by Mike Yarwood in impressions of Bygraves and
  taken up by Bygraves.

BY ROCKET TO THE MOON
German film 1928. Directed by Fritz Lang (1890–1976).

6   Five—four—three—two—one.
  Attrib
  Believed to be the origin of the reverse countdown for rocket
  launchings.

CABARET
Stage musical (1968), filmed (1972), with lyrics by Fred Ebb and music by John Kander.

1 Money Makes the World Go Around.
Song, 'Money, Money'

2 Tomorrow Belongs to Me.
Title of song.

3 Life is a cabaret, old chum.
Song, 'Cabaret'

CAGNEY, James
US actor (1899–1986)

4 □ You dirty rat!
The nearest he seems to have got to uttering the phrase with which he is most associated was in the films *Blonde Crazy* (1931) (where he says, 'You dirty, double-crossing rat') and *Taxi* (1931) (where he says, 'You dirty yellow-bellied rat'.)

5 Just don't make me mad, see!
Characteristic expression in gangster role
See also **WHITE HEAT 345:1.**

CAHN, Sammy
US lyricist (1913–93)

6 Love and marriage, love and marriage,
Go together like a horse and carriage.
Song 'Love and Marriage', *Our Town* (1955)

CAINE, Michael
British actor (1933–)

7 Not many people know that.
Characteristic expression, from 1970s onwards
His use of the phrase was revealed by Peter Sellers on the BBC TV chat show *Parkinson* on 28 October 1972.

CALLAGHAN, James (later Lord Callaghan)
British Labour Prime Minister (1912–)

8 □ A lie can be halfway round the world before the truth has got its boots on.
Speech, House of Commons, 1 November 1976
In fact he was misquoting the 19th century Baptist preacher, the Rev C. H. Spurgeon, who said: 'A lie travels round the world while truth is putting on her boots.' 'A lie can travel half way round the world while truth is putting on its shoes' has also been attributed to Mark Twain.

1   A *great debate* on education policy.

After speech, Ruskin College, Oxford, October 1976
In fact, he called for a 'national debate', but it became known as the
'great debate' using an old phrase.

2   Either back us or sack us.

Speech, Labour Party Conference, 5 October 1977

3   *On return from Guadaloupe summit to face widespread strikes:*
□ Crisis? What crisis?

Press conference, London airport, 10 January 1979
In answer to a reporter's question, 'What . . . of the mounting chaos in
the country at the moment?' Callaghan replied: 'I don't think that
other people in the world would share the view that there is mounting
chaos.' *The Sun* (11 January) encapsulated the remark in the given
form and used it as a headline.

CAMPBELL, Mrs Patrick

British actress (1865–1940)

4   *On a homosexual affair between two actors (1901):*
I don't care what people do, as long as they don't do it in the street
and frighten the horses.

Quoted in M. Peters, *The Life of Mrs Pat*

5   *To a man:*
Do you know why God withheld the sense of humour from women?
That we may love you instead of laughing at you.

Quoted in ibid

6   *On marriage:*
The deep, deep peace of the double-bed after the hurly-burly of the
chaise longue.

Quoted in ibid

7   When you were quite a little boy somebody ought to have said
'hush' just once.

Letter to Bernard Shaw, 1 November 1912

8   You are a terrible man, Mr. Shaw. One day you'll eat a beefsteak
and then God help all women.

Quoted in Arnold Bennett, *The Journals* (18 June 1919)

CAPONE, Al

US gangster (1899–1947)

9   I don't even know what street Canada is on.

Attrib

CAPOTE, Truman
US writer (1924–84)

1   *On Jack Kerouac:*
     That's not writing, that's typing.
     Attrib remark, 1959

2   Venice is like eating an entire box of chocolate liqueurs at one go.
     Quoted in the *Observer*, 26 November 1961

CARNEY, Don
US broadcaster (1897–1954)

3   *Thinking he was off the air after a children's radio show:*
     I guess that'll hold the little bastards.
     Attrib

CARNEGIE, Dale
US writer (1888–1955)

4   How to Win Friends and Influence People.
     Title of book (1938)

CARSON, Frank
Ulster comedian (1926–   )

5   It's the way I tell 'em . . . It's a cracker!
     Catchphrases, from 1970s onwards

CARSON, Rachel
US biologist (1907–64)

6   The Silent Spring.
     Title of book (1962)

7   Over increasingly large areas of the United States, spring now comes unheralded by the return of birds, and the early mornings are strangely silent where once they were filled with the beauty of bird song.
     ibid

CARTER, Howard
British archaeologist (1873–1939)

8   *On opening the tomb of Tutankhamun, 1921:*
     As my eyes grew accustomed to the light, details of the room within emerged slowly from the mist, strange animals, statues and gold—everywhere the glint of gold . . . Lord Carnavon, unable to stand the suspense any longer, inquired anxiously, 'Can you see anything?' It was all I could do to get out the words, 'Yes, wonderful things.'
     The Tomb of Tut-ankh-Amen (1933)

CARTER, Jimmy
US Democratic President (1924–   )

1   Why not the best?

Campaign slogan, 1976
From a question posed to Carter by Admiral Hyman Rickover in 1948
as to why Carter had not done his best at Naval Academy.

2   My name is Jimmy Carter and I'm running for President.

Stock phrase during campaign, 1976

3   I've looked on a lot of women with lust. I've committed adultery in
my heart many times. God recognises I will do this and forgives me.

Interview with *Playboy*, November 1976

4   *Of Bert Lance, government official:*
He is competent, honest, trustworthy, a man of integrity. Bert, I'm
proud of you.

Remark, 1977

5   *On a visit to the north-east of England, using trad. Geordie greeting
(meaning 'Come on, lads!'):*
Hawae the lads!

Speech, 1977

6   On a visit to Poland:
□ I desire the Poles carnally.

Quoted in the *Daily Mail*, 29 December 1978
This was the inadequate translation into Polish by an American
interpreter of Carter's 'I have come to learn your opinions and
understand your desires for the future.'

7   *Seeking to evoke the name of Hubert Horatio Humphrey:*
[The] great president who might have been—Hubert Horatio
Hornblower.

Speech accepting re-nomination, Democratic Convention, New York,
15 August 1980

CARTER, Mrs Lillian
US mother of President Carter (1898–1983)

8   Sometimes when I look at my children I say to myself, 'Lillian, you
should have stayed a virgin.'

Remark, 1980

CARTLAND, Barbara (later Dame Barbara)

British romantic novelist (1902–)

1   *When asked by interviewer whether she thought British class barriers had come down:*
Of course they have, or I wouldn't be sitting here talking to someone like you.

Attrib

CARUSO, Enrico

Italian singer (1873–1921)

2   *On watermelon:*
It is a good fruit. You eat, you drink, you wash your face.

Attrib

CASABLANCA

US film 1942. Script by Julius J. Epstein, Philip G. Epstein, Howard Koch, from an unproduced play *Everybody Comes To Rick's* by Murray Burnett and Joan Alison. With Humphrey Bogart as Rick, Ingrid Bergman as Ilsa, Dooley Wilson as Sam and Claude Rains as Capt. Louis Renaud.

3   □ *Rick/Ilsa:* Play it again, Sam.

Not said as such in the film. See following entries.

4   *Ilsa:* Play it once, Sam, for old times' sake.
Sam: I don't know what you mean, Miss Ilsa.
Ilsa: Play it, Sam. Play, 'As Time Goes By.'

Soundtrack

5   *Rick:* Of all the gin joints in all the towns in all the world, she walks into mine!

Soundtrack

6   *Rick:* You played it for her, and you can play it for me.
Sam: Well, I don't think I can remember it.
Rick: If she can stand it, I can. Play it.

Soundtrack

7   *Rick (to Ilsa):* Here's looking at you, kid.

Soundtrack

8   *Rick:* We'll always have Paris.

Soundtrack

9   □ *Rick:* Drop the gun, Louis.

Not spoken in the film but often used by Bogart impersonators. What he says is, 'Not so fast, Louis.'

10 *Rick:* Louis, I think this is the beginning of a beautiful friendship.

Last words of film.

'CASSANDRA' (William Connor)
British journalist (1909–67)

1   *On resuming his column after the Second World War:*
    As I was saying when I was interrupted, it is a powerful hard thing
    to please all the people all the time.

    Daily Mirror, September 1946
    See also **DAILY MIRROR 93:8.**

CASTLE, Ted (later Lord Castle)
British journalist (1907–79)

2   In Place of Strife.

    Title of White Paper on industrial relations legislation (1969)
    He suggested the title of this ill-fated proposal, put forward by his wife,
    Barbara.
    Compare **BEVAN 38:9.**

CASTLING, Harry
British songwriter

3   Let's all go down the Strand—have a banana!

    Song, 'Let's All Go Down the Strand', (1904)
    Written with C. W. Murphy. The words 'Have a banana' were
    interpolated by audiences. Although not part of the original lyrics, the
    words were included in later versions.

CATCHPHRASES
(in alphabetical order)

4   [Got] any gum, chum?

    Child's cry to American GIs in the Second World War.

5   Anyone for tennis?

    Other forms: 'Who's for tennis?', 'Tennis, anyone?' There is no single
    source for this popular phrase, often used to denote the light dramas
    of the 1920s and 30s. An early example of the form can be found in
    Shaw's *Misalliance* (1910).
    See also **BOGART 42:4.**

6   Are there any more at home like you?

    From the song, 'Tell Me, Pretty Maiden' in the musical comedy
    Floradora (written by Leslie Stuart, 1900).

7   Are we downhearted?—No!

    Popular at the start of the First World War, but current before. Also
    incorporated in a song.

8   'Arf a mo, Kaiser!

    Originally a caption on a First World War recruiting poster which
    showed a British 'Tommy' lighting his pipe prior to going into action.

1   Back to square one.

Meaning to go right back to the beginning—possibly derived from
BBC radio football commentators of the 1930s who would describe the
game in relation to a numbered plan of the pitch. Equally, it could
come from a board game like Snakes and Ladders.

2   Boom, boom!

Way of underlining the punchline of a joke, used by Billy Bennett,
Morecambe and Wise, Basil Brush and others.

3   The butler did it!

I.e. as the solution to a 'whodunit'. There is no obvious source for this
expression, though it was in use by 1916.

4   Cowabunga!

From the US film *Teenage Mutant Ninja Turtles* (1990), but known
earlier.

5   Goody, goody, gumdrops.

Phrase used by Humphrey Lestocq as host of children's TV series,
Whirligig, 1950s.

6   Heeeeere's Johnny!

Introduction to Johnny Carson on NBC-TV's *Tonight* show in the US,
from 1961. Spoken by the announcer Ed McMahon.

7   Here we go, here we go, here we go!

Chant beloved of British football fans since 1986—sung to the tune of
Sousa's 'Stars and Stripes for Ever'.

8   Hi-yo, Silver! Away!

Call to horse, by the Lone Ranger on US radio from 1933 and
subsequently in films and TV series.

9   Home, James, and don't spare the horses!

From the title of a song (1934) by Fred Hillebrand, though 'Home,
James!' had existed as such, in Thackeray, for example.

10 Hoots mon, there's a moose loose aboot this house./
    It's a braw bricht moonlicht nicht.

Cod Scotticisms used on the 1958 British hit 'Hoots Mon' (comp.
Robertson), performed by Lord Rockingham's XI.
See also **LAUDER 196:4.**

11 I'm sorry I'll read that again.

Customary BBC radio newsreader's apology for making an error. Also
used as the title of a radio comedy series, from 1964.

1 Is everybody happy?

Customary inquiry addressed to holiday-camp visitors. Also used by Ted Lewis (1892–1971), the 'Top Hatted Tragedian of Jazz' in vaudeville.

2 It's a bird! It's a plane! It's Superman!

Part of introduction to US radio version of the Superman comic strips (from 1940 onwards).

3 [Superman], disguised as Clark Kent, mild-mannered reporter for a great metropolitan newspaper, fights a never-ending battle for truth, justice, and the American way.

ibid

4 I was only obeying orders.

Often used as a defence by those charged with war crimes after the Second World War, this phrase became much parodied in skits thereafter. The defence of 'superior orders' was specifically ruled out by military tribunals, as at Nuremberg 1945–6.

5 Kookie, kookie, lend me your comb.

From the TV series *77 Sunset Strip* (late 1950s/ early 60s), in which 'Kookie' (Edd Byrnes) was always combing his hair. Also featured in a song (1960).

6 Let's get on with it!

Used in the variety act of Nat Mills (1900–) and Bobbie (*d*1955) from the early years of the Second World War onwards.

7 Loadsamoney!

Used by money-worshipping character, portrayed by Harry Enfield, in British TV shows 1987–8.

8 Nanu nanu!

'Goodbye' spoken by Robin Williams as Mork, an alien from Ork, in the US TV series *Mork and Mindy* (1978–81).

9 Nice legs, shame about her face.

From the title of a pop song performed by The Monks in 1979, giving rise to the format, 'Nice ——, shame about the ——.'

10 No comment.

Response to journalistic questioning, probably of American mid-century origin. Winston Churchill appeared only to become aware of it in 1946.

11 [That's the] sixty-four dollar question!

Meaning the question that would solve the problem if only we could answer it. Derived from CBS radio quiz *Take It or Leave It* (1941–8). Later, allowing for inflation, it became the title of TV quizzes, *The $64,000 Question, The $64,000 Challenge*, etc.

1   Some of my best friends are Jews/Jewish.

Possibly originated in untraced cartoon caption from the *New Yorker*, 1930s, but probably of earlier origin.

2   Take me to your leader.

Customary line spoken by Martian invaders, possibly originating in strip cartoons of the 1950s.

3   There's gold in them thar hills.

Possibly this phrase was established (from US gold-mining) by the end of the nineteenth century. It seems to have had a resurgence in the 1930s/40s, possibly through Western films. A Laurel and Hardy short called *Them Thar Hills* appeared in 1934. The melodrama *Gold in the Hills* by J. Frank Davis has been peformed every season since 1936 by the Vicksburg Theatre Guild in Mississippi.

4   This week's deliberate mistake.

A genuine error was covered up by saying this on the BBC radio show *Monday Night at Seven* (*c*1938) and the phrase has also been used in connection with deliberate errors.

5   Up there, Cazaly!

Crowd encouragement to Australian Rules footballer Roy Cazaly (1893–1963).

6   What's up, Doc?

From 'Bugs Bunny' cinema cartoons (1937–63).

7   Who shot J. R.?

Question posed by last episode of TV soap opera *Dallas*, in 1979–80 season, referring to character, J. R. Ewing.

8   Without hesitation, deviation or repetition.

In the radio panel game *Just a Minute* (1967–   ), people have to speak for sixty seconds without . . .

CAULFIELD, Mr Justice (Sir Bernard Caulfield)
British judge (1914–   )

9   Is Jeffrey Archer in need of cold, unloving, rubber-insulated sex? . . . Remember Mary Archer in the witness box. Your vision of her will probably not disappear. Has she elegance? Has she fragrance? Would she have, without the strain of this trial, a radiance?

Summing up, in libel case, 23 July 1987

CAVELL, Edith
British nurse (1865–1915)

1 *'Message to the world', given to Revd Stirling Gahan the day before Cavell was executed by the Germans for 'conducting soldiers to the enemy':*
This I would say, standing as I do in view of God and Eternity: I realize that patriotism is not enough; I must have no hatred and bitterness towards anyone.

11 October 1915

CHAMBERLAIN, Joseph
British Liberal, then Conservative, politician (1836–1914)

2 We are not downhearted. The only trouble is, we cannot understand what is happening to our neighbours.

Speech, 18 January 1906

CHAMBERLAIN, Neville
British Conservative Prime Minister (1869–1940)

3 In war, whichever side may call itself the victor, there are no winners, but all are losers.

Speech, Kettering, 3 July 1938

4 *On Czechoslovakia:*
How terrible, fantastic, incredible it is that we should be digging trenches and trying on gas-masks here because of a quarrel in a faraway country between people of whom we know nothing.

Radio broadcast, 27 September 1938

5 *On returning from signing the Munich agreement:*
This morning I had another talk with the German Chancellor, Herr Hitler, and here is the paper which bears his name upon it as well as mine . . . 'We regard the agreement signed last night—and the Anglo-German Naval Agreement—as symbolic of the desire of our two peoples never to go to war with one another again.'

Speech, Heston airport, 30 September 1938

6 My good friends, this is the second time in our history that there has come back from Germany to Downing Street peace with honour. I believe it is peace for our time. Go home and get a nice quiet sleep.

Remarks to crowd, Downing Street, London, 30 September 1938
He was alluding to Disraeli's 'Peace with honour'. Note, he did not say 'peace *in* our time'.

1   This morning the British Ambassador in Berlin handed the German Government a final note stating that, unless we heard from them by eleven o'clock that they were prepared at once to withdraw their troops from Poland, a state of war would exist between us. I have to tell you that no such undertaking has been received, and that consequently this country is at war with Germany.

Radio broadcast from Downing Street, London, 3 September 1939

2   Whatever may be the reason, whether it was that Hitler thought he might get away with what he had got without fighting for it, or whether it was that, after all, the preparations are not sufficiently complete, one thing is certain—he missed the bus.

Speech to Conservative Central Council, 5 April 1940

CHAMBERLAIN, Office of the Lord
British theatre censor until 1968

3   *Alterations ordered to script of **The Bed-Sitting Room** (by John Antrobus and Spike Milligan)(1963):*
Omit 'You get all the dirt off the tail of your shirt.' Substitute 'You get all the dirt off the front of your shirt . . .' Omit the song 'Plastic Mac Man' and substitute 'Oh you dirty young devil, how dare you presume to wet the bed when the po's in the room. I'll wallop your bum with a dirty great broom when I get up in the morning.'

Quoted in K. Tynan, *Tynan Right and Left*

CHANDLER, Raymond
US novelist (1888–1959)

4   The Big Sleep.

Title of novel (1939)
A synonym for death.

5   It was a blonde. A blonde to make a bishop kick a hole in a stained-glass window.

Farewell, My Lovely (1940)

6   She gave me a smile I could feel in my hip pocket.

ibid

7   [Hollywood] is a big hard-boiled city with no more personality than a paper cup.

The Little Sister (1949)

8   Down these mean streets a man must go who is not himself mean.

'The Simple Art of Murder', *Pearls Are a Nuisance* (1950)

CHAPLIN, Charles (later Sir Charles)
British-born film comedian (1889–1977)

1   All I need to make a comedy is a park, a policeman and a pretty girl.

    My Autobiography (1964)

CHAPMAN, F. Spencer
British soldier and writer (1907–71)

2   The Jungle is Neutral.

    Title of book, 1949

CHARLES (HRH the Prince of Wales)
Heir to the British throne (1948–)

3   The one advantage about marrying a princess—or someone from a royal family—is that they do know what happens.

    Attrib

4   I have fallen in love with all sorts of girls and I fully intend to go on doing so.

    Quoted in the *Observer*, 21 December 1975

5   *When asked if he was 'in love' upon getting engaged:*
    Yes . . . whatever that may mean.

    TV news interview, February 1981

6   *On a proposed extension to the National Gallery, London:*
    A kind of vast municipal fire station . . . I would understand better this type of high-tech approach if you demolished the whole of Trafalgar Square, but what is proposed is like a monstrous carbuncle on the face of a much-loved and elegant friend.

    Speech to the RIBA, 30 May 1984

7   *Of a planned Mies van der Rohe office building in the City of London:*
    A glass stump.

    ibid

8   I just come and talk to the plants, really—very important to talk to them, they respond I find.

    TV interview, 21 September 1986

9   You have to give this much to the Luftwaffe—when it knocked down our buildings it didn't replace them with anything more offensive than rubble. We did that.

    Speech to Corporation of London Planning and Communications Committee, 2 December 1987

1   Look at the National Theatre! It seems like a clever way of building a nuclear power station in the middle of London without anyone objecting.

TV film, *A Vision of Britain*, October 1988

CHARLIE BUBBLES

UK film 1968. Script by Shelagh Delaney. With Albert Finney as Charlie and Joe Gladwin as the waiter.

2   *Waiter:* Do you just do your writing now—or are you still working? *Charlie:* No . . . I just do the writing.

Soundtrack

CHASEN, Dave

US restaurateur (1899–1973)

3   Bogart's a helluva nice guy till 11.30 p.m. After that he thinks he's Bogart.

Quoted in L. Halliwell, *The Filmgoer's Book of Quotes*

CHEKHOV, Anton

Russian playwright (1860–1904)

4   *Irena:* If only we could go back to Moscow.

The Three Sisters (1901)

5   A distant sound is heard, coming out of the sky, like the sound of a string snapping, slowly and sadly dying. Silence ensues, broken only by the sound of an axe striking a tree in the orchard far away.

Stage direction at end of *The Cherry Orchard* (1903).

CHESTER, Charlie

British comedian (1914–   )

6   Don't force it, Phoebe.

Catchphrase, BBC radio series *Stand Easy*, 1940s

7   Down in the jungle,
     Living in a tent,
     Better than a pre-fab
     —No rent.

Chant from ibid

8   I say, what a smasher.

Catchphrase from ibid

9   Come to Charlie-ee!

Catchphrase, various BBC radio shows, 1950s

CHESTERTON, G. K.
British writer (1874–1936)

1 'My country, right or wrong' is a thing no patriot would ever think of saying except in a desperate case. It is like saying, 'My mother, drunk or sober.'
The Defendant (1901)

2 *Telegram to wife:*
Am in Market Harborough. Where ought I to be?
Quoted in M. Ward, *Return to Chesterton*
Other venues have been suggested, but this was the original and is
confirmed by his *Autobiography* (1936).

3 The human race, to which so many of my readers belong, has been playing at children's games from the beginning, and will probably do it till the end, which is a nuisance for the few people who grow up.
The Napoleon of Notting Hill (1904)
Opening words.

4 Individually, men may present a more or less rational appearance, eating, sleeping and scheming. But humanity as a whole is changeful, mystical, fickle and delightful. Men are men, but Man is a woman.
ibid

5 Mr [Bernard] Shaw is (I suspect) the only man on earth who has never written any poetry.
Orthodoxy (1908)

6 Thieves respect property; they merely wish the property to become their property that they may more perfectly respect it.
The Man Who Was Thursday (1908)

7 If a thing is worth doing it is worth doing badly.
'Folly and Female Education', *What's Wrong with the World* (1910)

8 Are they clinging to their crosses,
F. E. Smith?
Antichrist, or the Reunion of Christendom (1912)

9 Talk about the pews and steeples
    And the cash that goes therewith!
But the souls of Christian peoples . . .
    Chuck it, Smith!
ibid
Satirizing the pontificating of F. E. Smith on the Welsh
Disestablishment Bill.

1   Before the Roman came to Rye or out to Severn strode,
The rolling English drunkard made the rolling English road.

The Flying Inn (1914), 'The Rolling English Road'

2   For there is good news yet to hear and fine things to be seen,
Before we go to Paradise by way of Kensal Green.

ibid

3   The only way of catching a train I ever discovered is to miss the train before.

Attrib

4   Journalism largely consists in saying 'Lord Jones Dead' to people who never knew Lord Jones was alive.'

'The Purple Wig', *The Wisdom of Father Brown* (1914)

5   It is the test of a good religion whether you can joke about it.

Attrib

CHEVALIER, Maurice
French entertainer (1888–1972)

6   I prefer old age to the alternative.

Remark, 1960
Or 'Old age isn't so bad when you consider the alternative.'

CHILDERS, Erskine
British-born author and Irish patriot (1870–1922)

7   *Last words before being executed by firing squad, 24 November 1922:*
Take a step forward, lads. It will be easier that way.

Quoted in A. Boyle, *The Riddle of Erskine Childers*

CHRISTIE, Agatha (later Dame Agatha)
British detective novelist (1890–1976)

8   [Hercule Poirot] tapped his forehead. 'These little gray cells, It is "up to them"—as you say over here.'

The Mysterious Affair at Styles (1920)

9   I believe that a well-known anecdote exists to the effect that a young writer, determined to make the commencement of his story forcible and original enough to catch the attention of the most blasé of editors, penned the first sentence:
    '"Hell!" said the Duchess.'

The Murder on the Links (1923)

1   □ An archaeologist is the best husband any woman can have; the older she gets, the more interested he is in her.

News report, 8 March 1954, also quoted in the *Observer*, 2 January 1955
She denied having said it.

CHURCHILL, Caryl
British playwright (1938–   )

2   Serious Money.

Title of play (1987)

3   Sexy greedy *is* the late eighties.

In ibid

4   *On newspaper scandal in the age of AIDS:*
The more you don't do it, the more it's fun to read about.

ibid

CHURCHILL, Randolph
British politician and journalist (1911–68)

5   *While reading the Bible from cover to cover in response to a bet:*
Isn't God a shit.

Quoted in E. Waugh, *Diaries* (entry for 11 November 1944)

6   *During papal audience:*
I expect you know my friend, Evelyn Waugh, who, like you, your holiness, is a Roman Catholic.

Attrib

7   *In a letter to a hostess whose dinner party he had ruined with one of his displays of drunken rudeness:*
I should never be allowed out in private.

Quoted in B. Roberts, *Randolph*
See also **THE TIMES 328:1.**

CHURCHILL, Winston (later Sir Winston)
British Conservative Prime Minister (1874–1965)

8   *In response to the charge that the Government had brought the reputation of the country into contempt by describing the employment of Chinese indentured labour in South Africa as 'slavery':*
It cannot in the opinion of His Majesty's Government be classified as slavery in the extreme acceptance of the word without some risk of terminological inexactitude.

Speech, House of Commons, 22 February 1906
As a result, the phrase 'terminological inexactitude' is sometimes inaccurately used as a way of saying 'lie'.

1   *To Lady Astor who had said, 'If you were my husband, I'd poison your coffee',* c*1912:*
    If you were my wife, I'd drink it.

    Quoted in E. Langhorne, *Nancy Astor and Her Friends*

2   *In response to Bernard Shaw's offer of tickets for the first night of* **St Joan** *'for yourself and a friend, if you have one', Churchill expressed regret at being unable to attend and asked for tickets on the second night:*
    If there is one.

    Attrib

3   It is a good thing for an uneducated man to read books of quotations.

    My Early Life (1930)

4   *On Ramsay MacDonald:*
    [At Barnum's Circus] the exhibit on the programme I most desired to see was the one described as the Boneless Wonder. My parents judged that the spectacle would be too revolting and demoralizing for my youthful eyes, and I have waited fifty years to see the boneless wonder sitting on the Treasury bench.

    Speech, House of Commons, 28 January 1931

5   *When Gandhi was released from gaol to take part in a Round Table conference:*
    [It is] alarming and also nauseating to see Mr Gandhi, a seditious Middle Temple lawyer, now posing as a fakir of a type well-known in the East, striding half-naked up the steps of the vice-regal palace.

    Speech, Epping, 23 February 1931

6   *To A. P. Herbert, 1935:*
    Call that a maiden speech? I call it a brazen hussy of a speech.

    Quoted in L. Frewin, *Immortal Jester*

7   *On being asked by Somerset Maugham if he had ever had homosexual affairs:*
    Churchill: I once went to bed with a man to see what it was like.
    Maugham: Who was it?
    Churchill: Ivor Novello.
    Maugham: And what was it like?
    Churchill: Musical . . .

    Quoted in E. Morgan, *Somerset Maugham*
    (And, surely, of dubious veracity.)

8   I cannot forecast to you the action of Russia. It is a riddle wrapped in a mystery inside an enigma.

    Broadcast, 1 October 1939

1   *On becoming Prime Minister:*
     I would say to the House, as I said to those who have joined this
     Government: I have nothing to offer but blood, toil, tears and
     sweat.

     Speech, House of Commons, 13 May 1940

2   You ask, what is our aim? I can answer in one word: victory, victory
     at all costs, victory in spite of all terror, victory, however long and
     hard the road may be.

     ibid
     Compare **CLEMENCEAU 80:4.**

3   Come then, let us go forward together, with our united strength.

     ibid

4   *After the evacuation of Allied troops from Dunkirk:*
     We shall fight on the beaches, we shall fight on the landing
     grounds, we shall fight in the fields and in the streets, we shall fight
     in the hills; we shall never surrender.

     Speech, House of Commons, 4 June 1940

5   If we can stand up to [Hitler], all Europe may be free and the life
     of the world may move forward into broad, sunlit uplands.

     Speech, House of Commons, 18 June 1940
     'Broad, sunlit uplands' was an image often invoked by Churchill.

6   Let us therefore brace ourselves to our duties, and so bear ourselves
     that, if the British Empire and its Commonwealth last for a
     thousand years, men will say, This was their finest hour.

     ibid

7   *Instruction on the establishment of the Special Operations Executive to co-*
     ordinate acts of subversion against enemies overseas:
     Set Europe ablaze.

     Attrib, July 1940

8   *On RAF pilots in the Battle of Britain:*
     Never in the field of human conflict was so much owed by so many
     to so few.

     Speech, House of Commons, 20 August 1940

9   *On co-operation with the US:*
     Like the Mississippi, it just keeps rolling along. Let it roll. Let it roll
     on full flood, inexorable, irresistible, benignant, to broader lands
     and better days.

     ibid
     Alluding to **HAMMERSTEIN 150:6.**

1 *Français, c'est moi—Churchill—qui vous parle* ('French people, it is I—Churchill—who speaks to you').

Broadcast, London, 21 October 1940

2 *On 'crossing the floor' of the House of Commons more than once:*
They say you can rat, but you can't re-rat.

Reported in J. Colville, *The Fringes of Power*, Vol.1 (entry for 26 January 1941)

The remark may date from 1923/4 when Churchill rejoined the Conservatives, having earlier left them to join the Liberals.

3 Here is the answer which I will give to President Roosevelt . . . Give us the tools, and we will finish the job.

Broadcast, 9 February 1941

4 We must just KBO. ('Keep Buggering On'.)

Remark, December 1941, quoted in M. Gilbert, *Finest Hour*

5 What kind of people do they [the Japanese] think we are?

Speech to US Congress, 26 December 1941

6 When I warned [the French] that Britain would fight on alone . . . their General [Weygand] told their Prime Minister . . . in three weeks England will have her neck wrung like a chicken—some chicken, some neck.

Speech, Canadian Parliament, 30 December 1941

7 *On Charles de Gaulle:*
[He is] like a female llama surprised in her bath.

Attrib

He denied that he had ever said this.

8 *On Charles de Gaulle:*
□ The Cross of Lorraine is the heaviest cross I have had to bear.

Attrib

Churchill told Alexander Korda in 1948 that he had never said this.

9 I have not become the King's First Minister in order to preside over the liquidation of the British Empire.

Speech, Mansion House, London, 10 November 1942

10 Now this is not the end. It is not even the beginning of the end. But it is, perhaps, the end of the beginning.

ibid

11 This is your victory.

Speech to crowds, London, 8 May 1945

1   No socialist Government conducting the entire life and industry of the country could afford to allow free, sharp, or violently-worded expressions of public discontent. They would have to fall back on some form of Gestapo.

Party political radio broadcast, 4 June 1945

2   *On his defeat in the 1945 General Election, to his wife who had told him it might be a blessing in disguise:*
At the moment it seems quite effectively disguised.

Quoted in *The Second World War*, Vol. 6 (1954)

3   *On Soviet influence in post-war Europe:*
From Stettin in the Baltic to Trieste in the Adriatic, an iron curtain has descended across the Continent.

Speech, Fulton, Miss., 5 March 1946
The phrase 'iron curtain' in this context dates back to the 1920s and Churchill had already used it in telegrams to President Truman and in the House of Commons.

4   Neither the sure prevention of war, nor the continuous rise of world organization will be gained without what I have called the fraternal association of the English-speaking peoples. This means a special relationship between the British Commonwealth and Empire and the United States.

ibid

5   *When a proud mother said her baby looked like him:*
Madam, all babies look like me.

Attrib

6   One is a majority.

Attrib
On winning a parliamentary vote by only that amount, but quoting Disraeli.

7   *To Bessie Braddock MP who told him he was drunk:*
And you, madam, are ugly. But I shall be sober in the morning.

Attrib

8   *On Air Vice-Marshal Bennett who had joined the Liberals:*
It [is] the first time that [I have] heard of a rat actually swimming out to join a sinking ship.

Quoted in M. Muggeridge, *Like It Was* (diary entry for 14 February 1948)

1 *On Clement Attlee:*
☐ A sheep in sheep's clothing.

Attrib

Churchill told Sir Denis Brogan that he had said it not about Attlee but
about Ramsay MacDonald (perhaps echoing a 'Beachcomber'
remark.) Sir Edmund Gosse (*d*1928) is supposed to have said the same
of T. Sturge Moore.

2 *On Clement Attlee:*
☐ An empty taxi arrived at 10 Downing Street, and when the door
was opened Attlee got out.

Attrib

Churchill told John Colville he would never have made such a remark
about Attlee.

3 *On why Clement Attlee had not been to Moscow:*
He dare not absent himself from his Cabinet at home. He knows
full well that when the mouse is away the cats will play.

Quoted in H. Nicolson, *Diaries* (12 December 1946)

4 *On Sir Stafford Cripps:*
There, but for the grace of God goes God.

Attrib

5 *On Sir Alfred Bossom MP:*
Bossom? What an extraordinary name. Neither one thing nor the
other!

Quoted in L. Frewin, *Immortal Jester*

6 Do not criticize your government when out of the country. Never
cease to do so when at home.

Attrib

7 *On Ian Mikardo MP:*
He's not as nice as he looks.
Attrib

8 *On a long-winded memorandum by Sir Anthony Eden:*
☐ As far as I can see, you have used every cliché except 'God is love'
and 'Please adjust your dress before leaving.'

Quoted in M. Edelman, *The Mirror: A Political History*
Churchill commented: 'This offensive story is wholly devoid of
foundation.'

9 *Marginal comment on document:*
This is the sort of English up with which I will not put.

Quoted in Sir E. Gowers, *Plain Words*

1   In war, resolution; in defeat, defiance; in victory, magnanimity; in peace, goodwill.

'Moral of the Work', *The Second World War*, Vol. 1 (1948)
Originally devised as an inscription for a monument in France, but rejected.

2   *On becoming Prime Minister in 1939:*
I felt as if I were walking with destiny, and that all my past life had been but a preparation for this hour and this trial.

ibid

3   ***Quand je regarde mon derrière, je vois qu'il est divisé en deux parties.***
Attrib
What Churchill meant by *'mon derrière'* was not his backside but his past.

4   *On being asked what he would do if he saw Picasso walking ahead of him down Piccadilly:*
I would kick him up the arse, Alfred.

Quoted by Sir Alfred Munnings in speech at Royal Academy dinner, 1949
Munnings actually used the euphemism 'kick him up the something-something'.

5   *On his 75th birthday:*
I am ready to meet my Maker. Whether my Maker is ready for the ordeal of meeting me is another matter.

Speech, 30 November 1949

6   It is not easy to see how things could be worsened by a parley at the summit, if such a thing were possible.

Quoted in *The Times*, 15 February 1950
This was apparently the genesis of the phrase 'summit meeting/conference'.

7   *When someone said that Stanley Baldwin 'might as well be dead':*
Not dead . . . but the candle in that great turnip has gone out.

Quoted in H. Nicolson, *Diaries* (17 August 1950)

8   *On plans for commercial television in Britain:*
Why do we need this peep-show?

Attrib remark, *c*1951
Alternatively, ' . . . tuppenny Punch and Judy show'.

9   *To Stalin:*
In wartime, truth is so precious that she should always be attended by a bodyguard of lies.

Recounted in *The Second World War*, Vol. 5 (1952)

1   Here at the summit of our worldwide community is a lady whom we respect because she is our Queen, and whom we love because she is herself.

Broadcast, 2 June 1953

2   *On Field Marshal Montgomery:*
In defeat unbeatable; in victory unbearable.

Quoted in E. Marsh, *Ambrosia and Small Beer*

3   Talking jaw to jaw is better than going to war.

At White House lunch, 26 June 1954

4   *When, as an old man, a colleague told him his fly-buttons were undone:*
Dead birds don't fall out of nests.

Attrib
Also alluded to in *The Lyttelton Hart-Davis Letters*, Vol. 2 (for 1957).

5   *On his 80th birthday:*
I have never accepted what many people have kindly said, namely that I inspired the nation. It was the nation and the race dwelling all round the globe that had the lion heart. I had the luck to be called upon to give the roar.

Speech, Westminster Hall, 30 November 1954

6   *On being presented with his portrait painted by Graham Sutherland:*
The portrait is a remarkable example of modern art. It certainly combines force and candour. These are qualities which no active member of either house can do without or should fear to meet.

ibid
Churchill and especially his wife so disliked the portrait that she had it destroyed.

7   *On the same portrait:*
I look as if I was having a difficult stool.

Remark, quoted in E. Morgan, *Somerset Maugham*

8   I am not a pillar of the church but a buttress—I support it from the outside.

Recounted in M. Gilbert, *Never Despair* (1988)

9   *Last words:*
I'm so bored with it all.

Quoted in Mary Soames, *Clementine*
See also **BERNERS 37:3; BEVAN 39:2; GOLDWYN 140:5; HEALEY 157:3; KENNEDY 184:8; MURROW 236:6.**

CIANO, Count Galeazzo
Italian politician (1903–44)

1 As always, victory finds a hundred fathers, but defeat is an orphan.

Diary entry for 9 September 1942 (pub. 1946)

CITIZEN KANE
US film 1941. Script by Herman J. Mankiewicz and Orson Welles. With Orson Welles as Kane, Dorothy Comingore as Susan and George Couloris as Thatcher.

2 *Kane:* Rosebud!

Soundtrack
His last word, the first word in the film, and referred to *passim.*

3 *Thatcher (quoting Kane):* I think it would be fun to run a newspaper.

Soundtrack

4 *Kane:* I've talked to the responsible leaders of the Great Powers—England, France, Germany, and Italy. They're too intelligent to embark on a project which would mean the end of civilization as we now know it. You can take my word for it: there'll be no war!

Soundtrack
A good example of the Hollywood cliché, 'The end of civilization &c' in use.

5 *Kane, replying to a war correspondent's message, 'Could send you prose poems about scenery but . . . there is no war in Cuba':*
Dear Wheeler, you provide the prose poems. I'll provide the war.

Soundtrack
This is based on an 1898 exchange between the newspaper artist Frederic Remington and his proprietor, William Randolph Hearst. Remington asked to be allowed home from Cuba because there was no war for him to cover. Hearst cabled: 'Please remain. You furnish the pictures and I will furnish the war.'

6 *Susan:* I'm the one who has to do the singing. I'm the one who gets the raspberries.

Soundtrack

CLARK, Brian
British playwright (1932–)

7 Whose Life Is It Anyway?

Title of play (1978)

8 Don't half-quote me to reinforce your own prejudices.

Kipling (1984)

CLARK, Kenneth (later Lord Clark)
British art critic (1903–83)

1   What could be more agreeable?

   Remark attrib by *Private Eye* following TV series, *Civilisation* (1969)

2   One may be optimistic, but one can't exactly be joyful at the prospect before us.

   The end of *Civilisation*

CLEMENCEAU, Georges
French politician (1841–1929)

3   War is too serious a business to be left to the generals.

   Attrib
   One of his most famous observations (possibly dating from the last century.) Others have said similar things.
   See **BENN 32:7, DE GAULLE 97:6** *and* **MACLEOD 213:2.**

4   My home policy? I wage war. My foreign policy? I wage war. Always, everywhere, I wage war.

   Speech to the Chamber of Deputies, 8 March 1918

5   *To General Mordacq, 11 November 1918:*
   We have won the war: now we have to win the peace, and it may be more difficult.

   Quoted in D. R. Watson, *Clemenceau*

6   *On President Wilson's Fourteen Points (1918):*
   The good Lord has only ten.

   Attrib

7   *On David Lloyd George:*
   Ah, si je pouvais pisser comme il parle! ('If I could piss the way he speaks!')

   Attrib

8   America is the only country in history which miraculously has gone directly from barbarism to degeneration without the usual interval of civilization.

   Attrib, by 1945

THE COCOANUTS
US film 1929. Written by George S. Kaufman and Morrie Ryskind. With the Marx Brothers.

9   *Groucho:* Believe me, you have to get up early if you want to get out of bed.

   Soundtrack

COGGAN, Most Revd Donald (later Lord Coggan)
British Archbishop of Canterbury (1909–)

1   We listened to these words of Jesus [St Matthew 7:24] a few moments ago. How right he was!

Sermon, St Paul's Cathedral, London, 7 June 1977
At Queen Elizabeth II's Silver Jubilee.

COHAN, George M.
US songwriter and entertainer (1878–1942)

2   The Yanks are coming
And we won't come back till it's over
Over there!

Song, 'Over There' (1917)
Referring to the war in Europe.

3   I don't care what you say about me, as long as you say *something* about me, and as long as you spell my name right.

Quoted in J. McCabe, *George M. Cohan*

COHEN, Sir Jack
British supermarket trader (1898–1979)

4   Pile it high, sell it cheap.

Business motto

COLLINS, Norman
British broadcasting executive and novelist (1907–82)

5   London Belongs To Me.

Title of novel (1945)

6   Steam radio.

Coinage attrib by A. Briggs, *History of Broadcasting in the United Kingdom*, Vol. III

COLSON, Charles
US Watergate conspirator (1931–)

7   *To campaign staff, 1972:*
I would walk over my grandmother if necessary to get Nixon re-elected!

Recounted in *Born Again* (1976)

COMPTON-BURNETT, Ivy (later Dame Ivy)
British novelist (1884–1969)

8   *On a certain woman's age:*
Pushing forty? She's clinging on to it for dear life.

Attrib

CONABLE, Barber B., Jr
US Republican politician and banker (1922–   )

1   *Concerning a tape of President Nixon discussing (23 June 1972) how the FBI's investigation of the Watergate burglary could be limited:*
I guess we have found the smoking pistol, haven't we?
Remark, 1974
The term 'smoking gun' was also used in this connection.

CONN, Irving and SILVER, Frank
US songwriters (1898–1961) (1892–1960)

2   Yes, we have no bananas,
We have no bananas today.
Song 'Yes, We Have No Bananas' (1923)
The line came from a cartoon strip by Tad Dorgan and not, as the composers claimed, from a Greek fruit-store owner.

CONNOLLY, Cyril
British writer and critic (1903–74)

3   *On Sir Alec Douglas-Home at Eton:*
In the eighteenth century he would have become Prime Minister before he was thirty; as it was he appeared honourably ineligible for the struggle of life.
Enemies of Promise (1938)

4   Imprisoned in every fat man a thin one is wildly signalling to be let out.
The Unquiet Grave (1944)
See also **ORWELL 245:2.**

5   Whom the gods wish to destroy they first call promising.
ibid

6   The particular charm of marriage is the duologue, the permanent conversation between two people who talk over everything and everyone till death breaks the record. It is this back-chat which, in the long run, makes a reciprocal equality more intoxicating than any form of servitude or domination.
ibid

7   It is closing time in the gardens of the West and from now on an artist will be judged only by the resonance of his solitude or the quality of his despair.
In the final issue of *Horizon* magazine (1949)

1   *On V. Sackville-West:*
    She looked like Lady Chatterley above the waist and the gamekeeper below.
    Attrib

2   *On George Orwell:*
    He would not blow his nose without moralizing on conditions in the handkerchief industry.
    The Evening Colonnade (1973)

CONRAD, Joseph
Polish-born novelist (1857–1924)

3   The Heart of Darkness.
    Title of novel (1902)

4   The horror! The horror!
    ibid

5   Mistah Kurtz—he dead.
    ibid

6   I have lived, obscure, among the terrors and wonders of my time.
    Attrib

CONRAN, Shirley
British writer (1932–   )

7   Life is too short to stuff a mushroom.
    Epigraph, *Superwoman* (1975)

COOK, A. J.
British miners' leader (1885–1931)

8   Not a penny off the pay, not a minute on the day.
    Slogan prior to General Strike, 1926

COOK, Peter
British humorist (1937–   )

9   *Impersonating Harold Macmillan:*
    We exchanged many frank words in our respective languages.
    'T.V.P.M.', *Beyond the Fringe* (1961)

10 Yes, I could have been a judge but I never had the Latin, never had the Latin for the judging.
    'Sitting on the bench' in ibid

1   You know, I go to the theatre to be entertained . . . I don't want to see plays about rape, sodomy and drug addiction . . . I can get all that at home.

Cartoon caption in the *Observer*, 8 July 1962

2   *On the British satire boom of the early 1960s:*
[Britain must be] about to sink sniggering beneath the watery main.

Attrib 1962/3

3   Spotty Muldoon, Spotty Muldoon
He's got spots all over his face.
Spotty Muldoon, Spotty Muldoon,
He's got spots all over the place.

Song, 'The Ballad of Spotty Muldoon' (1965)

4   *On being told that the person sitting next to him at a dinner party was 'writing a book':*
Neither am I.

Attrib in 1984

COOL HAND LUKE

US film 1967. Script by Donn Pearce and Frank Pierson. With Strother Martin as Captain and Paul Newman as Luke.

5   *Captain to Luke:*
What we've got here is failure to communicate. Some men you just can't reach.

Soundtrack

COOLIDGE, Calvin

US Republican President (1872–1933)

6   *To the President of the American Federation of Labour:*
There is no right to strike against the public safety by anybody, anywhere, at any time.

Telegram, 14 September 1919
Coolidge was Governor of Massachussetts during the Boston police strike.

7   *On being asked to elaborate on a clergyman's sermon about sin:*
□ He was against it.

Attrib
A popular story from the 1920s—Coolidge denied it.

8   *Discussing the cancellation of the Allies' war debt, 1925:*
They hired the money, didn't they?

Attrib

1   The chief business of the American people is business.
     Speech to newspaper editors, 17 January 1925

2   I do not choose to run for President in 1928.
     Statement to newsmen, 2 August 1927

3   *When a girl told him her father had bet her she could not get more than two words out of Coolidge:*
     Poppa wins.
     Attrib

4   *When a woman said 'I could give you tit for tat any time':*
     Tat!
     Attrib

COREN, Alan
British writer (1938–)

5   *Of Salisbury, Southern Rhodesia:*
     A suburb without an urb.
     Quoted in the *Sunday Times Magazine*, 27 November 1977

6   Television is more interesting than people. If it were not, we should have people standing in the corners of our rooms.
     Attrib

CORNFORD, Frances
British poet (1886–1960)

7   A young Apollo, golden-haired,
     Stands dreaming on the verge of strife,
     Magnificently unprepared
     For the long littleness of life.
     Poems, 'Youth' (1910)
     Of Rupert Brooke.

8   O why do you walk through the fields in gloves,
     Missing so much and so much?
     O fat white woman whom nobody loves.
     'To a Fat Lady Seen from a Train' in ibid

COSTELLO, Lou
US comedian (1906–59)

9   I'm a ba-a-a-a-d boy.
     Catchphrase in films with Bud Abbott, from 1930s onwards

COTTON, Billy
British band leader (1900–69)

1   Wakey-wakey!

Catchphrase in broadcasts, from 1949 onwards

COUE, Emile
French psychologist (1857–1926)

2   Every day and in every way I am getting better and better (*'Tous les jours, à tous les points de vue, je vais de mieux en mieux'*).

Phrase for repeating, 1915
Part of his system of 'Self-Mastery Through Conscious Auto-Suggestion' or 'Couéism'.

COWARD, Noël (later Sir Noël)
British entertainer and writer (1899–1973)

3   *To Lady Diana Cooper who told him she had not laughed once at his comedy **The Young Idea**:*
How strange, when I saw you acting in *The Glorious Adventure* [a film about the Great Fire of London], I laughed all the time!

Quoted in *The Noël Coward Diaries* (note to 13 March 1946)
This is the original form of a much-told put-down.

4   *Requirements for acting:*
Just know your lines and don't bump into the furniture.

Attrib
Also attrib to Spencer Tracy.

5   I was photographed and interviewed and photographed again. In the street. In the park. In my dressing-room. At my piano. With my dear old mother. Without my dear old mother and on one occasion sitting up in an over-elaborate bed looking like a heavily-doped Chinese illusionist.

Quoted in D. Richards, *The Wit of Noël Coward*

6   Poor Little Rich Girl.

Title of song, *Charlot's Revue* (1926)
The phrase had been used for a Mary Pickford film in 1917, re-made in 1936.

7   A room with a view—and you
      And no one to worry us
   No one to hurry us.

Song, *This Year of Grace* (1928)

8   I'll see you again,
   Whenever spring breaks through again.

Song, *Bittersweet* (1929)

1   *In response to telegram from Gertrude Lawrence saying 'Nothing wrong that can't be fixed', concerning her part in **Private Lives:***
    Nothing to be fixed except your performance.
    Quoted in *Noël Coward and his Friends*

2   Very flat, Norfolk.
    Private Lives (1930)

3   Certain women should be struck regularly like gongs.
    ibid

4   Moonlight can be cruelly deceptive.
    ibid

5   You are looking very lovely in this damned moonlight, Amanda.
    ibid

6   Strange how potent cheap music is.
    ibid
    Some texts of the play employ 'extraordinary' instead of 'strange' but this is what Gertrude Lawrence says on the record she made with Coward in 1930.

7   Let's drink to the hope that one day this country of ours, which we love so much, will find dignity and greatness and peace again.
    The toast from *Cavalcade* (1931)
    See also **THATCHER 320:3.**

8   Twentieth Century Blues.
    Title of song in ibid

9   In spite of the troublous times we are living in, it is still pretty exciting to be English.
    His curtain speech at the first night of *Cavalcade*, Drury Lane Theatre, London, 1931

10 *Writing to T. E. Lawrence in the RAF:*
    Dear 338171 (May I call you 338?)
    Included in *Letters to T. E. Lawrence*

11 Mad dogs and Englishmen go out in the midday sun.
    Song, 'Mad Dogs and Englishmen', *Words and Music* (1932)

12 The Party's Over Now.
    Title of song in ibid
    'The Party's Over' was later (1956) the title of a song by Betty Comden and Adolph Green, to music by Jule Styne.

1   Mad about the Boy.

Title of song in ibid

2   I believe that since my life began
The most I've had is just
A talent to amuse.

Song, 'If Love Were All', *Bitter Sweet* (1932)

3   Don't put your daughter on the stage, Mrs Worthington.

Song, 'Mrs Worthington' (1935)

4   *On Randolph Churchill:*
Dear Randolph, utterly unspoiled by failure.

Attrib

5   The Stately Homes of England
How beautiful they stand,
To prove the upper classes
Have still the upper hand.

Song, 'The Stately Homes of England', *Operette* (1938)
Based on a song by Felicia Dorothea Hemans (*d*1835).

6   *Telegram to Gertrude Lawrence on her marriage to Richard S. Aldrich:*
Dear Mrs A., hooray hooray,
At last you are deflowered
On this as every other day
I love you. Noël Coward.

Attrib

7   Don't Let's Be Beastly to the Germans,

Title of song (1943)

8   Chase me, Charlie.

Title of song, *Ace of Clubs* (1950)

9   *On an American production of **The Cherry Orchard** set in the Deep South:*
A Month in the Wrong Country.

Diaries (4 September 1950)

10   *Watching the 1953 Coronation on TV, Coward was asked who the man
was riding in a carriage with the portly Queen of Tonga:*
Her lunch.

Attrib

11   *On the musical **Camelot:***
It's like *Parsifal* without the jokes.

Attrib

1   *On being told that a certain person had just blown his brains out:*
He must have been an incredibly good shot.
Quoted in D. Richards, *The Wit of Noël Coward*

2   Television is for appearing on, not looking at.
Attrib

3   Nescafé Society.
Quoted in Alec Guinness, *Blessings in Disguise.*

4   The only way to enjoy life is to work. Work is much more fun than fun.
Quoted in the *Observer*, 21 June 1963

5   *Directing Edith Evans in a revival of* **Hay Fever** *(1964), when she kept saying a line as, 'On a very clear day you can see Marlow':*
Edith, the line is 'On a clear day you can see Marlow. On a *very* clear day you can see Marlowe *and* Beaumont *and* Fletcher.
Quoted in the *Observer*, 1 April 1973

6   *She could eat an apple through a tennis racquet.*
Come Into the Garden, Maud (1966)

7   *On a child star, in a long-winded play:*
Two things should be cut: the second act and the child's throat.
Quoted in D. Richards, *The Wit of Noël Coward*

8   *On an inadequate portrayal of Queen Victoria:*
It made me feel that Albert had married beneath his station.
ibid

9   *To William Fairchild who wrote the dialogue for the part of Coward in the film* **Star:**
Too many Dear Boys, dear boy.
Quoted in C. Lesley, *The Life of Noël Coward*

10 *On child star Bonnie Langford in a musical of* **Gone with the Wind** *(1972), when a real horse messed up the stage:*
If they'd stuffed the child's head up the horse's arse, they would have solved two problems at once.
Quoted in N. Sherrin, *Cutting Edge*

11 *To Rex Harrison:*
If you weren't the best light comedian in the country, all you'd be fit for is selling cars in Great Portland Street.
Attrib

1   *To Laurence Olivier's five-year-old daughter, Tamsin, when she asked what two dogs were doing together:*
    The doggie in front has suddenly gone blind, and the other one has very kindly offered to push him all the way to St Dunstan's.
    Quoted by K. Tynan in the *Observer* (1 April 1973)

2   *Last words:*
    Goodnight, my darlings. I'll see you tomorrow.
    Quoted in C. Lesley, *The Life of Noël Coward*

CRICK, Francis
British scientist (1916–   )

3   *On discovering the structure of DNA, 1953:*
    We have discovered the secret of life!
    Recounted in J. D. Watson, *The Double Helix*

CRISP, Quentin
British celebrity (1908–   )

4   There was no need to do any housework at all. After the first four years the dirt doesn't get any worse.
    The Naked Civil Servant (1968)

5   I became one of the stately homos of England.
    ibid

CRITCHLEY, Julian
British Conservative politician and writer (1930–   )

6   I was told when a young man . . . that the two occupational hazards of the Palace of Varieties [Westminster] were alcohol and adultery. 'The Lords,' [a Knight of the Shires] said severely, 'has the cup for adultery' . . . The hurroosh that follows the intermittent revelation of the sexual goings-on of an unlucky MP has convinced me that the only safe pleasure for a parliamentarian is a bag of boiled sweets.
    Article in the *Listener*, 10 June 1982

7   She [Margaret Thatcher] cannot see an institution without hitting it with her handbag.
    Article in *The Times*, 21 June 1982

CROMPTON, Richmal
British writer (1890–1969)

1   'Anyway,' said Violet Elizabeth. 'It *ith* divorth an' I don't care if it ithn't. 'F you don' play houth with me. I'll thcream n'thcream till I'm thick. I can,' she added with pride.

'William the Match-Maker', *Still—William* (1925)

CRONKITE, Walter
US broadcaster (1916–   )

2   And that's the way it is.

Stock phrase
Concluding CBS TV news broadcasts, 1962–81.

CROSSMAN, Richard
British Labour politician (1907–74)

3   *Describing his first day in office as a Cabinet Minister, October 1964:*
Already I realize the tremendous effort it requires not to be taken over by the Civil Service. My Minister's room is like a padded cell, and in certain ways I am like a person who is suddenly certified a lunatic and put safely into this great vast room, cut off from real life . . . Of course, they don't behave *quite* like nurses because the Civil Service is profoundly deferential—'Yes, Minister! No, Minister! If you wish it, Minister!'

The Diaries of a Cabinet Minister 1964–70 Vol. 1 (1975)
Hence the title of the BBC TV series, *Yes, Minister.*

CUMMINGS, E. E.
US poet (1894–1962)

4   a politician is an arse upon
which everyone has sat except a man.

1 x 1 (1944), 'a politician'

CUNARD, Lady ('Emerald')
American-born society figure in Britain (1872–1948)

5   *To Somerset Maugham, who had said he was leaving a function early 'to keep his youth':*
Then why didn't you bring him with you? I should be delighted to meet him.

Quoted in D. Fielding, *Emerald and Nancy*

CURZON, George Nathaniel (later Marquis Curzon)
British Conservative politician (1859–1925)

6   Gentlemen do not take soup at luncheon.

Attrib remark, 1912

1   *On seeing soldiers bathing in the First World War:*
    I never knew the lower classes had such white skins.
    Quoted in K. Rose, *Superior Person* (1969)

2   *To fellow Cabinet-member on the clothes of a colleague:*
    Gentlemen never wear brown in London.
    Attrib

3   *To his second wife, on love-making:*
    Ladies never move.
    Attrib

DAD'S ARMY
UK TV comedy series (BBC), from 1968. Script by David Croft and Jimmy Perry. With Arthur Lowe as Captain Mainwaring, John Le Mesurier as Sergeant Wilson and Clive Dunn as Lance-Corporal Jones.

1   *Wilson:* Excuse me, sir, do you think that's wise?
    Catchphrase

2   *Jones:* Permission to speak, sir?
    Catchphrase

3   *Mainwaring:* Stupid boy!
    Catchphrase

DAILY EXPRESS
London newspaper

4   Britain will not be involved in a European war this year, or next year either.
    Headline, 30 September 1938
    Inspired by Lord Beaverbrook.

5   MARTIN BORMANN ALIVE
    Headline, 25 November 1972

6   CHARLES TO MARRY ASTRID—Official.
    Headline, 17 June 1977

DAILY MIRROR
London newspaper

7   Forward with the people.
    Slogan, from *c*1935–59.
    Later, 'Forward with Britain'.

8   'The price of petrol has been increased by one penny'—Official.
    Caption to cartoon by Philip Zec, 6 March 1942
    The cartoon showed a torpedoed sailor adrift on a raft. The caption was suggested by 'Cassandra' (William Connor). Together they led to the paper almost being suppressed by the Government.

9   'Here you are—don't lose it again.'
    Caption to cartoon by Philip Zec, 8 May 1945
    The cartoon showed a wounded soldier proferring 'Victory and peace in Europe.'

1   WHOSE FINGER?

Front page headline, 25 October 1951

This, on General Election day, was the culmination of a campaign.
Earlier, the paper had asked, 'Whose finger do you want on the trigger
when the world situation is so delicate?' The choice was between
Churchill and Attlee.

2   Enough is enough.

Front page headline, 10 May 1968

Headline on article by Cecil H. King, Chairman of the International
Publishing Corporation, referring to the government of Harold
Wilson.

3   *On Michael Foot, then Labour party leader:*
A good man fallen among politicians.

Editorial, 28 February 1983

DAILY TELEGRAPH

London newspaper

4   *On the premiership of Sir Anthony Eden:*
Most Conservatives, and almost certainly some of the wiser Trade
Union leaders, are waiting to feel the *smack of firm government.*

Editorial comment, 3 January 1956
Written by Donald McLachlan.

5   *Reviewing Alan Sillitoe's novel **Saturday Night and Sunday Morning:***
A novel of today with a freshness and raw fury that makes *Room at
the Top* look like a vicarage tea-party.

Book review, 1958
An early example of the 'makes . . . look like a . . . .' type of criticism
(not confined to this paper).

DALEY, Richard J.

US Democratic politician and Mayor of Chicago (1902–76)

6   *To the press, concerning riots during Democratic Convention, 1968:*
Gentlemen, get the thing straight once and for all. The policeman
isn't there to *create* disorder, the policeman is there to *preserve*
disorder.

Audio source

DANIELS, Paul

British entertainer (1938–   )

7   You'll like this. Not a lot, but you'll like it.

Catchphrase, by 1979

DANIELS, R. G.
British

1 The most delightful advantage of being bald—one can *hear* snowflakes.

Attrib, by 1977

DARLING
UK film 1965. Script by Frederic Raphael. With Dirk Bogarde as Robert Gold and Julie Christie as Diana Scott.

2 *Robert (to Diana):* Your idea of fidelity is not having more than one man in the bed at the same time . . . You're a whore, baby, that's all, just a whore, and I don't take whores in taxis.

Soundtrack

DARROW, Clarence
US lawyer (1857–1938)

3 I have never killed a man, but I have read many obituaries with a lot of pleasure.

Medley

4 When I was a boy I was told that anybody could become President; I'm beginning to believe it.

Attrib

DAUGHERTY, Harry
US Republican supporter (1860–1941)

5 *Prediction (February 1920) about the choosing of the Republican Party's Presidential candidate in Chicago (June 1920) if, as happened, the convention failed to make up its mind:*
[A group of senators]) bleary eyed for lack of sleep [will have to] sit down about two o'clock in the morning around a table in a *smoke-filled room* in some hotel and decide the nomination.

Quoted in W. Safire, *Political Dictionary*
Daugherty, however, denied he ever used the phrase 'smoke-filled'. To Associated Press reporter Kirke Simpson is ascribed a news report (12 June 1920): '[Warren] Harding of Ohio was chosen by a group of men in a smoke-filled room early today as Republican candidate for President'.

DAVIES, W. H.
British poet (1871–1940)

6 What is this life if, full of care,
We have no time to stand and stare?

Songs of Joy (1911) 'Leisure'

DAVIS, Bette
US film actress (1908–89)

1   *On a starlet:*
    I see—she's the original good time that was had by all.
    Attrib
    See also **ALL ABOUT EVE 3:8; THE LETTER 203:10.**

DAVIS, Sammy, Jnr
US entertainer (1925–90)

2   I'm a coloured, one-eyed Jew—do I need anything else?
    Yes I Can (1966)
    Sometimes reported as being in answer to the question, 'What's your golf handicap?'

DAWSON OF PENN, Viscount
British doctor (1864–1945)

3   *On his dying patient, George V:*
    The King's life is moving peacefully towards its close.
    Medical bulletin, 20 January 1936
    Taken up and broadcast by the BBC.

A DAY AT THE RACES
US film 1937. Script by Robert Pirosh, George Seaton and George Oppenheimer. With the Marx Brothers.

4   *Groucho:* Have the florist send some roses to Mrs Upjohn and write 'Emily I love you' on the back of the bill.
    Soundtrack

5   *Groucho (taking pulse):* Either this man is dead or my watch has stopped.
    Soundtrack

DE COUBERTIN, Baron Pierre
French founder of modern Olympics (1863–1937)

6   The most important thing in the Olympic Games is not winning but taking part, just as the most important thing in life is not the triumph but the struggle. The essential thing in life is not conquering but fighting well.
    Translation of speech, London, 24 July 1908

DEAN, John
US Presidential counsel (1938–)

1   *At White House meeting with President Nixon, 21 March 1973, on the Watergate scandal:*
We have a cancer within, close to the Presidency, that is growing. It is growing daily.

Revealed in *The White House Transcripts* (1974)

DEDERICH, Charles
US founder of Synanon anti-drug and alcohol centres (1913–)

2   Today is the first day of the rest of your life.

Attrib slogan *c*1969
Also known in the form 'Tomorrow is . . .' and as a wall-slogan, graffito, etc.

DE GAULLE, Charles
French General and President (1890–1970)

3   *Broadcast appeal from London to Frenchmen betrayed by Pétain's armistice with the Germans:*
I, General de Gaulle, now in London, call on all French officers and men who are at present on British soil, or may be in the future, with or without arms . . . to get in touch with me.

Translation of script broadcast 18 June 1940 (no recording exists)

4   ***La France a perdu une bataille! Mais la France n'a pas perdu la guerre!***
('France has lost a battle, but France has not lost the war!')

Proclamation dated 18 June 1940, circulated later in the month.
The phrase was not used in the broadcast, only in the proclamation.

5   *To his wife, at the burial of their mentally-retarded daughter, Anne:*
Come. Now she is like the others.

Quoted in B. Crozier, *De Gaulle The Statesman*

6   Politics is too important to be left to the politicians.

Quoted in C. Attlee, *A Prime Minister Remembers* (1961)
See also **BENN 32:7; CLEMENCEAU 80:3; MACLEOD 213:2.**

7   ***Toute ma vie je me suis fait une certaine idée de la France.*** ('All my life I have had a certain view of France'.)

Les Mémoires de Guerre (1954)

8   *On Marshal Pétain:*
La vieillesse est un naufrage. ('Old age is a shipwreck.')

ibid

1   How can you govern a country which produces 246 different kinds of cheese?

Quoted in E. Mignon, *Les Mots du Général* (1962)
Another source dates this as 1951 and has 265 as the number. Cf. De la Reyniere (*d*1838): *'On connoit en France 685 manières differentes d'accommoder les oeufs'.*

2   *On being compared with Robespierre:*
I always thought I was Jeanne d'Arc and Buonaparte—how little one knows oneself.

Quoted in *Figaro Littéraire* (1958)

3   *Je vous ai compris . . . Vive l'Algérie française!* ('I have understood you . . . Long live French Algeria!')

Speech to rally in Algiers, 4 June 1958
Here de Gaulle spoke with forked tongue—as he later led France out of its colonial link with Algeria.

4   *On why he had not arrested Jean-Paul Sartre for urging French troops in Algeria to desert:*
One does not arrest Voltaire.

Attrib remark *c*1960.

5   □ *Non!*

Press conference, Paris, 14 January 1963
His rejection of British attempts to join the European Common Market was not rendered so briefly, though this was the popular (British) way of characterizing his attitude.

6   *On Jackie Kennedy:*
I can see her in about ten years from now on the yacht of a Greek petrol millionaire.

Attrib after her husband's assassination
In Fallen Oaks (1972), André Malraux recalls de Gaulle as having said, rather, 'She is a star, and will end up on the yacht of some oil baron.'

7   *Vive le Québec libre!* ('Long live free Quebec!')

Speech, Montreal, 25 July 1967
The Federal Canadian government found these words offensive and de Gaulle had to cut short his visit.

8   *La réforme, oui; la chienlit, non.* ('Reform, yes; bed-shitting, no.')

Remark at Cabinet meeting, 19 May 1968, etc.
Referring to student protests. Reported to the press by his Prime Minister, Georges Pompidou.

DELLA FEMINA, Jerry
US advertising executive (1936–   )

1   *Suggested slogan for Panasonic:*
From those wonderful folks who gave you Pearl Harbor.

Recounted in book with that title (1970)

2   Advertising is the most fun you can have with your clothes on.

ibid

DE MANIO, Jack
British broadcaster (1914–88)

3   *Of Glenda Jackson:*
Her face could launch a thousand dredgers.

Attrib

DEMPSEY, Jack
US heavyweight boxer (1895–1983)

4   *To wife, on losing his World Heavyweight title to Gene Tunney, 23 September 1926:*
Honey, I just forgot to duck.

Recounted in his *Autobiography* (1977)
Quoted by President Reagan after an attempt on his life, 1981.

5   Kill the other guy before he kills you.

Motto, quoted in *The Times*, 2 June 1983

6   Keep punching.

ibid

DENNING, Lord
British lawyer (1899–   )

7   To every subject of this land, however powerful, I would use Thomas Fuller's words over three hundred years ago, 'Be ye never so high, the law is above you'.

In a High Court ruling against the Attorney-General, January 1977

8   *On the difference between a diplomat and a lady:*
When a diplomat says yes, he means perhaps. When he says perhaps he means no. When he says no, he is not a diplomat. When a lady says no, she means perhaps. When she says perhaps, she means yes. But when she says yes, she is no lady.

Speech at meeting of Magistrates Association, 14 October 1982
Based on a possibly apocryphal saying of Bismarck's.

DENNIS, Nigel
British writer (1912–89)

1   *Reviewing **Kennedy** by Theodore C. Sorensen (1965):*
A great American need not fear the hand of his assassin; his real demise begins only when a friend like Mr Sorensen closes the mouth of his tomb with a stone.

Attrib

DENT, Alan
British critic (1905–78)

2   [Hamlet is the tragedy of a] man who could not make up his mind.

Introduction to film *Hamlet* (1948)

DIAGHILEV, Serge
Russian ballet impresario (1872–1929)

3   *To Jean Cocteau, 1912:*
Etonne-moi! ('Astonish me!')

Quoted in J. Cocteau, *Journals*

DIANA (HRH the Princess of Wales)
British Royal (1961–   )

4   *When asked what her impression of Prince Charles was on first meeting her future husband in 1977:*
Pretty amazing.

Remark, 1981

5   I'm as thick as a plank.

Remark, quoted in *Sunday Today,* 25 January 1987

DIETZ, Howard
US writer and film executive (1896–1983)

6   *Motto of Metro-Goldwyn-Mayer, devised c 1916:*
Ars Gratia Artis ('Art for Art's sake').

Recalled in *Dancing in the Dark* (1974)

7   A day away from Tallulah [Bankhead] is like a month in the country.

ibid

8   *Slogan for MGM:*
More Stars Than There Are In Heaven.

Attrib

9   That's Entertainment.

Title of song, *The Band Wagon* (1953)

1   The world is a stage
     The stage is a world of entertainment.
     ibid

2   A ghost and a prince meet
     And everyone ends in mincemeat.
     ibid
     Summary of *Hamlet.*
     See also **GARBO 132:5.**

DINNER AT EIGHT

US film 1933. Script by Frances Marion and Herman J. Mankiewicz. Jean
Harlow as Kitty, Marie Dressler as Carlotta Vance.

3   *Kitty:* The guy said that machinery is going to take the place of
     every profession?
     Carlotta: That's something you need never worry about.
     Soundtrack

DISNEY, Walt

US film-maker (1901–66)

4   Girls bored me—they still do. I love Mickey Mouse more than any
     woman I've ever known.
     W. Wagner, *You Must Remember This*

DODD, Ken

British comedian (1927–   )

5   Freud never played the second house at Glasgow Empire on a
     Friday night.
     Quoted in the *Observer Magazine*, 16 December 1984
     His remark has appeared in several versions since 1965.

6   By Jove, I needed that!
     Catchphrase

7   Hello, Mrs!
     Catchphrase

8   How tickled I am!
     Catchphrase

9   Nikky, nokky, noo!
     Catchphrase

10   Where's me shirt?
     Catchphrase

DOUGLAS, Kirk

US film actor (1916–)

1   My kids never had the advantage I had: I was born poor.

Remark, in several interviews, early 1980s

DOUGLAS-HOME, Sir Alec (later Lord Home)

British Conservative Prime Minister (1903–)

2   When I have to read economic documents I have to have a box of matches and start moving them into position to illustrate and simplify the points to myself.

Interview in the *Observer*, 16 September 1962

3   As far as [being] the 14th Earl is concerned, I suppose Mr Wilson, when you come to think of it, is the 14th Mr Wilson.

TV interview, 21 October 1963
See also **WILSON 349:6.**

4   There are two problems in my life. The political ones are insoluble and the economic ones are incomprehensible.

Speech, January 1964

5   *On Stanley Baldwin:*
A large pipe and thick country tweeds gave the image of a yeoman squire living close to the soil. It was very clever, because in fact he was at his happiest in a room, preferably facing north, with the windows shut, reading Mary Webb.

The Way the Wind Blows (1976)

DOYLE, Sir Arthur Conan

British writer (1859–1930)

6   Come, Watson, come! The game is afoot.

'The Abbey Grange', *The Return of Sherlock Holmes* (1904)
See also **THE RETURN OF SHERLOCK HOLMES 273:1.**

DRAGNET

US radio series from 1949, TV series 1951–8, 1967–9. Starring, produced and directed by Jack Webb as Police Sergeant Joe Friday.

7   *Friday:* Ladies and gentlemen, the story you are about to hear/see is true. Only the names have been changed to protect the innocent . . . I'm a cop . . . My name's Friday.

Soundtrack
Standard preamble.

8   *Friday:* All we want is the facts, ma'am.

Stock phrase

DRAKE, Charlie
British comedian (1925–   )

1   Hello, my darlings.

Catchphrase, from 1950s onwards

DRAPER, Ruth
US entertainer (1884–1956)

2   *Of Dante:*
Of course he was a genius, wasn't he—like Shakespeare? . . . He and Dante seem to have known *everything* . . . known what would always be true . . . Wonderful, I imagine that we're going to find that this is *full* of quotations.

Sketch, 'The Italian Lesson'

DR WHO
UK TV science fiction series (BBC), from 1963. Script (originally) by Terry Nation.

3   Exterminate, exterminate!

Passim, cry of Daleks

DUBCEK, Alexander
Czechoslovakian politician (1921–92)

4   Socialism [or Communism] with a human face.

Translation of report in *Rudé právo*, 14 March 1968

DUCK SOUP
US film 1933. Script by various. With the Marx Brothers.

5   *Groucho:* I could dance with you till the cows come home. On second thoughts, I'd rather dance with the cows till you came home.

Soundtrack

6   *Groucho:* Go, and never darken my towels again!

Soundtrack

DULLES, John Foster
US politician (1888–1959)

7   When I was in Paris last week, I said that . . . the United States would have to undertake an *agonizing reappraisal* of basic foreign policy in relation to Europe.

Speech to National Press Club, Washington, December 1953

1   The ability to get to the verge without getting into the war is the necessary art. If you cannot master it, you inevitably get into war. If you try to run away from it, if you are scared to go to the brink, you are lost.

Quoted in *Life*, 16 January 1956
This was the origin of the term 'brinkmanship' popularized by Adlai Stevenson during the 1956 US Presidential campaign.

DU MAURIER, Daphne (later Dame Daphne)
British novelist (1907–89)

2   Last night I dreamt I went to Manderley again.

Rebecca (1938)
Opening words.

DUNCAN, Isadora
US dancer and choreographer (1878–1927)

3   *Last words:*
Adieu, mes amis. Je vais à la gloire ('Goodbye, my friends, I go on to glory').

Quoted in M. Desti, *Isadora Duncan's End* (1929)
She was about to test-drive a Bugatti and was strangled when the scarf she was wearing caught in the spokes of a wheel.

DURANT, Will
US teacher, philosopher and historian (1885–1982)

4   There is nothing in Socialism that a little age or a little money will not cure.

Attrib

DURANTE, Jimmy
US entertainer (1893–1980)

5   Dese [*or* dems] are de conditions dat prevail.

Catchphrase

6   Everybody wants to get into da act.

Catchphrase

7   Goodnight, Mrs Calabash—wherever you are.

Catchphrase
Referring to his late wife.

8   Stoppa da music!

Catchphrase
See also **JUMBO 180:1.**

DUROCHER, Leo
US baseball manager (1906–91)

1 *On the New York Giants:*
   Nice guys. Finish last.

   Remark, 6 July 1946
   Run together as 'Nice guys finish last.'

DURRELL, Lawrence
British writer (1912–90)

2 *Of the Mona Lisa:*
   She has the smile of a woman who has just dined off her husband.

   Attrib

DYLAN, Bob
US singer/songwriter (1941–   )

3 The answer, my friend, is blowin' in the wind.

   Song 'Blowin' in the Wind' (1962)

4 The Times They Are A-Changin'.

   Title of song (1963)

5 How does it feel
   To be without a home
   Like a complete unknown
   Like a rolling stone.

   Song, 'Like a Rolling Stone' (1965)

6 Keep a clean nose
   Watch the plain clothes
   You don't need a weather man
   To know which way the wind blows.

   Song, 'Subterranean Homesick Blues' (1965)

7 I ain't gonna work on Maggie's Farm no more.

   Song, 'Maggie's Farm' (1965)

8 All Along the Watch Tower.

   Title of song (1968)
   Alluding to Isaiah 21:5.

9 *When asked for 'a good quote' by a French journalist on a cold night:*
   If I had a good quote, I'd be wearing it.

   Quoted in *The Times*, July 1981

DYSON, Will
British cartoonist

1   *Clemenceau noticing a child bewailing the breakdown of the peace efforts at the Versailles conference:*
    Curious! I seem to hear a child weeping!

    Caption to cartoon in *Daily Herald*, 1919
    The child is prophetically labelled '1940 Class'.

E.T.
US film 1982. Script by Melissa Mathison. With Henry Thomas as Elliott.

1   *Elliott:* How do you explain school to a higher intelligence?
    Soundtrack

2   *The extra-terrestrial:* E.T., phone home!
    Soundtrack

EDEN, Sir Anthony (later 1st Earl of Avon)
British Conservative Prime Minister (1897–1977)

3   We are not at war with Egypt. We are in armed conflict.
    Quoted in the *Observer*, 4 November 1956

EDEN, Lady (Clarissa) (later Countess of Avon)
British wife of Sir Anthony Eden (1920–   )

4   During the past few weeks I have felt sometimes that the Suez Canal
    was flowing through my drawing-room.
    Speech, Gateshead, 20 November 1956

EDGAR, Marriott
British writer (1880–1951)

5   A grand little lad was young Albert,
        All dressed in his best; quite a swell
    With a stick with an 'orse's 'ead 'andle,
        The finest that Woolworth's could sell.
    'The Lion and Albert' (1932)
    Written with Wolseley Charles.

EDISON, Thomas Alva
US inventor (1847–1931)

6   Genius is one per cent inspiration and ninety-nine per cent
    perspiration.
    Quoted in *Life* (1932)
    Originally said *c*1903.

EDWARD VIII (later Duke of Windsor)
British Sovereign (1894–1972)

7   The young business and professional men of this country must get
    together round the table, adopt methods that have proved sound in
    the past, adapt them to the changing needs of the times and,
    whenever possible, improve them.
    Speech, British Industries Fair, Birmingham, 1927
    Adopted as the motto of the Round Table movement in the form
    'Adopt, adapt, improve'.

1 Perhaps one of the only positive pieces of advice that I was ever given was that supplied by an old courtier who observed: 'Only two rules really count. Never miss an opportunity to relieve yourself; never miss a chance to sit down and rest your feet.'

A King's Story (1951)
The 'old courtier' may have been his father, George V, to whom this advice has also been attributed.

2 *To official at Bessemer steel works, South Wales, where 9,000 men had been made unemployed:*
These works brought all these people here. Something must be done to find them work.

News reports, November 1936

3 I have found it impossible to carry the heavy burden of responsibility and to discharge my duties as King as *I* would wish to do without the help and support of the woman I love.

Radio broadcast after abdication, 11 December 1936

4 The thing that impresses me most about America is the way parents obey their children.

Quoted in *Look*, 5 March 1957

EHRLICHMAN, John D.
US Presidential aide (1925–   )

5 *Yardstick for judging whether policies would appeal to 'Middle America', 1968:*
It'll play in Peoria.

Quoted in W. Safire, *Political Dictionary*

6 *Of Patrick Gray, Acting Director of the CBI, who did not know his commission had been withdrawn:*
Let him twist slowly, slowly in the wind.

Telephone remark to John Dean, 7/8 March 1973

EHRMANN, Max
US writer (?–1945)

7 Go placidly amid the noise and haste, and remember what peace there may be in silence. As far as possible without surrender be on good terms with all persons. Speak your truth quietly and clearly; and listen to others, even the dull and ignorant; they too have their story. Avoid loud and aggressive persons, they are vexations to the spirit.

Desiderata (1927)
In the 1960s and 70s, these words were marketed anonymously as having come from Old St Paul's Church, Baltimore, and dating from 1692.

EINSTEIN, Albert
German-born US scientist (1879–1955)

1   $E=mc^2$ (Energy = mass x the speed of light squared.)

Statement (1905)

2   When a man sits with a pretty girl for an hour, it seems like a minute. But let him sit on a hot stove for a minute—and it's longer than any hour. That's relativity.

Attrib

3   [God] does not play dice with the universe.

In letter (4 December 1926)

EISENHOWER, Dwight D.
US General and Republican President (1890–1969)

4   I shall go to Korea and try to end the war.

Campaign promise, in speech, 24 October 1952

5   You have a row of dominoes set up. You knock over the first one and what will happen to the last one is that it will go over very quickly.

Remark at press conference, April 1954
The 'domino theory' had, however, first been applied to South-East
Asia by the columnist Joseph Alsop.

6   In the councils of government, we must guard against the acquisition of unwarranted influence, whether sought or unsought, by the military-industrial complex. The potential for the disastrous rise of misplaced power exists and will persist.

Farewell address, 17 January 1961

EKLAND, Britt
Swedish actress (1942–   )

7   I say I don't sleep with married men, but what I mean is that I don't sleep with happily-married men.

Attrib in January 1980

8   *When the Earl of Lichfield dropped her because she was 'no good in the country':*
And he's no good in bed.

Attrib

ELIOT, T. S.
American-born poet (1888–1965)

1   Let us go then, you and I
    When the evening is spread out against the sky
    Like a patient etherised upon a table.
    'The Love Song of J. Alfred Prufrock' (1917)

2   In the room the women come and go
    Talking of Michelangelo.
    ibid

3   The yellow fog that rubs its back upon the window panes.
    ibid

4   I have measured out my life with coffee spoons.
    ibid

5   No! I am not Prince Hamlet, nor was meant to be;
    Am an attendant lord, one that will do
    To swell a progress, start a scene or two.
    ibid

6   I grow old . . . I grow old . . .
    I shall wear the bottoms of my trousers rolled.
    Shall I part my hair behind? Do I dare to eat a peach?
    . . . I have heard the mermaids singing, each to each.
    I do not think that they will sing to me.
    ibid

7   Here I am, an old man in a dry month,
    Being read to by a boy, waiting for rain.
    'Gerontion' (1920)

8   The hippopotamus's day
    Is passed in sleep; at night he hunts;
    God works in a mysterious way—
    The Church can feed and sleep at once.
    'The Hippopotamus' (1920)

9   Webster was much possessed by death
    And saw the skull beneath the skin.
    'Whispers of Immortality' (1920)

10 April is the cruellest month, breeding
    Lilacs out of the dead land.
    The Waste Land (1922)

1 O O O O that Shakespeherian Rag
   It's so elegant
   So intelligent.

   ibid

   Based on 'That Shakespearian Rag' by Buck, Ruby and Stamper,
   published in the US, 1912

2 These fragments have I shored against my ruins.

   ibid

3 We are the hollow men
   We are the stuffed men
   Leaning together.

   The Hollow Men (1925)

4 This is the way the world ends
   Not with a bang but a whimper.

   ibid

5 Between the idea
   And the reality
   Between the motion
   And the act
   Falls the shadow.

   ibid

6 Pray for us now and at the hour of our birth.

   'Animula' (1929)

7 Time present and time past
   Are both perhaps present in time future,
   And time future contained in time past.

   'Burnt Norton', *Four Quartets* (1935)

8 At the still point of the turning world. Neither flesh nor fleshless;
   Neither from nor towards; at the still point, there the dance is,
   But neither arrest nor movement.

   ibid

9 Go go go said the bird.

   ibid

10 In my beginning is my end.

   'East Coker' in ibid (1940)

11 In my end is my beginning.

   ibid

1   We shall not cease from exploration
And the end of all our exploring
Will be to arrive where we started
And know the place for the first time.

'Little Gidding' (1942)

2   He always has an alibi, and one or two to spare:
At whatever time the deed took place—Macavity wasn't there.

'Macavity: The Mystery Cat', *Old Possum's Book of Practical Cats* (1939)

ELIZABETH THE QUEEN MOTHER, HM Queen
British Royal (1900–   )

3   *After the bombing of Buckingham Palace, September 1940:*
I'm glad we've been bombed. It makes me feel I can look the East End in the face.

Remark to policeman, 13 September 1940

4   *On whether her children would leave England after the bombing of Buckingham Palace:*
The children will not leave unless I do. I shall not leave unless their father does, and the King will not leave the country in any circumstances whatever.

Attrib

5   My favourite programme is 'Mrs Dale's Diary'. I try never to miss it because it is the only way of knowing what goes on in a middle-class family.

Untraced report from the London *Evening News*

6   *When a fishbone lodged in her throat:*
The salmon are striking back.

Attrib in November 1982

7   *On President Carter:*
He is the only man since my dear husband died, to have the effrontery to kiss me on the lips.

Attrib in February 1983

8   *To her daughter, when the Queen accepted a second glass of wine at lunch:*
Do you think it's wise, darling? You know you've got to rule this afternoon.

Attrib in 1984

ELIZABETH II, HM Queen
British Sovereign (1926–   )

1   *When a girl:*
    I should like to be a horse.
    Attrib

2   *To her sister, at end of radio talk to children evacuated to North America:*
    Come on, Margaret!
    Broadcast, 13 October 1940

3   *On her 21st birthday:*
    I declare before you all that my whole life, whether it be long or short, shall be devoted to your service, and the service of our great imperial family to which we all belong.
    Broadcast from South Africa, 21 April 1947

4   My husband and I left London a month ago . . .
    Christmas broadcast from New Zealand, 25 December 1953
    The phrase 'My husband and I' was used for many years.

5   *At Silver Wedding banquet:*
    I think everybody really will concede that on this, of all days, I should begin my speech with the words, 'My husband and I'.
    Speech, Guildhall, London, 20 November 1972

6   I have to be seen to be believed.
    Attrib

7   *On Princess Michael of Kent:*
    She's more royal than we are.
    Attrib in *Sunday* magazine, 14 April 1985
    Compare the saying from the time of Louis XVI: *'Il ne faut pas être plus royaliste que le roi'* ('You mustn't be more royalist than the king.')

ELLINGTON, Duke
US musician and composer (1899–1974)

8   Love you madly.
    Stock phrase

EMERY, Dick
British comedian (1917–83)

9   Oooh, you are awful . . . but I like you!
    Catchphrase
    As character 'Mandy'.

ENGLISH, Arthur
British comedian (1919–)

1 Mum, mum, they are laughing at me.

Catchphrase, from 1940s

2 Play the music and open the cage.

Catchphrase, from 1940s

EPITAPHS

3 *On Captain 'Titus' Oates, in the Antarctic, 1912:*
   Hereabouts died a very gallant gentleman.

Composed by E. L. Atkinson and Apsley Cherry-Garrard.

4 Their Name Liveth for Evermore.

Standard epitaph over lists of war dead, written after the First World
War by Rudyard Kipling and based on Ecclesiasticus 44:14.

5 A Soldier of the Great War Known unto God.

Standard epitaph over graves of the unknown dead from the First
World War.

6 They buried him among the kings because he had done good
   toward God and toward his house.

On the tomb of the Unknown Soldier in Westminster Abbey, buried
1920—echoing 2 Chronicles 24:16.

7 When you go home, tell them of us and say,
   'For your tomorrows these gave their today.'

From J. M. Edmonds, *Inscriptions Suggested for War Memorials* (1919)

ERWIN, Dudley
Australian politician (1917–)

8 *When asked the reason for his dismissal as Air Minister, 1969:*
   It is shapely, it wiggles, and its name is Ainslie Gotto.

Quoted in *Dictionary of Australian Quotations*
Ms. Gotto was the secretary of Prime Minister John Gorton, and was
said to exert undue influence.

EVANS, Dame Edith
British actress (1888–1976)

9 *On being told that Nancy Mitford had been lent a villa so that she could
   finish a book:*
   Oh really. What exactly is she reading?

Attrib

1   *To a salesgirl at Fortnum and Mason who insisted on giving her threepence change:*
    Keep the change, my dear. I trod on a grape as I came in.

    Quoted in B. Forbes, *Ned's Girl*

EVERETT, Kenny
British entertainer (1944–   )

2   It's all done in the best *possible* taste!

    Catchphrase, *The Kenny Everett Television Show* (from 1981 onwards)
    As American film-star 'Cupid Stunt'.

EWER, W. N.
British journalist (1885–1976)

3   How odd
    Of God
    To choose
    The Jews.

    Quoted in the *Week-end Book* (1924)
    In conversation at the Savage Club, London.

THE FACE OF FU MANCHU
UK film 1965. Script by Peter Welbeck. With Christopher Lee as Fu Manchu.

1   *Fu Manchu:* The world shall hear from me again!

Soundtrack
Last words of film, Fu Manchu having been blown up.

FAIRLIE, Henry
British journalist (1924–90)

2   I have several times suggested that what I call the 'Establishment' in
this country is today more powerful than ever before. By the
'Establishment' I do not mean only the centres of official power—
though they are certainly part of it—but rather the whole matrix of
official and social relations within which power is exercised . . . the
'Establishment' can be seen at work in the activities of, not only the
Prime Minister, the Archbishop of Canterbury and the Earl
Marshal, but of such lesser mortals as the Chairman of the Arts
Council, the Director-General of the BBC, and even the editor of
the *Times Literary Supplement,* not to mention dignitaries like Lady
Violet Bonham-Carter.

Article in *Spectator,* 23 September 1955
A. J. P. Taylor had also used the phrase 'Establishment' in its modern
sense in a review for the *New Statesman* in 1953.

FARJEON, Herbert
British writer (1887–1945)

3   Glory, glory, hallelujah!
I'm the luckiest of females!
For I've danced with a man
Who's danced with a girl
Who's danced with the Prince of Wales!

Song, 'I've Danced With a Man Who's Danced With a Girl', *Picnic*
(1927)

FARLEY, James
US Democratic politician (1888–1976)

4   As Maine goes, so goes Vermont.

Statement to press, 4 November 1936
Predicting that F. D. Roosevelt (whom he managed) would carry all but
two states in the presidential election. Alluding to an old saying, 'As
Maine goes, so goes the nation'.

FAROUK, King
Egyptian Royal (1920–65)

5   There will soon be only five kings left—the Kings of England,
Diamonds, Hearts, Spades and Clubs.

Remark to Lord Boyd-Orr, 1948

THE FATAL GLASS OF BEER
US film 1933. Script by W. C. Fields. With W. C. Fields.

1   *Fields:* 'Tain't a fit night out for man or beast.

Soundtrack
Fields had earlier used the phrase in a sketch, but did not claim to be the originator of the line.

FAULKNER, William
US novelist (1897–1962)

2   The Long Hot Summer.

Title of a film based on his short stories (1958) and of a TV series (1965–6)
He had used the phrase 'The Long Summer' in 1940.

3   *On Henry James:*
The nicest old lady I ever met.

Quoted in E. Stone, *The Battle and the Books*

FAWLTY TOWERS
UK TV comedy series (BBC), 1975–9. Script by John Cleese and Connie Booth. With John Cleese as Basil Fawlty and Andrew Sachs as Manuel, the Spanish waiter.

4   *On the shortcomings of Manuel:*
Basil: I'm sorry, he's from Barcelona.

Stock phrase (variable)

5   *Manuel:* ¿Qué?

Stock phrase

FELDMAN, Marty
British comedian and writer (1933–83)

6   Comedy, like sodomy, is an unnatural act.

In *The Times*, 9 June 1969

7   *To Judge Argyle in the **Oz** magazine obscenity trial, Summer 1971:*
Am I speaking loud enough for you, judge? Sorry, am I waking you up?

Quoted in T. Palmer, *The Trials of Oz* (1971)

FERBER, Edna
US writer (1887–1968)

8   Being an old maid is like death by drowning, a really delightful sensation after you cease to struggle.

Quoted in R. E. Drennan, *Wit's End*

FERLINGHETTI, Laurence
US poet (1919–)

1   The world is a beautiful place
       to be born into
    if you don't mind some people dying
       all the time
    or maybe only starving
       some of the time
    which isn't half so bad
       if it isn't you.

Pictures of the Gone World (1955)

2   Yes
       but then right in the middle of it
    comes the smiling
       mortician.

ibid

FIELDS, Dorothy
US lyricist (1904–74)

3   I Can't Give You Anything But Love.

Title of song, written for *Delmar's Revels* (1927)
but not performed till following year. Music by Jimmy McHugh.

FIELDS, W. C.
US comedian (1880–1946)

4   Never give a sucker an even break.

Quoted in *The Concise Oxford Dictionary of Proverbs* (1982)
Popularized by Fields, though attributed to various people including
Wilson Mizner. It was already associated with Fields by 1925 and may
have been used by him in the musical comedy *Poppy* (1923).

5   □ On the whole I'd rather be in Philadelphia.

What the comedian actually submitted as a suggested epitaph to *Vanity
Fair* magazine in 1925 was: 'Here lies W. C. Fields. I would rather be
living in Philadelphia.' It does not appear on his actual gravestone.
The saying evolved from an older expression 'Sooner dead than in
Philadelphia.'

6   I went to Philadelphia and found that it was closed.

Attrib
See also **ANONYMOUS 9:5.**

7   □ Any man who hates dogs and babies can't be all bad.

In fact, this was said by Leo Rosten (1908–) *about* Fields at a
Masquer's Club dinner, 16 February 1939. Often 'children' is
substituted for 'babies'.

1   *When asked why he did not drink water:*
    Fish fuck in it.
    Attrib

2   *When asked whether he liked children:*
    Boiled or fried?
    Attrib

3   *When a gambler asks, 'Is this a game of chance'?:*
    'Cuthbert J. Twillie': Not the way I play it.
    Film, *My Little Chickadee* (1939)

4   I was in love with a beautiful blonde once—she drove me to
    drink—'tis the one thing I'm indebted to her for.
    Film, *Never Give a Sucker an Even Break* (1941)

5   Horse sense is a good judgement which keeps horses from betting
    on people.
    Attrib

6   *During his last illness:*
    I have spent a lot of time searching through the Bible for
    loopholes.
    Attrib
    See also **THE FATAL GLASS OF BEER 117:1.**

FILM TITLES

7   Blonde Bombshell (US 1933)
    Title of a Jean Harlow vehicle (1933), known simply as *Bombshell* in the
    UK.

8   Close Encounters of the Third Kind (US 1977)
    Derived from categories (devised by J. Allen Hyhek) used by the US
    services to denote different types of UFO: the first 'kind' would be a
    simple sighting; the second, evidence of an alien landing; the third,
    actual contact with aliens.

9   The Days of Wine and Roses (US 1962)
    From Ernest Dowson (*d*1900), *Vitae Summa Brevis.*

10 Do Not Fold Spindle Or Mutilate (US 1971)
    From the instruction on punched cards, from 1930s.

11 A Fool There Was (US 1914)
    From Kipling's poem 'The Vampire' (1897). It was through this film
    that Theda Bara popularized the notion of the female 'vamp'.

1 **La Grande Illusion** (France 1937)

From the revised title of Norman Angell's book *The Great Illusion* (1910).

2 If It's Tuesday, This Must be Belgium (US 1969)

Title of film about US tourists rushing around Europe.

3 In Which We Serve (UK 1942)

From *The Book of Common Prayer*, 'Forms of Prayer to be Used at Sea'.

4 The Killing Fields (UK 1984)

From an unnamed American diplomat quoted in the *New York Times Magazine*, 20 January 1980, referring to scenes of Cambodian atrocities in 1975–8.

5 Love Pain and the Whole Damned Thing (US 1972)

Apparently an original coinage for Alan J. Pakula's film. Also used as the English title of short story collection by the German writer and film director, Doris Dorrie (1989).

6 Now Voyager (US 1942)

(And the original Olive Higgins Prouty novel), from Walt Whitman's line: 'Now voyager, sail thou forth to seek and find.'

7 An Officer and a Gentleman (US 1982)

See **PLAY TITLES 255:3.**

8 One Flew Over the Cuckoo's Nest (US 1975)

(And the original Ken Kesey novel), from the nursery rhyme 'One flew east, one flew west/One flew over the cuckoo's nest.'

9 **Les Quatre Cents Coups** ('The Four Hundred Blows') (France 1958)

From a French slang expression—*'faire les quatre cents coups'*—meaning either 'to paint the town red' or 'to be up to all sorts of tricks'.

10 She Done Him Wrong (1933)

Alluding to the traditional US ballad 'Frankie and Johnny' ('He was my man, but I done him wrong.')

11 Situation Hopeless But Not Serious (US 1965)

Probably derived from: 'The situation in Germany is serious but not hopeless; the situation in Austria is hopeless but not serious.' This is described as 'an Austrian proverb collected by Franklin Pierce Adams' in A. Andrews, *Quotations for Speakers and Writers*.

12 Straw Dogs (UK 1971)

'Heaven and Earth are not humane. They regard all things as straw dogs' (used in sacrifices)—Lao-tzu (*c*604–*c*531 BC).

1   *Tirez Sur Le Pianiste* (France 1960)

Translated as 'Shoot the Pianist/Piano-Player'—echoing the notice once reported by Oscar Wilde from a bar in the US Rocky Mountains—'Please do not shoot the pianist. He is doing his best.' (In 1972, Elton John had a record album entitled, 'Don't Shoot Me, I'm Only the Piano-Player'.)

2   A View To a Kill (UK 1985)

The title of Ian Fleming's original short story was 'From a View to a Kill', alluding more directly to the line 'From a view to a death' in the hunting song, 'D'ye Ken John Peel' (1832).

3   What's New Pussycat? (US/France 1965)

From a phrase associated with Warren Beatty for whom the film was originally written.

4   Where Were You When The Lights Went Out? (US 1968)

Alluding perhaps to the old (US?) rhyme 'Where was Moses when the lights went out? Down in the cellar eating sauerkraut.'

5   The Year of Living Dangerously (Australia 1982)

From the title of the source novel by Christopher Koch.

6   You Are What You Eat (US 1969)

A proverbial expression in several languages.

FISHER, Lord (Jacky)
British admiral (1841–1920)

7   The British Navy always travels first class.

Quoted in W. Churchill, *The Second World War*, Vol. 1

8   Fear God and Dread Nought.

His motto when elevated to the peerage

9   [Some day the Empire will go down because it is] Buggins's turn.

Letter (8 January 1917), reprinted in his *Memories* (1919)
He also used the expression in a letter in 1901, though he may not have originated it.

10   *On the ruinous cost of the Fleet and those responsible:*
You must be ruthless, relentless, and remorseless! *Sack the lot!*

Letter, *The Times*, 2 September 1919

11   Never explain. Never apologize.

Letter, *The Times*, 5 September 1919
Compare Benjamin Disraeli: 'Never complain and never explain.'

1   *Signing off correspondence:*
Yours till charcoal sprouts.

Quoted in C. Hassall, *Edward Marsh*
His other salutations included, 'Yours till hell freezes' (1909) and
'Yours to a cinder.'

FITZGERALD, F. Scott
US novelist (1896–1940)

2   Tales of the Jazz Age.

Title of book (1922)

3   Then wear the gold hat, if that will move her;
    If you can bounce high, bounce for her too,
Till she cry 'Lover, gold-hatted, high-bouncing lover,
    I must have you!'

Epigraph, *The Great Gatsby* (1925)
Attributed to 'Thomas Parke D'Invilliers'.

4   So we beat on, boats against the current, borne back ceaselessly
into the past.

ibid
Last line.

5   In a real dark night of the soul it is always three o'clock in the
morning.

The Crack-Up (1936)
The phrase *'Noche oscura'*—meaning a period of spiritual aridity
suffered by a mystic—had been used as the title of a Spanish work by St
John of the Cross in the sixteenth century.

FITZPATRICK, James A.
US travel film-maker (1902–   )

6   And so we say farewell.

Customary signing-off line in *Fitzpatrick Traveltalks*, from 1920s onwards

FITZSIMMONS, Bob
British boxer (1862–1917)

7   *Referring to an opponent of larger build (James L. Jeffries):*
    □ The bigger they come, the harder they fall.

Attrib 1900
Also attributed to John L. Sullivan. Probably of earlier proverbial origin
in any case.

FLANDERS, Michael
British entertainer (1922–75)

1   Mud, mud, glorious mud,
    Nothing quite like it for cooling the blood.
    'The Hippopotamus Song' (1953)

2   Eating people is wrong.
    Song, 'The Reluctant Cannibal', *At the Drop of a Hat* (1957)

3   Have Some Madeira, M'Dear.
    Song, 'Madeira, M'Dear' in ibid

4   Gnot a gnother gnu?
    Song, 'The Gnu' in ibid

5   If God had intended us to fly, he'd never have given us the railways.
    'By Air', *At the Drop of Another Hat* (1963)

6   It all makes work for the working man to do.
    'The Gas-Man Cometh' in ibid

7   The purpose of satire it has been rightly said is to strip off the
    veneer of comforting illusion and cosy half-truth and our job, as I
    see it, is to put it back again.
    ibid

8   Pee po belly bum drawers.
    Title of (a very rude) song (pub. 1977)
    Supposedly based on a traditional child's remark.

FLEMING, Ian
British novelist and journalist (1908–64)

9   '[My name's] Bond—James Bond.'
    Casino Royale (1953)
    Introduction, made well-known by more frequent use in the film
    versions on the Bond books.

10 You have a double-o number, I believe—007, if I remember right.
    The significance of that double-o number, they tell me, is that you
    have had to kill a man in the course of some assignment.
    Live and Let Die (1954)

11 The waiter brought the Martinis, shaken and not stirred, as Bond
    had stipulated.
    Diamonds are Forever (1956)
    This fad, although alluded to in the novel *Casino Royale* and in the first
    Bond film *Dr No* (1962), was not spoken in a film until *Goldfinger* (1964).

1   From Russia with Love.

Title of novel (1957)

2   The licence to kill for the Secret Service, the double-o prefix, was a great honour.

Dr No (1958)

3   'All you need is a course of TLC . . . Short for Tender Loving Care Treatment. It's what they write on most papers when a waif gets brought in to a children's clinic.'

Goldfinger (1959)

The phrase had existed before this, and in another context had been used by Shakespeare in *2 King Henry VI* (III.ii.279).

See also **FILM TITLES 121:2.**

FLETCHER, Cyril

British entertainer (1913–   )

4   I'm dreaming, oh my darling love, of thee.

Catchphrase, following broadcast in 1938
From poem 'Dreaming of Thee' by Edgar Wallace.

5   Pin back your lugholes.

Catchphrase
Preparing to recite one of his 'Odd Odes'.

FO, Dario

Italian playwright (1926–   )

6   Can't Pay? Won't Pay!

English title (1981) of his *Non Si Paga! Non Si Paga!* (1975)

FOCH, Ferdinand

French soldier (1851–1929)

7   *To General Joffre, during the second battle of the Marne (July/August 1918):*
Mon centre cède, ma droite recule, situation excellente. J'attaque! ('My centre gives way, my right retreats; situation excellent. I shall attack!')

Attrib

8   *On the Grand Canyon:*
What a marvellous place to drop one's mother-in-law.

Attrib

FOOT, Michael
British Labour politician and journalist (1913–   )

1   *Of Norman Tebbit:*
    Is it always his desire to give his imitation of a semi-house-trained polecat?

    Speech, Ebbw Vale, 8 June 1983
    Repeating a phrase he had earlier used in the House of Commons on 2 March 1978.

2   Guilty Men.

    Title of tract, July 1940
    Written with Frank Owen and Peter Howard.

FOOT, Paul
British journalist (1937–   )

3   If you don't know what's going on in Portugal, you must have been reading the papers.

    Attrib in 1975.

FORD, Gerald R.
US Republican President (1913–   )

4   *On becoming Vice-President:*
    I am a Ford, not a Lincoln. My addresses will never be as eloquent as Mr Lincoln's. But I will do my very best to equal his brevity and his plain speaking.

    Speech, Washington, 6 December 1973

5   *On becoming President:*
    I believe that truth is the glue that holds government together, not only our government but civilization itself . . . Our long national nightmare is over. Our Constitution works. Our great Republic is a government of laws and not of men. Here, the people rule.

    Speech, Washington, 9 August 1974

6   *Proposing a toast to Anwar Sadat:*
    [To] the great people and the government of Israel . . . Egypt, excuse me . . .

    Speech, Washington, December 1975

7   There is no Soviet domination of Eastern Europe and there never will be under a Ford administration.

    TV debate with Jimmy Carter, 6 October 1976

FORD, Henry

US industrialist (1863–1947)

1   *On the Model T Ford motor car (1909):*
People can have it any colour—so long as it's black.

Quoted in Hill & Nevins, *Ford: Expansion and Challenge*

2   We're going to try to get the boys out of the trenches before Christmas. I've chartered a ship, and some of us are going to Europe.

Statement, 1915
The *New York Tribune* put it this way: 'GREAT WAR ENDS CHRISTMAS DAY. FORD TO STOP IT.'

3   History is more or less bunk. It's tradition.

Interview with the *Chicago Tribune*, 25 May 1916
Popularly remembered as 'History is bunk.'

FORMBY, George (Jnr)

British entertainer (1904–61)

4   [It's] turned out nice again.

Catchphrase, from 1930s onwards
He starred in a film (UK 1941) with the title *Turned Out Nice Again.*

FORMBY, George (Snr)

British entertainer (1877–1921)

5   Coughin' well, tonight.

Catchphrase
He had a convulsive cough which eventually killed him.

6   John Willie, come on.

Catchphrase, from a monologue

FORSTER, E. M.

British novelist (1879–1970)

7   A Room With a View.

Title of novel (1908)
Noël Coward's song with the title did not appear until *This Year of Grace* (1928).

8   Only connect! That was the whole of her sermon. Only connect the prose and the passion, and both will be exalted, and human love will be seen at its height.

Howard's End (1910)
'Only connect' is also used as the novel's epigraph.

1   Personal relations are the important thing for ever and ever, and not this outer life of telegrams and anger.

ibid

2   It will generally be admitted that Beethoven's Fifth Symphony is the most sublime noise that has ever penetrated into the ear of man.

ibid

3   If I had to choose between betraying my country and betraying my friend, I hope I should have the guts to betray my country.

'What I Believe', in *The Nation*, 16 July 1938

4   I belong to the fag-end of Victorian liberalism.

Broadcast talk, 1946

FORSYTH, Bruce
British entertainer (1928–   )

5   I'm in charge!

Catchphrase in TV show, *Sunday Night at the London Palladium*, from *c*1958

6   Didn't he do well?

Catchphrase in TV show, *The Generation Game*, 1970s

7   Good game, good game!

Catchphrase in ibid

8   Nice to see you, to see you, nice!

Catchphrase in ibid

FORTY-SECOND STREET
US film 1933. Script by James Seymour and Rian James. With Warner Baxter as Julian Marsh, the theatre producer, and Ruby Keeler as Peggy Sawyer, the chorus girl.

9   *Julian (to Peggy):* You're going out a youngster—but you've got to come back a star!

Soundtrack

FRASER, Lady Antonia
British writer (1932–   )

10 *To Clive James:*
    I'm sorry, I only sleep with the first eleven.

Attrib by *Private Eye*, 1970s

FRASER, Malcolm
Australian Liberal Prime Minister (1930–)

1 Life is not meant to be easy.

Deakin lecture, 20 July 1971
Fraser said he derived it from Shaw, *Back to Methusaleh*, 'Life is not meant to be easy, my child; but take courage: it can be delightful.'

FREED, Alan
US broadcaster (1922–65)

2 Moondog's Rock 'n' Roll Party.

Title of radio programme, 1951
Freed is credited with taking the term 'rock 'n' roll' from black sexual slang and applying it to a type of music.

FRENCH, Marilyn
US novelist (1929–)

3 All men are rapists and that's all they are. They rape us with their eyes, their laws and their codes.

The Women's Room (1977)
Said by a character whose daughter has been raped.

FREUD, Sigmund
Austrian psychiatrist (1856–1939)

4 The artist has won—through his fantasy—what before he could only win *in* his fantasy: honour, power, and the love of women.

Introductory Lectures on Psycho-Analysis, No. 23 (1916)

5 *On phallic dream symbolism:*
Sometimes a cigar is just a cigar.

Attrib

FRIEDMAN, Milton
US economist (1912–)

6 □ There's no such thing as a free lunch.

The concept of the 'free lunch' is an old US expression, dating back to 1840 at least. 'There ain't no such thing as a free lunch' was popular by 1966, and Friedman gave it new life in the 1970s, using it in articles, lectures, and as the title of a book, to support his monetarist theories.

FROHMAN, Charles
US theatre producer (1860–1915)

7 Why fear death? It is the most beautiful adventure of life.

Quoted in I. F. Marcosson & D. Frohman, *Charles Frohman* (1916)
Last words before going down with the *Lusitania*, echoing the words from the play *Peter Pan* (*see* **BARRIE 24:7**) which he had produced.

THE FRONT PAGE
US play 1928. Written by Charles MacArthur and Ben Hecht.

1   The son of a bitch stole my watch!

   Last line.

FROST, Lady Carina
(wife of David) (1952–   )

2   *On being asked if her husband was a religious man:*
   Oh, yes, he thinks he's God.

   Quoted in *TV Times*, 6 June 1987

FROST, David (later Sir David)
British broadcaster (1939–   )

3   *After satirical attack on a person:*
   Seriously, though, he's doing a grand job.

   Catchphrase, TV show, *That Was The Week That Was* (1962)

4   Hello, good evening, and welcome.

   Catchphrase, first used on ITV, *The Frost Programme* (1966)

5   The sexual chemistry thing is really important.

   Remark, 1983
   Endorsing a suggestion from a reporter about an element in the on-screen relationship of presenters at the breakfast television station, TV-am.

6   We have been on a working honeymoon.

   Remark to reporters, March 1983
   Returning with his second wife from Venice.

FROST, Robert
US poet (1874–1963)

7   Something there is that doesn't love a wall.

   'Mending Wall', *North of Boston* (1914)

8   Good fences make good neighbours.

   ibid

9   Home is the place where, when you have to go there,
   They have to take you in.

   'The Death of the Hired Man', in ibid

10   Two roads diverged in a wood, and I—
   I took the one less travelled by,
   And that has made all the difference.

   'Road Not Taken', *Mountain Interval* (1916)

1   The woods are lovely, dark and deep.
     But I have promises to keep,
     And miles to go before I sleep,
     And miles to go before I sleep.

     'Stopping by Woods on a Snowy Evening' (1923)

FRYE, David
US impressionist and comedian (1934–   )

2   *On Gerald R. Ford:*
     He looks like the guy in a science fiction movie who is the first to
     see the Creature.

     Attrib in 1975

FUCHIDA, Mitsuo
Japanese pilot (1902–   )

3   Tora-tora-tora.

     Radio message, 7 December 1941
     Fuchida was leading the Japanese attack on Pearl Harbor. This was the
     signal to confirm that the fleet was being taken by surprise. 'Tora'
     means 'tiger'.

FUKUYAMA, Francis
US State Department official (1953–   )

4   What we may be witnessing is not the end of the Cold War but the
     end of history as such; that is, the end point of man's ideological
     evolution and the universalization of Western liberal democracy.

     Article in *National Interest*, Summer 1989

FULLER, R. Buckminster
US architect (1895–1983)

5   I am a passenger on the spaceship, Earth.
     Operating Manual for Spaceship Earth (1969)

FUNK, Walther
German Nazi minister (1890–1960)

6   ***Kristallnacht*** ('Night of Broken Glass').
     Attrib
     Euphemism to describe Nazi pogrom against Jews in Germany on the
     night of 9/10 November 1938.

FYLEMAN, Rose
British poet (1877–1957)

7   There are fairies at the bottom of our garden!
     'The Fairies', in *Punch*, 23 May 1917

GABOR, Zsa Zsa
Hungarian-born film actress (1919–   )

1   *In answer to the question 'How many husbands have you had?':*
You mean apart from my own?

Attrib, by 1976

GAITSKELL, Hugh
British Labour politician (1906–63)

2   *Attempting to persuade his party not to adopt a policy of unilateral disarmament:*
There are some of us . . . who will fight and fight and fight again to save the party we love.

Speech, Labour Party Conference, 3 October 1960

3   *On Britain joining the European Community:*
It does mean, if this is the idea, the end of Britain as an independent European state . . . it means the end of a thousand years of history.

Speech, Labour Party Conference, 3 October 1962

GALBRAITH, John Kenneth
US economist (1908–   )

4   The Affluent Society.

Title of book (1958)

5   The conventional wisdom.

In ibid
Phrase devised to describe 'the beliefs that are at any time assiduously, solemnly and mindlessly traded between the pretentiously wise.'

6   The Great Wall, I've been told, is the only man-made structure on earth that is visible from the moon. For the life of me I cannot see why anyone would go to the moon to look at it, when, with almost the same difficulty, it can be viewed in China.

Article in the *Sunday Times Magazine*, 1970s

GALSWORTHY, John
British novelist (1867–1933)

7   Nobody tells me anything.

Stock phrase of 'James Forsyte' in *The Man of Property* (1906) and *In Chancery* (1920)

GANDHI, Indira
Indian Prime Minister (1917–84)

1   Even if I die in the service of this nation, I would be proud of it. Every drop of my blood, I am sure, will contribute to the growth of this nation and make it strong and dynamic.

Speech, Bhubaneswar, Orissa, 31 October 1984
Twenty-four hours later she was assassinated. The wording varied from report to report.

GANDHI, Mahatma
Indian politician (1869–1948)

2   *When asked what he thought of Western civilization:*
I think it would be a good idea.

Attrib remark, 1930

GARBO, Greta
Swedish-born film actress (1905–90)

3   □ I think I go home.

Attrib remark
Much-beloved by Garbo imitators, this line is sometimes said to have been used as a negotiating ploy when Garbo was seeking a pay-rise from Louis B. Mayer. However, her 'interpreter', Sven-Hugo Borg, stated that she said to him 'Borg, I think I shall go home now. It isn't worth it, is it?' after her fellow-Swede, the director Mauritz Stiller, was fired (1926).

4   □ I want to be alone.

She 'said' the line in the 1929 silent film *The Single Standard* and in later 'talkies', but when referring to herself she tended to say 'I like to be alone'.

5   *Declining Howard Dietz's invitation to dine with him 'on Monday':*
How do I know I'm going to be hungry on Monday?

Attrib
See also ANNA CHRISTIE 7:3–4.

GARDNER, Ava
US actress (1922–90)

6   □ *On the Beach* is a story about the end of the world, and Melbourne sure is the right place to film it.

Attrib in 1959
In fact, an invention of Melbourne journalist Neil Jillett.

GARNER, John Nance
US Democratic Vice-President (1868–1937)

1   *On the Vice-Presidency:*
    [It] isn't worth a pitcher of warm piss.

    Attrib
    Usually bowdlerised to 'spit'. He also said the job 'didn't amount to a
    hill of beans.'

GARROD, Heathcote William
British academic (1878–1960)

2   *On being asked why he was not fighting to defend civilization in the First
    World War:*
    I am the civilization they are fighting for.

    Attrib

GEDDES, Sir Eric
British Conservative politician (1875–1937)

3   I have personally no doubt we will get everything out of her
    [Germany] that you can squeeze out of a lemon and a bit more . . .
    I will squeeze her until you can hear the pips squeak . . . I would
    strip Germany as she has stripped Belgium.

    Speech Cambridge Guildhall, 9 December 1918

GELDOF, Bob (later Hon. KBE)
Irish singer/musician (1952–   )

4   I'm into pop because I want to get rich, get famous and get laid.

    Attrib remark, by 1977

GEORGE V, HM King
British Sovereign (1865–1936)

5   □ Wake up England!.

    Speech, Guildhall, London, 5 December 1901
    On returning from an Empire tour, as Duke of York, he said: 'I venture
    to allude to the impression which seemed generally to prevail among
    our brethren overseas, that the old country must wake up if she intends
    to maintain her old position of pre-eminence in her Colonial trade
    against foreign competitors.'

6   Today, 23 years ago, dear Grandmama died. I wonder what she
    would have thought of a Labour Government.

    Diary, 22 January 1924
    He had just asked Ramsay MacDonald to form the first Labour
    Government.

1 After you've met one hundred and fifty Lord Mayors, they all begin to look the same.

Attrib

2 My father was frightened of his mother. I was frightened of my father, and I'm damned well going to make sure that my children are frightened of me.

Quoted in R. Churchill, *Life of the Earl of Derby*

3 Never miss an opportunity to relieve yourself; never miss a chance to sit down and rest your feet.

Attrib
See also **EDWARD VIII 108:1.**

4 *On the pact between Sir Samuel Hoare, Foreign Secretary, and Pierre Laval over Abyssinia, 1935:*
No more coals to Newcastle, no more Hoares to Paris.

Quoted in K. Rose, *George V*

5 *To the suggestion that his favourite watering place be dubbed Bognor Regis, c1929:*
Bugger Bognor!

ibid
Not his last words, as often supposed.

6 *To members of the Privy Council at Sandringham:*
Gentlemen. I am sorry for keeping you waiting like this—I am unable to concentrate.

20 January 1936. Quoted in H. Nicolson, *George V*
Sometimes called his last words.

7 *To his secretary, Lord Wigram:*
How is the Empire?

Quoted by S. Baldwin in broadcast, 21 January 1936
Sometimes quoted as his last words.

GEORGE VI, HM King
British Sovereign (1895–1952)

8 A former President of the United States [Abraham Lincoln] used to tell of a boy who was carrying an even smaller boy up a hill. Asked whether the heavy burden was not too much for him, the boy answered, 'It's not a burden, it's my brother!'

Christmas broadcast, 25 December 1942
Cf. the title of the later song 'He Ain't Heavy, He's My Brother', sung by the Hollies (1969).
See also **HASKINS 156:1.**

'GEORGE, Boy'
British singer (1961–)

1   I'd rather have a cup of tea than go to bed with someone—any day.

Remark, variously expressed, 1983

GEORGE, David Lloyd (later Earl Lloyd George of Dwyfor)
British Liberal Prime Minister (1863–1945)

2   *On Conservative use of a majority in the House of Lords to block legislation:*
□ This is the leal and trusty mastiff which is to watch over our interests, but which runs away at the first snarl of the trade unions? A mastiff? It is the right hon. Gentleman's Poodle. It fetches and carries for him. It barks for him. It bites anybody that he sets it on to.

Speech, House of Commons, 26 June 1907
Summarized by the phrase 'Mr Balfour's poodle'. A. J. Balfour was the
Conservative leader.

3   Sporting terms are pretty well understood wherever English is spoken . . . Well, then. The British soldier is a good sportsman . . . Germany elected to make this a finish fight with England . . . The fight must be to a finish—to a knock out.

Interview in *The Times*, 29 September 1915
In his memoirs, Lloyd George entitled one chapter 'The Knock-out
Blow'—which was how this notion was popularly expressed.

4   What is our task? To make Britain a fit country for heroes to live in.

Speech, Wolverhampton, 24 November 1918
This turned into the slogan 'A land fit for heroes' or 'A country fit for
heroes.'

5   The world is becoming like a lunatic asylum run by lunatics.

In the *Observer*, 8 January 1933
See also **STALLINGS 311:5.**

6   *On Neville Chamberlain:*
A good mayor of Birmingham in an off-year.

Attrib
Also attributed to Lord Hugh Cecil in the form 'No better than a
Mayor of Birmingham, and in a lean year at that.'

7   *On Sir John Simon:*
He has sat so long upon the fence that the iron has entered into his soul.

Attrib

1   *On Herbert Samuel:*
    When they circumcised Herbert Samuel they threw away the wrong
    bit.
    Attrib

2   *On Sir Douglas Haig:*
    He was brilliant to the top of his army boots.
    Attrib
    See also **SLOGANS 300:13.**

GERSHWIN, Ira
US lyricist (1896–1983)

3   I got rhythm,
    I got music,
    I got my man—
    Who could ask for anything more.
    Song, 'I Got Music', *Girl Crazy* (1930)

4   I Got Plenty o' Nuthin.
    Title of song, *Porgy and Bess* (1935)

5   It Ain't Necessarily So.
    Title of song in ibid

6   Nice Work, If You Can Get It.
    Title of song, *A Damsel in Distress* (1937)

7   You like potato and I like po-tah-to,
    You like tomato and I like to-mah-to . . .

    So, if you like pajamas and I like pa-jah-mas . . .
    Let's call the whole thing off!
    Song, 'Let's Call the Whole Thing Off',
    Shall We Dance (1937)

8   They Can't Take That Away From Me
    Title of song in ibid

9   In time the Rockies may crumble,
    Gibraltar may tumble
    (They're only made of clay),
    But our love is here to stay.
    Song, 'Love Is Here to Stay', *The Goldwyn Follies* (1937)

GETTY, J. Paul
US oil tycoon (1892–1976)

1   *Explaining why he refused to pay ransom money to secure the release of his grandson:*
I have fourteen other grandchildren and if I pay one penny now, then I'll have fourteen kidnapped grandchildren.
Attrib remark, 26 July 1973

2   The meek shall inherit the earth, but not the mineral rights.
Attrib

3   If you can actually count your money, you are not really rich.
Attrib

4   *Last words:*
I want my lunch.
Attrib

GIBBONS, Stella
British novelist (1902–89)

5   Something nasty in the woodshed.
Passim in *Cold Comfort Farm* (1933)

GIBBS, Wolcott
US writer (1902–58)

6   *Parody of **Time** magazine style:*
Backward ran sentences until reeled the mind.
More in Sorrow (1958)

7   Where it will all end, knows God.
ibid

GILLIATT, Penelope
British writer and critic (1933–   )

8   One of the most characteristic sounds of the English Sunday is the sound of Harold Hobson barking up the wrong tree.
Encore, Nov.–Dec. 1959
Hobson was for many years drama critic of the *Sunday Times*.

9   Sunday Bloody Sunday.
Title of film (1971)

GILMOUR, Sir Ian (later Lord Gilmour)
British Conservative politician (1926–)

1 *On being sacked as Deputy Foreign Secretary by Margaret Thatcher:*
It does no harm to throw the occasional man overboard, but it does not do much good if you are steering full speed ahead for the rocks.
Quoted in *Time*, September 1981

GINSBERG, Allen
US poet (1926–)

2 Liverpool is at the present moment the centre of the consciousness of the human universe.
Attrib *c*1964

GIRAUDOUX, Jean
French playwright (1882–1944)

3 Only the mediocre are always at their best.
Attrib
This saying has also been credited to Max Beerbohm and W. Somerset Maugham (the latter specifically referring to writers).

GISCARD D'ESTAING, Valéry
French president (1926–)

4 During my seven years in office, I was in love with seventeen million French women . . . I know this declaration will inspire irony and that English language readers will find it very French.
Le Pouvoir et la Vie (1988)

GLEASON, Jackie
US comedian (1916–87)

5 And awa-a-aay we go.
Catchphrase on TV show, from 1950s onwards

6 How sweet it is.
Saying in ibid

GODARD, Jean-Luc
French film director (1930–)

7 Photography is truth. And cinema is truth twenty-four times a second.
Film, *Le Petit Soldat* (1960)

8 Every film should have a beginning, a middle and an end—but not necessarily in that order.
Quoted in L. Deighton, *Close Up*

GOEBBELS, Joseph
German Nazi leader (1897–1945)

1 We can do without butter, but, despite all our love of peace, not without arms. One cannot shoot with butter, but with guns.

Translation of speech, Berlin, 17 January 1936
Possible origin of the phrase 'Guns or butter' or 'Guns before butter'.
See also **GOERING** *below.*

GOERING, Hermann
German Nazi leader (1893–1946)

2 Guns will make us powerful; butter will only make us fat.

Radio broadcast, late 1936
See also **JOHST 178:2.**

GOGARTY, Oliver St John
Irish writer (1878–1957)

3 I said, 'It is most extraordinary weather for this time of year.' He replied, 'Ah, it isn't this time of year at all.'

It Isn't This Time of Year at All

4 If a queen bee were crossed with a Fresian bull, would not the land flow with milk and honey?

Attrib

GOLDMAN, William
US screenwriter (1931–)

5 *Dictum on Hollywood film-making:*
Nobody knows anything.

Adventures in the Screen Trade (1983)

GOLDSMITH, Sir James
British businessman (1933–)

6 □ If you pay peanuts, you get monkeys.

This remark—in connection with the pay given to journalists on his short-lived news magazine *Now!* (c1980)—is not original. The modern proverb was in use by 1966.

7 When you marry your mistress, you create a job vacancy.

Attrib

GOLDWATER, Barry M.
US Republican politician (1909–   )

1   *Accepting his party's nomination for the Presidency:*
I would remind you that extremism in the defence of liberty is no vice. And let me remind you also that moderation in the pursuit of justice is no virtue.

Speech, San Francisco convention, 16 July 1964
Goldwater disclaimed any originality, saying the idea could be found in Cicero and in Greek authors.

2   In your heart you know I'm right.

Campaign slogan, 1964

GOLDWYN, Samuel
Polish-born US film producer (1882–1974)

3   *On Louis B. Mayer's funeral:*
The reason so many people showed up at his funeral was because they wanted to make sure he was dead.

Quoted in B. Crowther, *Hollywood Rajah*
Probably apocryphal, if only because the funeral was in fact sparsely attended.

4   *To Jack L. Warner, when Goldwyn discovered that one of his directors was moonlighting for Warner Bros.:*
How can we sit together and deal with this industry if you're going to do things like that to me? If this is the way you do it, gentlemen, include me out!

Quoted by S. Goldwyn Jnr, *TV Times*, 13 November 1982
One of the few genuine Goldwynisms.

5   An oral contract is not worth the paper it's written on.

ibid
In 1955, Winston Churchill said, 'I heard it said that an extemporare speech was not worth the paper it was written on.'

6   Let's have some new clichés.

Quoted in the *Observer*, 24 October 1948

7   □ In two words—impossible.

ibid
Unlikely to be genuine, according to his son.

8   The trouble with this business is the dearth of bad pictures.

Attrib, but probably apocryphal

9   They're always biting the hand that lays the golden egg.

Ditto

1   We have all passed a lot of water since then.
    Ditto

2   Anyone who goes to a psychiatrist needs to have his head
    examined.
    Ditto

3   *Waving from liner to friends on the quayside:*
    Bon Voyage!
    Quoted in L. Hellman, *Pentimento*

4   *On films with a 'message':*
    Messages are for Western Union.
    Attrib

GONE WITH THE WIND
US film 1939. Script by Sidney Howard, based on the novel by Margaret
Mitchell. With Vivien Leigh as Scarlett O'Hara and Clark Gable as Rhett Butler.

5   *Scarlett:* Where shall I go? What shall I do?
    Rhett: Frankly, my dear, I don't give a damn.
    Soundtrack

6   *Concluding words:*
    Scarlett: After all, tomorrow is another day.
    Soundtrack

7   The Greatest Motion Picture Ever Made.
    Slogan
    See also **BOOK TITLES 44:3.**

THE GOON SHOW
UK radio comedy series (BBC), from 1951. Also called *The Goons.*
Script by Spike Milligan and Larry Stephens. With Spike Milligan as Little Jim,
Harry Secombe as Seagoon, Peter Sellers as Bluebottle, and Wallace
Greenslade (announcer).

8   And there's more where that came from.
    Catchphrase

9   And this is where the story really begins.
    Catchphrase

10 Damn clever these Chinese.
    Catchphrase

11 *Q.* Do you come here often?
    A. Only in the mating season.
    Catchphrase

1 The dreaded lergy.
Catchphrase
Pronounced 'lurgy'.

2 *Seagoon:* Hello folks, and what about the workers?
Catchphrase

3 *Little Jim:* He's fallen in the water.
Catchphrase

4 He's very good, you know.
Catchphrase

5 *Greenslade:* It's all in the mind, you know.
Catchphrase

6 I've been sponned.
Catchphrase

7 Needle, nardle, noo.
Catchphrase

8 Time for your OBE, Neddie.
Catchphrase

9 You can't get the wood, you know.
Catchphrase

10 *Bluebottle:* You dirty rotten swine, you.
Catchphrase

11 You silly twisted boy.
Catchphrase

GRABLE, Betty
US film actress (1916–73)

12 There are two reasons why I'm in show business, and I'm standing on both of them.
Attrib

GRADE, Lew (later Lord Grade)
Russian-born British media tycoon (1906–)

13 All my shows are great. Some of them are bad. But they are all great.
Quoted in the *Observer*, 14 September 1975

1   *To Franco Zeffirelli who explained that the high cost of the film **Jesus of Nazareth** was partly because there had to be twelve apostles:*
Twelve! So who needs *twelve?* Couldn't we make do with *six?*
Quoted in *Radio Times*, October 1983

2   *When it was revealed that the actor playing Christ in the film was living with a woman to whom he was not married:*
What about it? Do you want to crucify the boy?
Attrib

3   *On the film he produced called **Raise the Titanic:***
□ It would have been cheaper to lower the Atlantic.
Attrib
What he actually said was, 'I didn't raise the *Titanic* high enough.'

GRAHAM, Dr Billy
US evangelist (1918–   )

4   Decide for Christ.
Slogan, from 1940s onwards

5   I want you to get up out of your seats.
Frequent exhortation, by 1966

GRAHAM, Philip L.
US newspaper publisher (1915–63)

6   News [journalism] is the first rough draft of history.
Attrib remark in *Washington Post*, 29 September 1991
Also attributed to Ben Bradlee (*b*1921), an editor of the *Washington Post*.

GRAHAME, Kenneth
British writer (1859–1932)

7   There is *nothing*—absolutely nothing—half so much worth doing as simply messing about in boats.
The Wind in the Willows (1908)

8   O bliss! O poop-poop! O my! O my!
ibid
'Toad' on the joys of motoring.

9   The clever men at Oxford
   Know all there is to be knowed.
But they none of them know one half as much
   As intelligent Mr Toad.
ibid

1   The Piper at the Gates of Dawn.

Chapter heading in ibid

GRAVES, Robert
British poet (1895–1985)

2   Goodbye To All That.

Title of autobiography (1929)

3   The remarkable thing about Shakespeare is that he is really very good—in spite of all the people who say he is very good.

Quoted in the *Observer*, 6 December 1964

4   Far away is close at hand
     Close joined is far away,
     Love shall come at your command
     Yet will not stay.

'Song of Contrariety', *Collected Poems* (1975)

GRAYSON, Larry
British comedian (1930–   )

5   Shut that door!

Catchphrase, from 1970 onwards

6   What a gay day!

Catchphrase

7   *Of contestant:*
     He seems like a nice boy, doesn't he?

Catchphrase on TV show *The Generation Game*, from 1978 onwards

GRAYSON, Victor
British Labour politician (1881–?1920)

8   Never explain: your friends don't need it and your enemies won't believe it.

Attrib
Compare **HUBBARD 167:1.**

GREEN, Benny
British writer and broadcaster (1927–   )

9   Live music is an anachronism, and now is the winter of our discothèque.

Remark, by 1976

GREENE, Graham
British novelist (1904–91)

1   Fame is a powerful aphrodisiac.
     Quoted in *Radio Times*, 10 September 1964

GREEN, Hughie
British broadcaster (1920–)

2   I mean that most sincerely, friends.
     Stock phrase, TV shows, 1950s–70s

3   It's make your mind up time.
     Stock phrase on TV show *Opportunity Knocks*, from 1960s onwards

GREER, Germaine
Australian-born writer and feminist (1939–)

4   *When Ned Sherrin claimed that **Laugh-In** was a spin-off of **That Was The Week That Was:***
     Like Concorde is a spin-off of the Tiger Moth, darling.
     On *Quote . . . Unquote*, BBC Radio, 7 March 1976

5   No sex is better than bad sex.
     Attrib

GRENFELL, Joyce
British entertainer (1910–80)

6   George—*don't* do that.
     'Nursery Sketches', (1953)

7   *Quoting an Irish woman:*
     When you've got over the disgrace of the single life, it's more airy.
     Remark, 1970

8   If I should go before the rest of you
     Break not a flower nor inscribe a stone,
     Nor when I'm gone speak in a Sunday voice
     But be the usual selves that I have known.
         Weep if you must,
         Parting is hell,
         But life goes on,
         So sing as well.
     Poem (date unknown), quoted in *Joyce By Herself and Her Friends* (1980)
     See also **STOPPARD 314:5.**

GREY, Sir Edward (later Viscount Grey of Fallodon)
British Liberal politician (1862–1933)

1   *In his room at the Foreign Office, 3 August 1914:*
The lamps are going out all over Europe; we shall not see them lit
again in our life-time.

Recounted in *Twenty-five Years* (1925)

GRIFFITH, D. W.
US film director (1874–1948)

2   Out of the cradle endlessly rocking.

Film script, *Intolerance* (1916)
This repeated sub-title quotes the title of a poem by Walt Whitman.

3   *Directing an epic film:*
Move those ten thousand horses a trifle to the right. And that mob
out there, three feet forward.

Attrib

GRIFFITH-JONES, Mervyn
British lawyer (1907–79)

4   *To jury, as prosecuting counsel at trial of Penguin Books Ltd who were
accused of publishing an obscene work in D. H. Lawrence's **Lady
Chatterley's Lover**, October 1960:*
Is it a book that you would have lying around in your own house? Is
it a book that you would even wish your wife or your servants to
read?

Quoted in C. H. Rolph, *The Trial of Lady Chatterley*

GRIFFITHS, Trevor
British playwright (1935–   )

5   *Captain Oates:*
Call of nature, Birdie!

TV play, *The Last Place on Earth*, 1985
Avoiding use of the actual **OATES 243:1.**

GRIMOND, Jo (later Lord Grimond)
British Liberal politician (1913–   )

6   In bygone days, commanders were taught that when in doubt, they
should march their troops towards the sound of gunfire. I intend to
march my troops towards the sound of gunfire.

Speech, Liberal Party Assembly, Llandudno, 14 September 1963

7   *On the chance of a pact with the Labour Government:*
Our teeth are in the real meat.

Speech, Liberal Party Assembly, 1965

GROMYKO, Andrei
Soviet politician (1909–89)

1   *Proposing Mikhail Gorbachev as Soviet Communist Party leader:*
This man has a nice smile, but he has got iron teeth.

Speech, 11 March 1985

GUEDALLA, Philip
British writer (1889–1944)

2   The cheerful clatter of Sir James Barrie's cans as he went round with the milk of human kindness.

Supers and Supermen (1920), 'Some Critics'

3   History repeats itself; historians repeat each other.

'Some Historians' in ibid
Has also been ascribed to A. J. Balfour.

GUINAN, Texas
US nightclub hostess (1884–1933)

4   *Greeting to clients:*
Hello, sucker!

Quoted in W. & M. Morris, *Dictionary of Word and Phrase Origins*

5   *Description of small-town businessman trying to prove himself a big shot in the city:*
Big butter-and-egg man.

ibid

6   *When refused entry to France with her troupe in 1931:*
It goes to show that fifty million Frenchmen *can* be wrong.

See also **ANONYMOUS 8:8.**

GUINNESS, Sir Alec
British actor (1914–   )

7   Always remember before going on stage, wipe your nose and check your flies.

Attrib
Time (11 May 1987) prefers 'Blow your nose and check your fly'.

GULBENKIAN, Nubar
British industrialist and philanthropist (1896–1972)

8   The best number for a dinner party is two: myself and a damn good head waiter.

Quoted in the *Daily Telegraph*, 14 January 1965

GURNEY, Dorothy Frances
British poet (1858–1932)

1   The kiss of the sun for pardon,
       The song of the birds for mirth,
   One is nearer God's Heart in a garden
       Than anywhere else on earth.

   Poems (1913), 'God's Garden'

GWENN, Edmund
British actor (1875–1959)

2   *When someone said to him, on his deathbed, that dying 'must be very hard':*
   It is. But not as hard as farce.

   Quoted in *Time*, 30 January 1984

HAIG, Alexander
US General and Republican politician (1924–   )

1   *After an assassination attempt on President Reagan:*
As of now, I am in charge at the White House.
Quoted in *The Times*, 1 April 1981

HAIG, Sir Douglas (later Earl Haig)
British soldier (1861–1928)

2   *On Lord Derby:*
A very weak-minded fellow, I'm afraid, and, like the feather pillow, bears the marks of the last person who has sat on him!
Letter to wife, 14 January 1918

3   *To British troops on the Western Front:*
Every position must be held to the last man: there must be no retirement. With our *backs to the wall*, and believing in the justice of our cause, each one of us must fight on to the end.
Order, 12 April 1918

HAILSHAM, Viscount (later Quintin Hogg, later Lord Hailsham)
(British Conservative politician) (1907–   )

4   *On the Profumo Affair:*
A great party is not to be brought down because of a squalid affair between a woman of easy virtue and a proved liar.
Interview, BBC TV, 13 June 1963

5   *On Labour policies during a General Election:*
If the British public falls for this, I say it will be stark, staring bonkers.
Press conference, London, 12 October 1964

HALDANE, J. B. S.
British scientist (1892–1964)

6   My suspicion is that the universe is not only queerer than we suppose, but queerer than we *can* suppose.
Possible Worlds (1927)

HALDEMAN, H. R.
US government official (1929–   )

7   Once the toothpaste is out of the tube, it is awfully hard to get it back in.
Remark on Watergate affair, 8 April 1973
The remark has also been attributed to his colleague, John D. Erlichman, and to President Nixon.

HALL, Archibald
British butler (1924–)

1 *On being convicted of five murders:*
It was easy after the first one. After that I was trying for the *Guinness Book of Records.*
Quoted in the *Observer,* 5 November 1978

HALL, Henry
British band leader (1898–1989)

2 Here's to the next time.
Stock phrase, from 1930s onwards

3 This *is* Henry Hall speaking and tonight is my guest night.
Stock phrase, from 1934 onwards

HALL, Jerry
US model (1956–)

4 My mother said it was simple to keep a man—you must be a maid in the living-room, a cook in the kitchen and a whore in the bedroom. I said I'd hire the other two and take care of the bedroom bit.
Attrib remark, by 1985

HAMMARSKJOLD, Dag
Swedish UN official (1905–61)

5 Never let success hide its emptiness from you, achievement its nothingness, toil its desolation. And so . . . keep alive the incentive to push on further, that pain in the soul which drives us beyond ourselves . . . Do not look back. And do not dream about the future, either. It will neither give you back the past, nor satisfy your other daydreams. Your duty, your reward—your destiny—are *here* and *now.*
Markings (1965)

HAMMERSTEIN II, Oscar
US lyricist (1895–1960)

6 Ol' Man River
He just keeps rollin' along.
'Ol Man River', *Show Boat* (1927)
Music by Jerome Kern, as for the following:

7 The last time I saw Paris, her heart was warm and gay,
I heard the laughter of her heart in every street café.
Song, 'The Last Time I saw Paris', *Lady Be Good* (1941)

1   The corn is as high as an elephant's eye.

Song, 'Oh, What a Beautiful Mornin'', *Oklahoma!* (1943)
Music by Richard Rodgers, as for the following:

2   June is Bustin' Out All Over.

Title of song, *Carousel* (1945)

3   You'll Never Walk Alone.

Title of song in ibid

4   There Is Nothin' Like a Dame.

Title of song, *South Pacific* (1949)

5   Some enchanted evening . . .
    You may see a stranger across a crowded room.

Song, 'Some Enchanted Evening' in ibid

6   Fools give you reasons, wise men never try.

ibid

7   I'm Gonna Wash That Man Right Out of My Hair.

Title of song in ibid

8   Hello, Young Lovers (Wherever You Are).

Title of song, *The King and I* (1951)

9   The hills are alive with the sound of music.

Title song, *The Sound of Music* (1959)

10 These are a few of my favourite things.

Song, 'My Favourite Things', in ibid

HAMMOND, Percy
US theatre critic (1873–1936)

11 I have knocked everything but the knees of the chorus-girls, and
    Nature has anticipated me there.

Quoted in *The Frank Muir Book*

HAMPTON, Christopher
British playwright (1946–   )

12 Masturbation is the thinking man's television.

The Philanthropist (1970)

13 *Philip (bewildered):* I'm sorry. *(Pause.)* I suppose I am indecisive.
    (Pause.) My trouble is, I'm a man of no convictions. *(Longish pause.)*
    At least, I think I am.

ibid

1   Asking a working writer what he thinks about critics is like asking a lamp-post how it feels about dogs.

   Quoted in the *Sunday Times Magazine*, 16 October 1977

HANCOCK'S HALF-HOUR

UK radio and TV series (BBC), from 1954 onwards (also called simply *Hancock* on TV). Scripts by Alan Simpson and Ray Galton. With Tony Hancock (1924–68).

2   Ha-harr, Jim, lad.

   Stock routine
   Impersonating Robert Newton as Long John Silver in the film *Treasure Island* (1950).

3   Mis-ter *Chris*-tian . . . I'll have you *hung* from the *high*-est *yard*-arm in the *Navy*.

   Stock routine
   Impersonating Charles Laughton as Captain Bligh in the film *Mutiny on the Bounty* (1935).

4   A man of my cal-i-bre.

   Stock phrase.

5   I thought my mother was a bad cook but at least her gravy used to move about a bit.

   'A Sunday Afternoon at Home' (radio), 22 April 1958

6   A pint? That's very nearly an armful.

   'The Blood Donor' (TV), 23 June 1961
   See also **WILLIAMS 347:5.**

HANFF, Minnie Maud

US advertising copywriter (1880–1942)

7   Vigor, Vim, Pefect Trim;
     Force made him, Sunny Jim.

   Jingle for Force breakfast cereal (1903)
   The name 'Sunny Jim' was invented by Miss Hanff and a Miss Ficken.

8   High o'er the fence leaps Sunny Jim,
     Force is the food that raises him.

   Ditto (1920)

HANRAHAN, Brian
British journalist (1949–   )

1   *Of British attack on Port Stanley airport, during the Falklands war:*
I'm not allowed to say how many planes [Harrier jets from HMS *Hermes*] joined the raid, but I counted them all out and I counted them all back.

Report broadcast by BBC, 1 May 1982
'An elegant way of telling the truth without compromising the exigencies of military censorship'—Alasdair Milne.

HARBACH, Otto
US lyricist (1873–1963)

2   She didn't say yes,
She didn't say no.

Song, 'She Didn't Say Yes', *The Cat and the Fiddle* (1931)

3   Smoke Gets in Your Eyes.

Title of song, *Roberta* (1933)

HARBURG, E. Y.
US lyricist (1898–1981)

4   It's only a paper moon,
Sailing over a cardboard sea,
But it wouldn't be make-believe
If you believed in me.

Song, 'It's Only a Paper Moon', *The Great Magoo* (1932)
Written with Harold Arlen and Billy Rose.

5   Once I built a rail-road,
Now it's done.
Brother, can you spare a dime?

Song, 'Brother Can You Spare a Dime', *New Americana* (1932)
Music by Jay Gorney.

6   Somewhere over the rainbow, skies are blue,
And the dreams that you dare to dream really do come true.

Song, 'Over the Rainbow', *The Wizard of Oz* (1939)
Music by Harold Arlen.

7   Follow the Yellow Brick Road.

Title of song in ibid

8   Happiness is a Thing Called Joe.

Title of song (1942)
Music by Harold Arlen.

HARDING, Gilbert
British broadcaster (1907–60)

1   *In written answer to US immigration question, 'Is it your intention to overthrow the government of the United States by force?':*
Sole purpose of visit.

Attrib

2   *To Mae West's manager who had suggested he might sound a bit more 'sexy' when interviewing her for the BBC:*
If, sir, I possessed the power of conveying unlimited sexual attraction through the potency of my voice, I would not be reduced to accepting a miserable pittance from the BBC for interviewing a faded female in a damp basement.

Quoted in *Gilbert Harding by His Friends* (1961)

HARDING, Warren G.
US Republican President (1865–1923)

3   America's present need is not heroics but healing, not nostrums but normalcy.

Speech, Boston, 14 May 1920
Giving rise to the slogans 'Back to Normalcy' and 'Return to Normalcy with Harding.'

HARDY, Oliver
US film comedian (1892–1957)

4   *To Stan Laurel:*
Here's another fine mess you've gotten me into.

Catchphrase in films from the 1930s onwards
Another Fine Mess was the title of one of their shorts in 1930.

HARE, Robertson
British comedy actor (1891–1979)

5   Indubitably!

Catchphrase

6   Oh, calamity!

Catchphrase

HARGREAVES, William
British songwriter (1846–1919)

1   I'm Burlington Bertie
    I rise at ten thirty and saunter along like a toff,
    I walk down the Strand with my gloves on my hand,
    Then I walk down again with them off.

    Song, 'Burlington Bertie from Bow' (1915)
    Not to be confused with 'Burlington Bertie'(1900) by Harry B. Norris.

2   They made me a present of Mornington Crescent—
    They threw it a brick at a time.

    Song, 'The Night I Appeared as Macbeth' (1922)

HART, Lorenz
US lyricist (1895–1943)

3   With a Song in my Heart.

    Title of song (1930)
    Music by Richard Rodgers, as for all the following:

4   When love congeals
    It soon reveals
    The faint aroma of performing seals
    The double-crossing of a pair of heels.

    Song, 'I Wish I Were in Love Again', *Babes in Arms* (1937)

5   That's why the lady is a tramp.

    Song, 'The Lady Is a Tramp', in ibid

6   Bewitched, Bothered and Bewildered.

    Title of song, *Pal Joey* (1940)

7   I Didn't Know What Time It Was.

    Title of song in ibid

8   My Funny Valentine.

    Title of song in ibid (originally in *Babes in Arms*)

HARTLEY, L. P.
British novelist (1895–1972)

9   The past is a foreign country: they do things differently there.

    The Go-Between (1953)

HASKINS, Minnie Louise
British poet (1875–1957)

1   And I said to the man who stood at the Gate of the Year, 'Give me a light that I may tread safely into the unknown.' And he replied, 'Go out into the darkness, and put your hand into the hand of God. That shall be to you better than light, and safer than a known way.'

The Desert (Introduction) (1908)

Quoted by King George VI in Christmas broadcast, 1939.

HASSALL, Christopher
British writer (1912–63)

2   *On Edith Sitwell:*
She's genuinely bogus.

Attrib

HATTON, Will
British comedian

3   *To partner Ethel Manners:*
Don't you know there's a war on?

Catchphrase, 1940s

HAVERS, Sir Michael (later Lord Havers)
British Conservative politician (1923–92)

4   *On the immunity from prosecution offered to the spy, Sir Anthony Blunt, in 1964:*
He maintained his denial. He was offered immunity from prosecution. He sat in silence for a while. He got up, looked out of the window, poured himself a drink and after a few minutes confessed. Later he co-operated, and he continued to co-operate. That is how the immunity was given and how Blunt responded.

Speech, House of Commons, 21 November 1979
As Attorney-General.

'HAW-HAW, Lord' (William Joyce)
US-born propagandist for German Nazis (1906–46)

5   Germany calling, Germany calling.

Radio broadcasts to Britain, during the Second World War

HAY, Ian
British novelist and playwright (1876–1952)

6   The First Hundred Thousand.

Title of novel (1915)

7   What do you mean, funny? Funny-peculiar, or funny ha-ha?

Play, *The Housemaster* (1936)

HAYES, J. Milton
British writer (1884–1940)

1 There's a one-eyed yellow idol to the North of Khatmandu.

'The Green Eye of the Yellow God' (1911)

HEALEY, Denis (later Lord Healey)
British Labour politician (1917–   )

2 I warn you there are going to be howls of anguish from the 80,000 people who are rich enough to pay over 75% on the last slice of their income.

Speech to Labour Party Conference, 1 October 1973

3 *On being attacked by Sir Geoffrey Howe in parliamentary debate over his Budget proposals:*
That part of his speech was rather like being savaged by a dead sheep.

Speech, House of Commons, 14 June 1978
Earlier, Sir Roy Welensky had said of Iain Macleod that being attacked by him was like being 'bitten by a dead sheep'. Healey later claimed he had taken the line from what Winston Churchill had said about being attacked by Clement Attlee, that it was like 'being savaged by a pet lamb'.

4 *On US politicians having got themselves into a hole over the arms race:*
When you are in a hole, stop digging.

Remark, September 1983

5 I plan to be the Gromyko of the Labour party for the next thirty years.

Remark, on several occasions, 1984

6 Silly Billy!

Catchphrase
Invented for him by the impressionist, Mike Yarwood, and then sometimes used by him.

7 You mustn't take out a man's appendix while he's moving a grand piano.

Quoted as a 'favourite aphorism' in P. Ziegler, *Mountbatten* (1985)

HEATH, Edward (later Sir Edward)
British Conservative Prime Minister (1916–   )

8 Nor would it be in the interests of the [European] Community that its enlargement should take place except with the full-hearted consent of the Parliament and people of the new member countries.

Speech to the Franco-British Chamber of Commerce, Paris, 5 May 1970

1   *On tax cuts and a freeze on prices by nationalized industries:*
☐ This would, at a stroke, reduce the rise in prices, increase productivity and reduce unemployment.

Press release (No. G.E.228), from Conservative Central Office, 16 June 1970
Never actually spoken by Heath.

2   We were returned to office to change the course of history of this nation—nothing less. If we are to achieve this task we will have to embark on a change so radical, a revolution so quiet and yet so total, that it will go far beyond the programme for a parliament to which we are committed and on which we have already embarked, far beyond the decade and way into the 80s.

Speech, Conservative Party Conference, October 1970

3   *On the Lonrho affair (involving tax avoidance):*
It is the unpleasant and unacceptable face of capitalism, but one should not suggest that the whole of British industry consists of practices of this kind.

Speech, House of Commons, 15 May 1973
His draft had 'unacceptable facet'.

4   I entered the House in 1950 having fought an election on Mr Churchill's theme that Conservatives were to set the people free. It was not a theme that we were to set the people free to do what we tell them.

Speech, House of Commons, 17 January 1984

'HEATHERTON, Fred'
Pseudonym of British and US songwriters
Desmond Cox and Elton Box

5   Big ones, small ones, some as big as your head.

Song, 'I've Got a Lovely Bunch of Cocoanuts' (1944)

HELLER, Joseph
US novelist (1923–   )

6   Orr was crazy and could be grounded. All he had to do was ask; and as soon as he did, he would no longer be crazy and would have to fly more missions . . . Yossarian was moved very deeply by the absolute simplicity of this clause of Catch-22 and let out a respectful whistle.

Catch-22 (1961)

HELLMAN, Lillian
US playwright and writer (1905–84)

1 *Letter to Chairman, House Committee on Un-American Activities, Washington, 19 May 1952:*
To hurt innocent people whom I knew many years ago in order to save myself is, to me, inhuman and indecent and dishonorable. I cannot and will not cut my conscience to fit this year's fashions.

Quoted in *Scoundrel Time* (1976)

HELL'S ANGELS
US film 1930. Script by Howard Estabrook and Harry Behn. With Jean Harlow as Helen.

2 *About to exchange her fur wrap for a dressing-gown:*
Helen: Would you be shocked if I put on something more comfortable?

Soundtrack

HELMSLEY, Leona
US hotelier (*c*1920–)

3 Only the little people pay taxes. We don't pay taxes.

Remark, quoted 1989

HELPMANN, Sir Robert
Australian dancer and choreographer (1909–86)

4 *After the opening night of **Oh, Calcutta!**:*
The trouble with nude dancing is that not everything stops when the music stops.

Quoted in *The Frank Muir Book*
Also in the form: 'There are portions of the human anatomy which would keep swinging after the music had finished.'

HEMINGWAY, Ernest
US novelist (1899–1961)

5 The Sun Also Rises.

Title of novel (1926)
After quotation from Ecclesiastes 1:5: 'The sun also ariseth and the sun goeth down, and hasteth to his place where he arose.'

6 *Definition of 'guts':*
Grace under pressure.

Interview in the *New Yorker*, 30 November 1929
Based on Latin *'fortiter in re, suaviter in modo'*, and later invoked by John F. Kennedy in *Profiles in Courage*.

1   *In response to the remark 'The very rich are different from you and me':*
    □ Yes, they have more money.

    Discussed in T. Burnam, *More Misinformation* (1980)
    F. Scott Fitzgerald had written 'Let me tell you about the very rich.
    They are different from you and me' in 1926 and the exchange is
    sometimes given as having been between the two writers. In fact, the
    response came from the critic Mary Colum who told Hemingway in
    1936 'The only difference between the rich and other people is that
    the rich have more money.'

2   Did thee feel the earth move?

    For Whom the Bell Tolls (1940)

3   Where do the noses go? I always wondered where the noses would
    go.

    ibid

4   Across the River and Into the Trees.

    Title of novel (1950)
    Probably alluding to the last words of General Stonewall Jackson
    (killed in error by his own troops in 1863): 'Let us cross over the river,
    and rest under the trees.'

5   If you are lucky enough to have lived in Paris as a young man, then
    wherever you go for the rest of your life, it stays with you, for Paris is
    a moveable feast.

    Epigraph to *A Moveable Feast* (1964)

HENDERSON, Leon
US economist (1895–1986)

6   Having a little inflation is like being a little pregnant.

    Attrib

HENDRIX, Jimi
US rock musician (1942–70)

7   Once you're dead, you're made for life.

    Attrib

'HENRY, O.'
US writer (1862–1910)

8   *Last words:*
    Turn up the lights [*or* put up the shades], I don't want to go home
    in the dark.

    Attrib
    Alluding to the song 'I'm Afraid to Go Home in the Dark.'

HEPBURN, Katharine
US film actress (1909–)

1   *In response to query, 'Hey, you used to be Joan Crawford, didn't you?'*
    Not any more I'm not.

    Attrib
    See also **STAGE DOOR 311:1.**

HERBERT, A. P. (later Sir Alan)
British writer and politician (1890–1971)

2   Holy Deadlock.

    Title of novel on divorce (1934)

3   The critical period in matrimony is breakfast-time.

    Uncommon Law (1935)

HERFORD, Oliver
US humorist (1863–1935)

4   Actresses will happen in the best-regulated families.

    Attrib

HEWART, Gordon (later Lord Hewart)
British lawyer (1870–1943)

5   *When taunted by F. E. Smith about the size of his stomach with, 'What's it
    to be—a boy or a girl?':*
    If it's a boy I'll call him John. If it's a girl I'll call her Mary. But if, as
    I suspect, it's only wind, I'll call it F. E. Smith.

    Attrib
    This story can also be found in US and Australian folklore involving
    other pairs.

6   *In case of Rex v. Sussex Justices, 9 November 1923:*
    A long list of cases shows that it is not merely of some importance
    but is of fundamental importance that justice should not only be
    done, but should manifestly be seen to be done.

    King's Bench Reports (1924)

HIGHWAY PATROL
US TV police series, 1955–9. With Broderick Crawford.

7   *Into radio, signifying agreement:*
    Ten-four.

    Catchphrase

HILL, Charles (later Lord Hill)

British doctor, politician, broadcaster (1904–89)

1   Black-coated workers.

Description of prunes as laxatives, used in broadcasts as 'The Radio
Doctor', 1940s.

HILL, Joe

Swedish-born songwriter and industrial organizer in US (1879–1915)

2   Work and pray, live on hay,
You'll get pie in the sky when you die.

'The Preacher and the Slave' (1911)

HILL, Patty Smith

US teacher (1868–1946)

3   Happy Birthday to You.

Title of song (copyrighted 1935)

Originally entitled 'Good Morning to All' and published in *Song Stories
for Children* (1893). The music was written by her sister, Mildred
(1859–1916).

HILLARY, Edmund (later Sir Edmund)

New Zealand mountaineer (1919–   )

4   *On being (with Tenzing Norgay) the first persons to climb Mount Everest,
29 May 1953:*
Well, we knocked the bastard off!

Recounted in *Nothing Venture, Nothing Win* (1975)

HILLINGDON, Alice, Lady

Wife of 2nd Baron Hillingdon (1857–1940)

5   ☐ I am happy now that Charles calls on my bedchamber less
frequently than of old. As it is, I now endure but two calls a week
and when I hear his steps outside my door I lie down on my bed,
close my eyes, open my legs and think of England.

Journal (1912), cited in E. Partridge, *A Dictionary of Catch Phrases*
The original remains untraced and the woman's name may be
'Hillingham'.

HILLS, Denis

British teacher (1913–   )

6   *On President Amin of Uganda:*
A village tyrant . . . a black Nero.

The White Pumpkin (1975)
Hills was sentenced to death for treason on account of these words but
was freed after the intervention of the Queen and the Foreign
Secretary.

HIROHITO, Emperor
Japanese Head of State and former divinity (1901–89)

1   The war situation has developed not necessarily to Japan's advantage.

Announcing Japan's surrender, 15 August 1945

HITCHCOCK, Alfred
British-born film director (1899–1980)

2   Actors are cattle.

In *Saturday Evening Post*, 22 May 1943
He later denied this: 'What I said was actors should be treated like cattle'

HITLER, Adolf
German Nazi leader (1889–1945)

3   With a suitcase full of clothes and underwear in my hand and an indomitable will in my heart, I set out for Vienna . . . I too hoped to become 'something'.

Mein Kampf (1925)

4   The great masses of the people . . . will more easily fall victims to a big lie than to a small one.

ibid

5   It was no secret that this time the revolution would have to be bloody . . . When we spoke of it, we called it 'The Night of the Long Knives' (*'Die Nacht der Langen Messer'*).

Speech to the Reichstag, 13 July 1934
Referring to the events of 29 June/2 July when, aided by the SS, Hitler liquidated the leadership of the SA.

6   I go the way that Providence dictates with the assurance of a sleepwalker.

Speech, Munich, 15 March 1936

7   And now before us stands the last problem that must be solved and will be solved. It is the *last territorial claim* which I have to make in Europe, but it is the claim from which I will not recede and which, God willing, I will make good . . . With regard to the problem of the Sudeten Germans, *my patience is now at an end.*

Speech, Berlin Sportpalast, 26 September 1938

8   *On Neville Chamberlain:*
Well, he seemed such a nice old gentleman, I thought I would give him my autograph as a souvenir.

Attrib

1   A Last Appeal to Reason.

Title of leaflet translating his Reichstag speech of 19 July 1940, and dropped over England.

2   **Nacht und Nebel** ('Night and Fog').

Title of decree, issued 1941
Hitler's euphemism for the way in which people suspected of crimes against occupying forces would be dealt with. They would be spirited away into the night and fog. The phrase derives from Wagner, *Das Rheingold*.

3   The Final Solution of the Jewish Problem (*'Endloesung'*).

Term used used by Nazi officials from the summer of 1941 onwards
G. Reitlinger in *The Final Solution* (1953), suggests that the choice of phrase was probably, though not certainly, Hitler's own.

4   This war . . . is one of those elemental conflicts which usher in a new millennium and which shake the world *once in a thousand years.*

Speech, Reichstag, 26 April 1942

5   *To Jodl at Oberkommando der Wehrmacht, 25 August 1944, after the recapture of Paris by the Allies:*
Is Paris burning? (*'Brennt Paris?'*)

Quoted in A. Crawley, *De Gaulle*
He received no reply.

HOFFNUNG, Gerard
British cartoonist and tuba-player (1925–1959)

6   *Advice to tourists visiting Britain for the first time:*
Have you tried the famous echo in the Reading Room of the British Museum?

Speech, Oxford Union debating society, 4 December 1958
On the motion 'Life begins at 38'.

7   There is a French widow in every bedroom (affording delightful prospects).

In ibid

1   Never Explain—your Friends do not need it and your Enemies will not believe you anyway.

The Note Book of Elbert Hubbard (1927)
Compare **GRAYSON 144:8.**

HUBBARD, Frank McKinney ('Kin')
US humorist (1868–1930)

2   If there's one thing above all a vulture can't stand, it's a glass eye.

Attrib

HUGHES, Ted
British Poet Laureate (1930–   )

3   It took the whole of Creation
    To produce my foot, each feather:
    Now I hold Creation in my foot.

'Hawk Roosting', *The Hawk in the Rain* (1957)

4   The helicopter picked you up,
    The pilot it was me.

'The Honey Bee and the Thistle' (1986)
Written to mark the wedding of the Duke and Duchess of York.

HUMPHREY, Hubert H.
US Democratic Vice President (1911–78)

5   The Politics of Joy.

Campaign slogan, 1964

6   It was once said that the moral test of government is how that government treats those who are in the dawn of life, the children; those who are in the twilight of life, the elderly; and those who are in the shadows of life, the sick, the needy and the handicapped.

Speech, 1 November 1977

HUMPHRIES, Barry
Australian entertainer (1934–   )

7   *As 'Edna Everage', on seeing a Morris Traveller in Stratford-upon-Avon:*
    Why, even the cars are half-timbered here!

TV show, 1970s

8   *As 'Edna Everage':*
    Wave your gladdies, possums!

Stock phrase, 1970s onwards

'HUNTER, Evan'
US writer (1926–   )

1   The Blackboard Jungle.

Title of novel (1954, film US 1955)

HUPFELD, Herman
US songwriter (1894–1951)

2   You must remember this, a kiss is still a kiss,
A sigh is just a sigh;
The fundamental things apply,
As time goes by.

Song, 'As Time Goes By', *Everybody's Welcome* (1931)
Also in the film *Casablanca* (1943).

HUSSEIN, Saddam
Iraqi President (1937–   )

3   *At the start of the Gulf War, 6 January 1991:*
The great, the jewel and the mother of battles has begun.

Quoted in *The Independent*, 19 January 1991

HUTCHINS, Robert M.
US educator (1899–1977)

4   Whenever I feel like exercise, I lie down until the feeling passes.

Attrib

HUXLEY, Aldous
British novelist and writer (1894–1964)

5   The proper study of mankind is books.

Crome Yellow (1921)

6   Christlike in my behaviour,
Like every good believer,
I imitate the Saviour,
And cultivate a beaver.

Antic Hay (1923)

7   *On a discovery made using mescaline:*
I looked down by chance, and went on passionately staring by
choice, at my own crossed legs. Those folds in the trousers—what a
labyrinth of endlessly significant complexity! And the texture of the
grey flannel—how rich, how deeply, mysteriously sumptuous!

The Doors of Perception (1954)

IBARRURI, Dolores ('La Pasionaria')
Spanish communist (1895–1989)

1   Fascism will not pass, the executioners of October will not pass.

> Translation of radio speech, Madrid, 18 July 1936
> Later, *'No pasarán'* ('They shall not pass') was used as a Republican
> slogan in the Spanish Civil War (1936–9).
> *Compare* **PETAIN 252:5.**

2   It is better to die on your feet than to live on your knees.

> Translation of radio speech, Paris, 3 September 1936
> According to her autobiography (1966), she had also used these words
> on 18 July when broadcasting in Spain. Emilio Zapata, the Mexican
> guerilla leader, had used the expression before her in 1910.

I COVER THE WATERFRONT
US film 1933. Written by Wells Root, Jack Jevne and Max Miller.

3   I Cover the Waterfront.

> Title of film

4   □ Not tonight, Josephine.

> This film has been credited with launching the phrase, though it
> merely popularized it. A British song with the title had appeared in
> 1915 and an American one probably earlier. Indeed, the catchphrase
> may have been established in music hall and vaudeville by the end of
> the previous century.

INGHAM, Bernard (later Sir Bernard)
British civil servant (1932–   )

5   *Of John Biffen MP:*
     A semi-detached member of the Cabinet.

> Remark, 1986
> Said as Prime Minister Margaret Thatcher's Press Secretary.

INGRAMS, Richard
British writer and editor of *Private Eye*, the satirical magazine (1937–   )

6   *On the prospect of having to go to gaol, 1976:*
     The only thing I really mind about going to prison is the thought of
     Lord Longford coming to visit me.

> Attrib
> Ingrams has no recollection of having made this remark but is happy
> to accept authorship.

7   *Suggested personal motto:*
     Publish and be sued.

> On *Quote . . . Unquote*, BBC Radio, 4 May 1977

INNES, Hammond
British novelist (1913–   )

1   *On growing trees:*
I'm replacing some of the timber used up by my books. Books are just trees with squiggles on them.

Interview, *Radio Times*, 18 August 1984

INSCRIPTIONS

2   *In the forest of Compiègne, France, where the Armistice was signed at the end of the First World War:*
Here on 11 November 1918 succumbed the criminal pride of the German Reich, vanquished by the free peoples which it tried to enslave.

3   Kilroy was here.

The most widely-known piece of graffiti. The phrase may have originated with James J. Kilroy, a shipyard inspector in Quincy, Mass., who would chalk it up to indicate a check had been made. Brought to Europe by GIs, *c*1942.

4   *Plaque left on moon by US crew of Apollo XI space mission:*
HERE MEN FROM THE PLANET EARTH
FIRST SET FOOT UPON THE MOON
JULY 1969 AD
WE CAME IN PEACE FOR ALL MANKIND.

IN TOWN TONIGHT
UK radio magazine programme (BBC), from 1933–60.

5   *Voice 1:* Stop!
Voice 2: Once again we stop the mighty roar of London's traffic and from the great crowds we bring you some of the interesting people who have come by land, sea and air to be In Town Tonight.

Introductory announcement

6   Carry on, London!

Concluding announcement

IRISH REPUBLICAN ARMY

7   Our day will come (*'Tiocfaidh Ar La'*)
Slogan
Also the title of a song by Ruby and the Romantics, 1963.

1   Thatcher will now realize that Britain cannot occupy our country, torture our prisoners and shoot our people in their own streets and get away with it. Today we were unlucky. But remember, we only have to be lucky once. You will have to be lucky always.

Quoted in *Irish Times*, 13 October 1984
This message was contained in an anonymous telephone call to a
Dublin radio station following the unsuccessful IRA attempt to blow up
Margaret Thatcher and other government leaders at a Brighton hotel.

IRMA LA DOUCE

UK stage musical 1958, adapted from the French original of Alexandre Breffort and Marguerite Monnot. (Later filmed in US.)

2   *Opening words:*
Don't worry, it's quite suitable for the children. This is a story about passion, bloodshed, desire and death—everything in fact that makes life worth living.

Preamble to song 'Valse Milieu'

ISHERWOOD, Christopher

British-born writer (1904–86)

3   I am a camera with its shutter open, quite passive, recording, not thinking.

'A Berlin Diary', *Goodbye to Berlin* (1939)

ITMA

UK radio comedy show (BBC), 1939–49. The title means 'It's that man again'— a phrase derived from the frequent newspaper appearances by Adolf Hitler in the 1930s. Script by Ted Kavanagh and Tommy Handley. With Tommy Handley; Clarence Wright; Horace Percival as Ali Oop, Cecil and the Diver; Jack Train as Claude, Colonel Chinstrap, Lefty and Funf; Hugh Morton as Sam Fairfechan; Sydney Keith as Sam Scram; Dorothy Summers as Mrs Mopp; Joan Harben as Mona Lott; and Fred Yule as George Gorge.

4   *Cecil:* After you, Claude . . .
Claude: No, after you, Cecil.

Catchphrase

5   *Sam Fairfechan:* As if I cared!

Catchphrase

6   *Sam Scram:* Boss, boss, sumpin terrible's happened.

Catchphrase

7   *Mrs Mopp:* Can I do you now, sir?

Catchphrase

1   *The Diver:* Don't forget the diver.

    Catchphrase

    Based on the saying of an actual one-legged man who dived off New
    Brighton pier for pennies in the 1920s.

2   *Wright:* Good morning . . . nice day.

    Catchphrase

3   *Colonel Chinstrap (accepting what he thought to be the offer of a drink):*
    I don't mind if I do.

    Catchphrase

4   *Ali Oop:* I go—I come back.

    Catchphrase

5   *The Diver:* I'm going down now, sir.

    Catchphrase

6   *Mona Lott:* It's being so cheerful as keeps me going.

    Catchphrase

7   *Lefty:* It's me noives [nerves].

    Catchphrase

8   *George Gorge:* Lovely grub, lovely grub.

    Catchphrase

9   *Ali Oop:* No likey, oh crikey!

    Catchphrase

10 *Funf (German spy):* This is Funf speaking.
    Catchphrase

JACOBS, Joe
US boxing manager (1896–1940)

1   *Believing that his client, Max Schmeling, had been cheated of a heavyweight title by Jack Sharkey, 21 June 1932:*
We wuz robbed!

Attrib

2   *Losing a bet on the World baseball series, October 1935:*
I should have stood in bed.

Quoted in J. Lardner, *Strong Cigars and Lovely Women*

JAGGER, Mick and RICHARD, Keith
British rock musicians and songwriters (1943–   ) and (1943–   )

3   I can't get no satisfaction.

Song, 'Satisfaction' (1965)

4   It's Only Rock 'n' Roll.

Title of song (1974)

JAMES, Henry
US novelist (1843–1916)

5   *After having a stroke (2 December 1915), he said he had heard a voice saying:*
So here it is at last, the distinguished thing.

Quoted in E. Wharton, *A Backward Glance*
Not his dying words.

JAMES, William
US psychologist (1842–1910)

6   The moral flabbiness born of the exclusive worship of the bitch-goddess Success.

Letter to H. G. Wells, 11 September 1906

JAY, Douglas (later Lord Jay)
British Labour politician (1907–   )

7   Fair Shares for All, is Labour's Call.

Slogan, Battersea North by-election, June 1946

8   For in the case of nutrition and health, just as in the case of education, the gentleman in Whitehall really does know better what is good for people than the people know themselves.

The Socialist Case (1947)

JAY, Peter

British journalist and diplomat (1937–   )

1   As we walked the White Cliffs overlooking the English Channel during the weekend he [James Callaghan] was taking over the Government . . . [he said] he saw his role as being like that of Moses—to lead the people away from the fleshpots of Egypt into the desert and in the direction of the promised land . . . even if it were never to be given to him to see that land . . . [It was] the language of realism and statesmanship.

Speech as British Ambassador, Washington, August 1977
Callaghan was his father-in-law.

2   A mission to explain.

IBA public meeting, Croydon, 1980 and many times thereafter
Phrase encapsulating his programme philosophy for the TV-am
breakfast television station.

3   Remember above all that together we can—being so nice and so talented—work it out.

Pep-talk to TV-am staff, November 1982, quoted in M. Leapman,
Treachery
See also **BIRT 41:3.**

JENKIN, Patrick (later Lord Jenkin)

British Conservative politician (1926–   )

4   *Advice to members of the public as Energy Minister, during the Three-Day Week, 1974:*
You don't even need to do your teeth with the light on. You can do it in the dark.

Interviewed on BBC Radio *Newsbeat*, 15 January 1974

JENKINS, Rt Revd David

British Anglican Bishop (1925–   )

5   *On the Resurrection:*
A conjuring trick with bones.

In discussion, BBC Radio, 29 October 1984

JENKINS, Roy (later Lord Jenkins)

British Labour, then Social Democrat, then Liberal Democrat politician (1920–   )

6   The permissive society has been allowed to become a dirty phrase. A better phrase is the civilized society.

Speech, Abingdon, 19 July 1969

1 *On the possibility of the creation of a new centre party:*
The experimental plane may well finish up a few fields from the end of the runway. If that is so, the voluntary occupants will have only inflicted bruises or worse upon themselves. But the reverse may occur and the experimental plane soar into the sky.

Speech, Commons Press Gallery lunch, 8 June 1980

2 The politics of the left and centre of this country are frozen in an out-of-date mould which is bad for the political and economic health of Britain and increasingly inhibiting for those who live within the mould. Can it be broken?

ibid

Later, when the Social Democratic Party was established in 1981, there was much talk of 'breaking the mould of British politics'—i.e. doing away with the traditional system of a Government party and one chief Opposition party. This was by no means a new way of describing political change and getting rid of an old system for good, in a way that prevents it being reconstituted. However, Jenkins had quoted Andrew Marvell's 'Horatian Ode Upon Cromwell's Return from Ireland' (1650): 'And cast the kingdoms old,/Into another mould' in his book *What Matters Now* as early as 1972.

JENNINGS, Paul
British humorist (1918–89)

3 Wembley, adj. Suffering from a vague *malaise*. 'I feel a bit w. this morning.'

'Ware, Wye, Watford', *The Jenguin Pennings* (1963)

JESSEL, George
US entertainer (1898–1981)

4 *On the large number of mourners at Harry Cohn's funeral:*
Same old story: you give 'em what they want and they'll fill the theatre.

Quoted in L. Hellman, *Scoundrel Time*
Also attributed to Red Skelton.

JOAD, C. E. M.
British broadcaster (1891–1953)

5 It all depends what you mean by . . .

Passim on *Brains Trust*, BBC radio, 1940s

JOFFRE, Joseph Jacques Césaire
French soldier (1852–1931)

1   *Order for the start of the first Battle of the Marne:*
We are about to engage in a battle on which the fate of our country depends and it is important to remind all ranks that the moment has passed for looking to the rear; all our efforts must be directed to attacking and driving back the enemy. Troops that can advance no farther must, at any price, hold on to the ground they have conquered and die on the spot rather than give way. Under the circumstances which face us, no act of weakness can be tolerated.
Recounted in *The Memoirs of Marshal Joffre* (1932)

JOHN XXIII
Italian-born Pope (1881–1963)

2   It often happens that I wake at night and begin to think about a serious problem and decide I must tell the Pope about it. Then I wake up completely and remember I am the Pope.
Quoted in H. Fesquet, *The Wit and Wisdom of Good Pope John* (1964)

3   Anybody can be Pope; the proof of this is that I have become one.
In ibid

JOHN, Augustus
British artist (1878–1961)

4   *To Nina Hamnett:*
We have become, Nina, the sort of people our parents warned us about.
Attrib

JOHNSON, Hiram
US all-party Senator (1866–1945)

5   The first casualty when war comes is truth.
Speech, US Senate, *c*1917

JOHNSON, Lyndon B.
US Democratic President (1908–73)

6   Come now, let us reason together.
Frequent exhortation
Based on Isaiah 1:18.

7   *When Senate Majority leader:*
I've got his pecker in my pocket.
Quoted in D. Halberstam, *The Best and the Brightest*

1   *On becoming President following the assassination of John F. Kennedy:*
    All I have, I would have given gladly not to be standing here today.
    Speech to Congress, 27 November 1963

2   In your time we have the opportunity to move not only toward the
    rich society and the powerful society but upward to the Great
    Society.
    Speech, University of Michigan, May 1964

3   We are not about to send American boys nine or ten thousand
    miles away from home to do what Asian boys ought to be doing for
    themselves.
    Broadcast address, 21 October 1964

4   *On Vietnam:*
    You let a bully come into your front yard, the next day he'll be on
    your porch.
    Quoted in *Time*, 15 April 1984
    A remark he made on several occasions.

5   That Gerald Ford. He can't fart and chew gum at the same time.
    Quoted in J. K. Galbraith, *A Life in Our Times*
    Correct version of the oft-misquoted: 'He couldn't walk and chew gum
    at the same time.'

6   *On why he kept J. Edgar Hoover at the FBI:*
    I'd much rather have that fellow inside my tent pissing out, than
    outside my tent pissing in.
    Quoted in ibid

7   Did y'ever think, Ken, that making a speech on economics is a lot
    like pissing down your leg? It seems hot to you, but it never does to
    anyone else.
    Quoted in ibid

8   *When told by an officer that he was walking towards the wrong helicopter,
    with the words, 'That's your helicopter over there, sir':*
    Son, they are all my helicopters.
    Attrib

9   I want *loyalty*. I want him to kiss my ass in Macy's window at high
    noon and tell me it smells like roses. I want his pecker in my
    pocket.
    Quoted in D. Halberstam, *The Best and the Brightest*

1   *Announcing his intention not to stand again as President:*
It is true that a house divided against itself is a house that cannot
stand. There is a division in the American house now and believing
this as I do, I have concluded that I should not permit the
Presidency to become involved in the partisan divisions that are
developing in this political year. Accordingly, I shall not seek, and I
will not accept, the nomination of my party for another term as
your President.

Broadcast address, 31 March 1968

JOHST, Hanns
German Nazi playwright (1890–1978)

2   *Storm-trooper:* When I hear the word 'culture', I reach for my
revolver.

Translation from *Schlageter* (1933)
A more accurate translation would be: ' . . . I release the safety catch of
my Browning' (automatic rifle). A saying often attributed to Hermann
Goering.

JOLSON, Al
US entertainer (1888–1950)

3   You ain't heard nothin' yet.

Soundtrack, *The Jazz Singer* (1927)
Ad-lib introduction to song. He did not add 'folks'.

JONES, Spike
US musician (1911–1965)

4   *After eccentric rendering of classic theme:*
Thank you, music-lovers.

Catchphrase, from 1940s

JONG, Erica
US novelist (1942–   )

5   The zipless fuck is the purest thing there is. And it is rarer than the
unicorn. And I have never had one.

Fear of Flying (1973)

6   My response . . . was . . . to evolve my fantasy of the Zipless Fuck . . .
Zipless because when you come together zippers fell away like
petals.

ibid

JOSEPH, Michael
British publisher (1897–1958)

1   Authors are easy enough to get on with—if you are fond of children.

Quoted in the *Observer*, 29 May 1949

JOYCE, James
Irish novelist (1882–1941)

2   Snow was general all over Ireland . . . [Michael Furey's] soul swooned slowly as he heard the snow falling faintly through the universe and faintly falling, like the descent of their last end, upon all the living and the dead.

'The Dead', *Dubliners* (1916)

3   The snotgreen sea. The scrotumtightening sea.

Ulysses (1937)

4   riverrun, past Eve and Adam's, from swerve of shore to bend of bay.

Finnegans Wake (1939)

5   *When a young man accosted him in Zurich and asked, 'May I kiss the hand that wrote* **Ulysses***?'*
No, it did a lot of other things, too.

Quoted in R. Ellman, *James Joyce*

6   Love me, love my umbrella.

Attrib

JUDGE, Jack
British entertainer (1878–1938)

7   It's a long way to Tipperary
It's a long way to go;
It's a long way to Tipperary
To the sweetest girl I know!
Goodbye Piccadilly! Farewell, Leicester Square!
It's a long, long way to Tipperary,
But my heart's right there.

Song, 'Tipperary' (1912)
Written with Harry Williams.

JUMBO

US film 1962. With Jimmy Durante. Joke specifically credited to Charles
Lederer.

1   *Sherriff:* Where are you going with that elephant?
    Durante: What elephant?

    Soundtrack
    The film was based on the 1935 Rodgers-Hart-Hecht-MacArthur stage
    show *Jumbo* in which Durante delivered the same joke.

JUNG, Carl

Swiss psychologist (1875–1961)

2   [Man's] psyche should be studied because we are the origin of all
    coming evil.

    Interview, *Face to Face*, BBC TV, 22 October 1959

3   *Describing a dream he once had:*
    I had a vision of unearthly beauty and that was why I was able to live
    at all. *Liverpool is the 'pool of life'.* The 'liver', according to an old
    view, is the seat of life—that which 'makes to live'.

    Memories, Dreams, Reflections (1963)
    Comment based on fanciful etymology. 'Liverpool' means 'pool with
    clotted water' and not 'pool of life'.

KAEL, Pauline
US film critic (1919–   )

1   Kiss Kiss Bang Bang.

> Title of book (1968)
> From the wording on an Italian film poster seen by her, 'perhaps the briefest statement imaginable on the basic appeal of movies.'

2   *Of Barbra Streisand in* **What's Up, Doc?**
She's playing herself—and it's awfully soon for that.

> *Deeper into Movies* (1973)

KAUFMAN, George S.
US playwright (1889–1961)

3   Everything I've ever said will be credited to Dorothy Parker.

> Quoted in S. Meredith, *George S. Kaufman and the Algonquin Round Table*

4   *At rehearsal for the Marx Brothers film* **Animal Crackers** *for which he wrote the script:*
Excuse me for interrupting but I actually thought I heard a line I wrote.

> In ibid

5   *Of Raymond Massey's off-stage interpretation of Abraham Lincoln:*
Massey won't be satisfied until somebody assassinates him.

> In ibid

6   *When stopped at the stage door and asked if he was 'with the show':*
Well, let's say I'm not against it . . .

> In ibid

7   *Of an actor called Guido Nadzo:*
Guido Nadzo is nadzo guido.

> In ibid
> Also attributed to Brooks Atkinson.

8   Satire is what closes Saturday night.

> In ibid

9   *Of a dead waiter:*
God finally caught his eye.

> In ibid
> Also attributed to D. McCord, among others.

10 *When a poor bridge partner asked how he should have played a hand:*
Under an assumed name.

> In ibid

1 You Can't Take It With You.

Title of play (written with Moss Hart) (1936)

KEATS, John (C.)
US writer (1920–)

2 Americans have plenty of everything and the best of nothing.

You Might As Well Live (1970)

KENNEDY, Edward F.
US Democratic politician (1932–)

3 *Failing to win his party's nomination for the Presidency:*
For me, a few hours ago, this campaign came to an end. For all those whose cares have been our concern, the work goes on, the cause endures, the hope still lives, and the dream shall never die.

Speech at Democratic Convention, 13 August 1980

4 I am a Pole.

Statement, Gdansk, 1987

5 *On George Bush:*
The man who was never there [when controversial issues were discussed in the Reagan administration] . . . Where was George?

Speech, Democratic Convention, Atlanta, July 1988
Congressman Tony Coelho also hit upon this taunt.

KENNEDY, Jimmy
Ulster songwriter (1902–84)

6 If you go down in the woods today
You're sure of a big surprise . . .
For every bear that ever there was
Will gather there for certain because
Today's the day the teddy bears have their picnic.

Song, 'The Teddy Bears' Picnic' (1932)
Written to earlier music by John W. Bratton.

KENNEDY, John F.
US Democratic President (1917–63)

7 I just received the following wire from my generous Daddy—'Dear Jack. Don't buy a single vote more than necessary. I'll be damned if I'm going to pay for a landslide'.

Speech, Washington, 1958

1   *Accepting the Democratic nomination:*
    We stand today on the edge of a New Frontier . . . But the New
    Frontier of which I speak is not a set of promises—it is a set of
    challenges. It sums up not what I intend to offer the American
    people, but what I intend to ask of them.
    Speech, Los Angeles Convention, 1960

2   Do you realize the responsibility I carry? I'm the only person
    standing between Nixon and the White House.
    Remark, 13 October 1960, quoted in A. M. Schlesinger Jr, *A Thousand
    Days*

3   *When asked how he became a war hero:*
    They sank my boat.
    ibid

4   Let the word go forth from this time and place, to friend and foe
    alike, that the torch has been passed to a new generation of
    Americans, born in this century, tempered by war, disciplined by a
    hard and bitter peace, proud of our ancient heritage, and unwilling
    to witness or permit the slow undoing of those human rights to
    which this nation has always been committed, and to which we are
    committed today at home and around the world.
        Let every nation know, whether it wishes us well or ill, that we
    shall pay any price, bear any burden, meet any hardship, support
    any friend, oppose any foe to assure the survival and the success of
    liberty.
    Inaugural address, Washington, 20 January 1961

5   Let us never negotiate out of fear, but let us never fear to negotiate.
    ibid

6   Together let us explore the stars . . .
    ibid

7   All this will not be finished in the first one hundred days. Nor will it
    be finished in the first one thousand days, nor in the life of this
    Administration, nor even perhaps in our lifetime on this planet.
    But let us begin.
    ibid

1   Now the trumpet summons us again—not as a call to bear arms, though arms we need; not as a call to battle, though embattled we are; but a call to bear the burden of a long twilight struggle, year in and year out, 'rejoicing in hope, patient in tribulation' a struggle against the common enemies of man: tyranny, poverty, disease and war itself.

    ibid

2   And so, my fellow Americans, ask not what your country can do for you; ask what you can do for your country.

    ibid

3   I believe that this nation should commit itself to achieving the goal, before this decade is out, of landing a man on the moon and returning him safely to earth.

    Supplementary State of the Union message to Congress, 25 May 1961

4   *To Harold Macmillan:*
    I wonder how it is with you, Harold? If I don't have a woman for three days, I get a terrible headache.

    Remark, quoted in A. Horne, *Macmillan 1957–1986*

5   Some men are killed in a war and some men are wounded, and some men never leave the country . . . It's very hard in military or personal life to assure complete equality. Life is unfair.

    Remark at news conference, 21 March 1962

6   I think it's the most extraordinary collection of talent, of human knowledge, that has ever been gathered together at the White House—with the possible exception of when Thomas Jefferson dined alone.

    Speech at dinner for Nobel Prizewinners, 29 April 1962

7   We don't see the end of the tunnel, but I must say I don't think it is darker than it was a year ago, and in some ways lighter.

    Press conference, 12 December 1962
    Numerous politicians had earlier used the expression 'The light at the end of the tunnel', but it became a catchphrase of the Vietnam War.

8   *Conferring honorary US citizenship on Winston Churchill:*
    He mobilized the English language and sent it into battle.

    Speech, 9 April 1963
    See also **MURROW 236:6.**

9   All free men, wherever they may live, are citizens of Berlin, and, therefore, as a free man, I take pride in the words *'Ich bin ein Berliner'*.

    Speech, Berlin City Hall, 26 June 1963

1   *On the Test Ban Treaty:*
    Yesterday, a shaft of light cut into the darkness . . . For the first
    time, an agreement has been reached on bringing the forces of
    nuclear destruction under international control.
    Broadcast address, 26 July 1963

2   Forgive but never forget.
    Remark attributed to him by Ted Sorensen in 1968 TV interview

KENNEDY, Joseph P.
US politician, businessman, and father of JFK (1888–1969)

3   When the going gets tough, the tough get going.
    Quoted in J. H. Cutler, *Honey Fitz*
    Probably not original.

4   Don't get mad, get even.
    Quoted in B. Bradlee, *Conversations with Kennedy*
    Attributed to 'the Boston Irish political jungle'.

5   If you want to make money, go where the money is.
    Quoted in A. M. Schlesinger Jr, *Robert Kennedy and His Times*

6   Kennedys don't cry.
    ibid
    Family rendering of his 'We don't want any crying in this house.'

KENNEDY, Robert F.
US Democratic politician (1925–68)

7   One fifth of the people are against everything all the time.
    Speech at University of Pennsylvania, 6 May 1964

8   *After winning California primary:*
    My thanks to all of you. And now it's on to Chicago and let's win
    there.
    Speech, Los Angeles, 4 June 1968
    His last public remark before being murdered.
    See also **SHAW 291:1.**

KENYATTA, Jomo
Kenyan President (?1891–1978)

1 Originally, the Africans had the land and the English had the Bible. Then the missionaries came to Africa and got the Africans to close their eyes and fold their hands and pray. And when they opened their eyes, the English had the land and the Africans had the Bible.

Attrib on *Quote . . . Unquote*, BBC Radio, 13 October 1984

The *Observer* 'Sayings of the Week' (16 December 1984) had Bishop Desmond Tutu saying it. A version relating to the American Indians had earlier been said by Chief Dan George (*d*1982).

KEPPEL, Mrs Alice
British mistress of King Edward VII

2 *On the day of King Edward VIII's abdication:*
Things were done better in my day.

Attrib

Also attributed to Maxine Elliott, another former mistress of the King's, in the form, 'They managed things better in our day'.

KEROUAC, Jack
US writer (1922–69)

3 You know, this is really a beat generation.

Recalled in *The Origins of the Beat Generation*

Phrase borrowed from a broken-down drug addict called Herbert Huncke. Others have also been credited with the coinage.

KEYNES, John Maynard (Lord Keynes)
British economist (1883–1946)

4 In the long run we are all dead.

Tract on Monetary Reform (1923)

5 *On being asked what happened when David Lloyd George was alone in a room:*
When he's alone in a room, there's nobody there.

Quoted by Baroness Asquith, *As I Remember*, BBC TV, 30 April 1967

KHRUSCHEV, Nikita S.
Soviet Communist Party leader (1894–1971)

6 *On the likelihood of the Soviet Union rejecting Communism:*
Those who wait for that must wait until a shrimp learns to whistle.

Attrib remark, 1955

7 *Denouncing Stalin:*
[He promoted a] cult of personality.

Speech to 20th Party Congress, 25 February 1956

1   *To Western diplomats at Moscow reception:*
    Whether you like it or not, history is on our side. We will bury you.

    Reported in *The Times*, 19 November 1956
    Khruschev later attempted to explain that he meant 'we will outlive
    you' in the sense of 'outstrip' economically, rather than anything more
    threatening.

2   If you cannot catch a bird of paradise, better take a wet hen.

    Quoted in *Time*, 6 January 1958

3   Politicians are the same all over. They promise to build a bridge
    even when there is no river.

    Remark, Glen Cove, New York, 1960

4   If you start throwing hedgehogs under me, I shall throw two
    porcupines under you.

    Quoted in the *Observer*, 10 November 1963

KILMER, Joyce
US poet and journalist (1886–1918)

5   I think that I shall never see
    A poem lovely as a tree.

    'Trees' (1913)
    Compare **NASH 238:4.**

KING, Rev Dr Martin Luther, Jnr
US Civil Rights leader (1929–68)

6   I have a dream.

    Speech, Washington civil rights demonstration, 28 August 1963
    He had used this theme in other speeches that summer.

7   Free at last, free at last, thank God Almighty, we are free at last!
    ibid
    Quoting an old negro spiritual.

8   I've been to the mountain top . . . I've looked over, and I've seen
    the promised land. I may not get there with you, but I want you to
    know tonight that we as a people will get to the promised land. So,
    I'm happy tonight. Mine eyes have seen the glory of the coming of
    the Lord.

    Speech, Memphis, 3 April 1968
    The next day he was assassinated.

KING, Philip
British playwright (1904–79)

1 *To policeman confronting a horde of vicars:*
Sergeant, arrest most of these people!

See How They Run (1944)
Sometimes misquoted as 'Arrest several of these vicars!'

KING KONG
US film 1933. Script by James Creelman and Ruth Rose. With Robert Armstrong.

2 *Last line:*
Oh no, it wasn't the airplanes. It was beauty killed the beast.

Soundtrack

KING KONG
US film 1976. Script by Lorenzo Semple Jnr. With Jeff Bridges as Jack Prescott and Jessica Lange as Dwan.

3 *Jack (to Dwan) about King Kong:* He's bigger than both of us, know what I mean?

Soundtrack

KING'S ROW
US film 1941. Script by Casey Robinson. With Ronald Reagan as Drake McHugh and Ann Sheridan as Randy Monaghan.

4 *Drake:* Randy—where's the rest of me?

On waking to find that his legs have been amputated by a sadistic doctor. Used by Reagan as the title of an early autobiography.

KINGSMILL, Hugh
British writer (1889–1949)

5 It is difficult to love mankind unless one has a reasonable private income and when one has a reasonable private income one has better things to do than loving mankind.

Quoted in R. Ingrams, *God's Apology*

6 Friends are God's apology for relations.

In ibid

KINNOCK, Neil
British Labour politician (1942–)

7 *In reply to heckler's comment, 'At least Mrs Thatcher has got guts':*
And it's a pity that people had to leave theirs on the ground at Goose Green in order to prove it.

TV election programme, 5 June 1983

1   *To militants within the Labour Party:*
    You don't play politics with people's jobs.
    Speech, Labour Party Conference, October 1985

2   I would die for my country . . . but I could never let my country die
    for me.
    Speech on nuclear disarmament, Labour Party Conference,
    30 September 1986

3   Why am I the first Kinnock in a thousand generations to be able to
    go to university?
    Party Political Broadcast, 21 May 1987
    From a speech later plagiarized by US Senator Joe Biden.

KIPLING, Rudyard
British poet and novelist (1865–1936)

4   The flannelled fools at the wicket or the muddied oafs at the goals.
    'The Islanders' (1902)

5   I keep six honest serving men
    (They taught me all I knew):
    Their names are What and Why and When
    And How and Where and Who.
    'The Elephant's Child', *The Just-So Stories* (1902)

6   The Cat That Walked By Himself.
    Title of story in ibid

7   Watch the wall, my darling, while the Gentlemen go by!
    'A Smuggler's Song', *Puck of Pook's Hill* (1906)

8   If you can keep your head when all about you
    Are losing theirs and blaming it on you . . .
    'If', *Rewards and Fairies* (1910)

9   If you can meet with Triumph and Disaster
    And treat those two impostors just the same . . .
    ibid

10 If you can talk with crowds and keep your virtue,
    Or walk with Kings—nor lose the common touch . . .
    ibid

1   If you can fill the unforgiving minute
    With sixty seconds' worth of distance run,
    Yours is the Earth and everything that's in it,
    And—which is more—you'll be a Man, my son!
    ibid

2   For the female of the species is more deadly than the male.
    'The Female of the Species' (1911)

3   Our England is a garden, and such gardens are not made
    By singing:—'Oh, how beautiful!' and sitting in the shade.
    'The Glory of the Garden' (1911)

4   So when the world is asleep, and there seems no hope of her
        waking
      Out of some long, bad dream that makes her mutter and moan,
    Suddenly, all men arise to the noise of fetters breaking,
        And every one smiles at his neighbour and tells him his soul is
        his own!
    'The Dawn Wind' (1911)
    See also **BALDWIN 21:6.**

KISSINGER, Henry
US Republican Secretary of State (1923–   )

5   *Diagnosing his success as a 'swinger':*
    Power is the ultimate aphrodisiac.

    Attrib
    Also, in the form 'great aphrodisiac', quoted in the *New York Times*,
    19 January 1971.

6   There cannot be a crisis next week. My schedule is already full.

    Quoted in *Time*, 24 January 1977
    See also **BOOK TITLES 43:1.**

KITCHEN, Fred
British entertainer (1872–1950)

7   Meredith, we're in!

    Sketch, 'The Bailiff' (1907)
    Performed with Fred Karno's music-hall troupe and possibly written by
    Karno.

KITCHENER, Lord
British soldier (1850–1916)

1   *To soldiers of the British Expeditionary Force:*
You are ordered abroad as a soldier of the King to help our French comrades . . . In this new experience you may find temptations both in wine and women. You must entirely resist and, while treating all women with perfect courtesy, you should avoid any intimacy. Do your duty bravely. Fear God. Honour the King.

Message, August 1914

KNOX, Ronald
British priest and writer (1888–1957)

2   *Definition of a baby:*
A loud noise at one end and no sense of responsibility at the other.

Attrib

KNUTE ROCKNE—ALL AMERICAN
US film 1940. Script by Robert Buckner, based on reminiscences. With Pat O'Brien as Knute Rockne and Ronald Reagan as George Gipp.

3   *Rockne:* 'Rock,' he said, 'some time when the team is up against it and the breaks are beating the boys, tell them to go out there with all they got and win just one for the Gipper.'

Soundtrack

Based on the words of the real Rockne at half-time in a 1928 army game, recalling what the real Gipp (a football star who died young in 1920) had said to him: 'Rock, someday when things look real tough for Notre Dame, ask the boys to go out there and win one for me.' 'Win this one for the Gipper' became a slogan of Ronald Reagan's supporters when he went into politics.

KOCH, Ed
US politician and Mayor of New York City (1924–   )

4   How'm I doing?

Catchphrase from *c*1977

KOESTLER, Arthur
Hungarian-British writer (1905–83)

5   Darkness at Noon.

Title of book (1940)
Compare Milton, 'Dark amid the blaze of noon', *Samson Agonistes* (1671).

KOJAK

US TV police drama series, from 1973–7. With Telly Savalas as Kojak.

1 Who loves ya, baby?

Stock phrase

KOVACS, Ernie

US entertainer (1919–62)

2 *On television:*
A medium, so called because it is neither rare nor well done.

Attrib
Compare ACE 1:1.

KREISLER, Fritz

Austrian-born US violinist (1875–1962)

3 *To a society hostess who had jibbed at his fee of $5,000 for a recital, adding that he would not be expected to mingle with the guests:*
In that case, madam, my fee will be only two thousand dollars.

Attrib
Also ascribed to other famous musicians and singers.

KUBRICK, Stanley

US film director (1928–)

4 The great nations have always acted like gangsters, and the small nations like prostitutes.

In *The Guardian*, 5 June 1963

KUNDERA, Milan

Czech writer (1929–)

5 The Unbearable Lightness of Being.

Title of novel (1984), originally called in Czech *Nesnesitelná lehkost bytí*.

KURNITZ, Harry

US screenwriter (*c*1907–68)

6 *On the wife (with whom he was having a feud) of Frank Loesser:*
Lynn is the evil of two Loessers.

Quoted in the *Observer*, 31 March 1968

LABOUR PARTY
British political organization

1 To secure for the workers by hand or by brain the full fruits of their industry and the most equitable distribution thereof that may be possible upon the basis of the common ownership of the means of production, distribution, and exchange.

Clause 4 of the party's Constitution (Party Objects), adopted 1918/1926
The words 'socialisation of the means of production &c.' had appeared in the 1900 Labour Party manifesto.

LAMPEDUSA, Giuseppe Di
Italian writer (1896–1957)

2 If we want everything to remain as it is, it will be necessary for everything to change.

The Leopard (1958)

3 *Of marriage:*
One year of flames and thirty of ashes.

Attrib

LANCASTER, Osbert (later Sir Osbert)
British cartoonist (1908–86)

4 Stockbroker's Tudor.

Pillar to Post (1938)
Term for bogus Tudor architecture.

5 *'Maudie Littlehampton' (on the Lady Chatterley trial):*
It's an odd thing, but now one knows it's profoundly moral and packed with deep spiritual significance a lot of the old charm seems to have gone.

Caption to cartoon in the *Daily Express* (1961)

LANCE, Bert
US Democratic politician (1931–   )

6 *On government reorganization as President Carter's Director of the Office of Management:*
If it ain't broke, don't fix it.

Quoted in *The Nation's Business*, 27 May 1977
What may be the first appearance of a modern proverb.
See also **CARTER 59:4.**

LANCHESTER, Elsa
British film actress (1902–86)

1   *On Maureen O'Hara:*
She looked as though butter wouldn't melt in her mouth. Or anywhere else.
Attrib

LANDOWSKA, Wanda
Hungarian harpsichordist (1877–1959)

2   *Remark to fellow musician:*
Oh, well, you play Bach *your* way. I'll play him *his.*
Attrib

LANG, Andrew
British poet (1844–1912)

3   He uses statistics as a drunken man uses lamp-posts—for support rather than illumination.
Attrib

LANG, Julia
British broadcaster (1921–   )

4   *As prelude to telling a story:*
Are you sitting comfortably? Then I'll begin.
Passim in *Listen with Mother*, BBC radio, from 1950

LARKIN, Philip
British librarian and poet (1922–85)

5   Nothing, like something, happens anywhere.
'I Remember, I Remember', *The Less Deceived* (1955)

6   Why should I let the toad work
      Squat on my life?
Can't I use my wit as a pitchfork
      And drive the brute off?
'Toads' in ibid

7   Give me your arm, old Toad;
Help me down Cemetery Road.
'Toads Revisited', *The Whitsun Weddings* (1964)

8   Get stewed:
Books are a load of crap.
'A Study of Reading Habits' in ibid

1   What will survive of us is love.
    'An Arundel Tomb', in ibid

2   Perhaps being old is having lighted rooms
    Inside your head, and people in them, acting.
    People you know, yet can't quite name.
    'The Old Fools', *High Windows* (1974)

3   Sexual intercourse began
    In nineteen sixty-three
    (Which was rather late for me)—
    Between the end of the *Chatterley* ban
    And the Beatles' first LP.
    'Annus Mirabilis', in ibid

4   They fuck you up, your mum and dad.
        They may not mean to, but they do.
    They fill you up with the faults they had
        And add some extra, just for you.
    'This Be the Verse' in ibid

5   Man hands on misery to man.
        It deepens like a coastal shelf.
    Get out as early as you can,
        And don't have any kids yourself.
    ibid

6   Deprivation is for me what daffodils were for Wordsworth.
    Interview in the *Observer*, 1979

7   *He described himself as:*
    Looking like a balding salmon.
    Attrib

THE LAST FLIGHT
US film 1931. Script by John Monk Saunders. With Richard Barthelmess.

8   *On why some American airmen in Europe had gone bull-fighting, with the
    result that one was gored to death:*
    RB: It seemed like a good idea at the time.
    Soundtrack
    L. Halliwell in *The Filmgoer's Book of Quotes*, (1978) suggests that this was
    the first time the film catchphrase was used.

THE LAST REMAKE OF BEAU GESTE
US film 1977. Script by Marty Feldman and Chris J. Allen. With Terry-Thomas and Ann-Margret.

1   *Prison governor (T-T) to woman (A-M) who has slept with him in order to secure an escape:*
Delighted you came, my dear, and I'd like you to know that you made a happy man feel very old.
Soundtrack

LAUDER, Sir Harry
Scots entertainer (1870–1950)

2   I Love a Lassie.
Title of song (1905)

3   Roamin' in the gloamin',
By the bonny banks of Clyde.
Song, 'Roamin' In the Gloamin'' (1911)

4   □ It's a braw brecht moonlicht nicht.
Song, 'Just a Wee Deoch-an-Doris' (1912)
In fact, the words are by R. F. Morrison, to music by Whit Cunliffe.

5   Oh, it's nice to get up in the mornin'
But it's nicer to lie in bed.
Song, 'It's Nice to Be in Bed' (1913)

6   (Keep Right On to) the End of the Road.
Title of song (1924)

7   □ Bang went saxpence (sixpence).
Joke repopularized by Lauder. Originated by Charles Keene in *Punch* (1868)—'Mun, a had na' been the-erre abune two hours when—bang—went saxpence!!!'

LAUGH-IN (ROWAN AND MARTIN'S)
US television comedy series 1967–73. Script by various. With Dan Rowan, Dick Martin, Judy Carne, Goldie Hawn, Arte Johnson, Gary Owens, Lily Tomlin, and Dewey 'Pigmeat' Markham.

8   The Flying Fickle Finger of Fate.
Stock phrase
Based on an armed forces expression, 'Fucked by the fickle finger of fate', from the 1930s.

9   Here come de judge!
Catchphrase
An old vaudeville catchphrase of Dewey 'Pigmeat' Markham's. He was brought along to utter it again.

1   *Tomlin (as telephone operator):* Is this the party to whom I am speaking?
    Catchphrase

2   Look that up in your Funk and Wagnalls.
    Catchphrase

3   *Carne:* Sock it to me!
    Catchphrase
    Derived from Aretha Franklin song, 'Respect' (1968).

4   *Owens (announcer):* This is beautiful downtown Burbank.
    Catchphrase

5   You bet your sweet bippy!
    Catchphrase

6   *Johnson (as German soldier):* Very interesting . . . (but stupid)!
    Catchphrase

LAW, Andrew Bonar
British Conservative Prime Minister (1858–1923)

7   I must follow them; I am their leader.

> Quoted in E. Raymond, *Mr Balfour*
> Usually this is ascribed to Alexandre Auguste Ledru-Rollin, who said it as a mob passed by in the 1848 Paris revolution (*'Eh, je suis leur chef, il fallait bien les suivre'*).

LAWRENCE, D. H.
British novelist (1885–1930)

8   *On a publisher's rejection of Sons and Lovers:*
    Curse the blasted, jelly-boned swines, the slimy, the belly-wriggling invertebrates, the miserable sodding rotters, the flaming sods, the snivelling, dribbling, dithering, palsied, pulseless lot that make up England today.

> Letter to Edward Garnett, 3 July 1912

9   *On James Joyce:*
    Nothing but old fags and cabbage-stumps of quotations from the Bible and the rest, stewed in the juice of deliberate, journalistic dirty-mindedness.

> Letter to Aldous Huxley, 15 August 1928

10 Some things can't be ravished. You can't ravish a tin of sardines.

> *Lady Chatterley's Lover* (1928)

1 John Thomas says good-night to Lady Jane, a little droopingly, but with a hopeful heart.

ibid
Closing words.

2 How beastly the bourgeois is
especially the male of the species.

'How Beastly the Bourgeois Is' (1929)

3 The dirty little secret [attitude to sex] is most difficult to kill.

Pornography and Obscenity (1929)

4 *Homo sum!* the Adventurer.

Essay, 'Climbing Down Pisgah' (pub. 1936)
This is the text on his memorial in Westminster Abbey.

LAWRENCE, T. E.
British soldier and writer (1888–1935)

5 I loved you, so I drew these tides of men into my hands
    and wrote my will across the sky in stars
to earn you freedom, the seven pillared worthy house,
    that your eyes might be shining for me
when we came.

Epigraph 'To S.A.', *The Seven Pillars of Wisdom* (1926)

6 All men dream: but not equally. Those who dream by night in the dusty recesses of their minds wake in the day to find that it was vanity; but the dreamers of the day are dangerous men, for they may act their dream with open eyes, to make it possible. This I did.

Introductory Chapter to ibid

LAWTON, Lord Justice
British judge (1911–   )

7 Wife beating may be socially acceptable in Sheffield but it is a different matter in Cheltenham.

Attrib

LEACOCK, Stephen
US writer (1869–1944)

8 He flung himself from the room, flung himself upon his horse and rode madly off in all directions.

Nonsense Novels (1911), 'Gertrude the Governess'

LEARY, Dr Timothy
US hippie guru (1920–   )

1   Turn on, tune in, drop out.

Title of lecture, 1966
Later Leary ascribed the phrase to Marshall McLuhan.

'LE CARRÉ, John'
British novelist (1931–   )

2   The Spy Who Came In from the Cold.

Title of novel (1963)

'LE CORBUSIER'
French architect (1887–1965)

3   A house is a machine for living in (*'Une maison est une machine-à-habiter'*).

Vers une architecture (1923)

LEE, Gypsy Rose
US entertainer (1913–1970)

4   God is love—but get it in writing.

Attrib

LEHMAN, Ernest
US writer (1920–   )

5   Sweet Smell of Success.

Title of novel and film (1957)

LEHMANN, Rosamond
British writer (1901–90)

6   *On Ian Fleming:*
The trouble with Ian is that he gets off with women because he can't get on with them.

Quoted in J. Pearson, *The Life of Ian Fleming*
Borrowing a line from Elizabeth Bowen.

LEHRER, Tom
US songwriter and entertainer (1928–   )

7   Life is like a sewer. What you get out of it depends on what you put in.

On record album, *An Evening Wasted with Tom Lehrer* (1953)

8   He was into animal husbandry—until they caught him at it.

ibid

1   It is a sobering thought . . . that when Mozart was my age he had been dead for two years.

On record album *That Was the Year That Was* (1965)

LEIBER, Jerry and STOLLER, Mike
US songwriters (1933–   ) and (1933–   )

2   You ain't nothin' but a hound dog,
Cryin' all the time.

Song, 'Hound Dog' (1956)

3   I (Who Have Nothing).

Title of song (*c*1963)
Credited to 'Donida; Leiber, Stoller, Mogol'.

LEJEUNE, C. A.
British film critic (1897–1973)

4   *On the film I Am a Camera:*
Me no Leica.

Attrib

5   *On Charlton Heston's performance as a doctor:*
It makes me want to call out, Is there an apple in the house?

Attrib

LEMAY, Curtis E.
US General and Air Force chief (1906–90)

6   *On the North Vietnamese:*
My solution to the problem would be to tell them frankly that they've got to draw in their horns and stop their aggression, or we're going to bomb them back into the Stone Age.

Mission with LeMay (1965)
See also **SLOGANS 296:10.**

'LENIN, N.'
Russian revolutionary and Soviet leader (1870–1924)

7   One Step Forward, Two Steps Back.

Translation of book title (1904)

8   Communism is Soviet power plus the electrification of the whole country.

Report to 8th Congress, 1920

9   It is true that liberty is precious—so precious that it must be rationed.

Quoted in S. & B. Webb, *Soviet Communism* (1936)

1   *Question to show that there are two categories of people — those who do and those to whom it is done:*
    Who, whom? We or they?
    Quoted in F. Maclean, *Disputed Barricade*

2   *On Bernard Shaw:*
    A good man fallen among Fabians.
    Quoted in A. Ransome, *Six Weeks in Russia in 1919* (1919)

3   Give us a child for eight years and it will be a Bolshevist forever.
    Remark to the Commissars of Education, Moscow, 1923
    Possibly apocryphal. Compare the Jesuit saying: 'Give us a child until it is seven and it is ours for life'.
    See also **BEVAN 39:5.**

LENNON, John
British singer and songwriter (1940–80)

4   *To audience at Royal Variety Performance:*
    Would the people in the cheaper seats clap your hands. And the rest of you—could you just rattle your jewellery.
    TV soundtrack, 15 November 1963

5   Christianity will go. It will vanish and shrink. I needn't argue about that. I'm right and I'll be proved right. We're more popular than Jesus now.
    Interview with the London *Evening Standard*, 4 March 1966

6   WAR IS OVER! If you want it.
    Slogan, Christmas 1969

7   Whatever Gets You Thru the Night.
    Title of song (1974)

8   Imagine there's no heaven
    It's easy if you try
    No hell below us
    Above us only sky
    Imagine all the people
    Living for today.
    Song 'Imagine' (1975)

9   You shoulda been there.
    Slogan promoting rock'n'roll album, 1975

1 □ Life is what happens to you while you're making other plans.

Song, 'Beautiful Boy' (1980)
This is a quotation which Laurence J. Peter in *Quotations for Our Time*
ascribes to 'Thomas La Mance'.

2 *On the split-up of the Beatles and the end of the 'sixties:*
And so, dear friends, you'll just have to carry on. The dream is over
. . . nothing's changed. Just a few of us are walking around with
longer hair.

Attrib
*See also **next entry**:*

LENNON, John and McCARTNEY, Paul
British songwriters (1940–80) and (1942–   )

3 Yeh-yeh-yeh.

'She Loves You' (1963)

4 It's been a hard day's night.

Song, 'A Hard Day's Night' (1964)
The use of the phrase as a film title is said to have been suggested by
Ringo Starr, though Lennon may have used it earlier in a poem.

5 Yesterday, all my troubles seemed so far away.

Song, 'Yesterday' (1965)

6 It was twenty years ago today, that
Sgt. Pepper taught the band to play.

Song, 'Sgt. Pepper's Lonely Hearts Club Band' (1967)

7 4,000 holes in Blackburn.

'A Day In the Life', in ibid

8 Waits at the window, wearing the face that she keeps in a jar by the
door
Who is it for?
All the lonely people, where do they all come from?

Song 'Eleanor Rigby' (1967)

9 Will you still need me, will you still feed me
When I'm sixty-four?

Song, 'When I'm Sixty-Four' (1967)

10 I get by with a little help from my friends.

Song, 'With a Little Help from My Friends' (1967)

11 All You Need is Love.

Title of song (1967)

1   Magical Mystery Tour.
    Title of film (1967)

2   (All we are saying is) Give Peace a Chance
    Title of song (1969)

3   Let It Be.
    Title of song (1970)

LERNER, Alan Jay
US lyricist and playwright (1918–86)

4   Why can't a woman be more like a man?
    Song, 'A Hymn to Him', *My Fair Lady* (1956)
    Music by Frederick Loewe, *as for the following:*

5   Ah, yes, I remember it well.
    Song, 'I Remember It Well', *Gigi* (1958)

6   Thank heaven for little girls,
    For little girls get bigger every day.
    Song, 'Thank Heaven for Little Girls' in ibid

7   Don't let it be forgot
    That once there was a spot
    For one brief shining moment that was known
    As Camelot . . .
    Title song, *Camelot* (1960)

8   You write a hit the same way you write a flop.
    Attrib

9   The female sex has no bigger fan than I, and I have the bills to prove it.
    The Street Where I Live (1978)

THE LETTER
US film 1940. Script by Howard Koch, from the story by W. Somerset Maugham. With Bette Davis.

10   □ Yes, I killed him. And I'm glad, I tell you. Glad, glad, glad!
    Although associated with Bette Davis and the film, this line is not uttered in it.

LEVANT, Oscar
US pianist and actor (1906–72)

1   Strip the phoney tinsel off Hollywood and you'll find the real tinsel underneath.

Attrib

2   *Romance on the High Seas* was Doris Day's first picture; that was before she became a virgin.

Memoirs of an Amnesiac (1965)
Compare **G. MARX 220:7.**

LEVERHULME, 1st Viscount
British industrialist (1851–1925)

3   Half the money I spend on advertising is wasted, and the trouble is I don't know which half.

Quoted in D. Ogilvy, *Confessions of an Advertising Man* (1963)

'LIBERACE'
US pianist (1919–87)

4   When the reviews are bad I tell my staff that they can join me as I cry all the way to the bank.

Liberace: An Autobiography (1973)

LINKLATER, Eric
British writer (1899–1974)

5   At my back I often hear Time's winged chariot changing gear.

Juan in China (1937)

LINLEY, Viscount
British Royal and furniture designer (1961–   )

6   *When asked in November 1983 what he would give his worst enemy as a present:*
Dinner with Princess Michael.

Quoted in *Daily Mail*, 16 April 1985

LITTLE CAESAR
US film 1930. Script by various. With Edward G. Robinson as Rico.

7   *Rico (dying words):*
Mother of Mercy, is this the end of Rico?

Soundtrack

LITVINOV, Maxim
Soviet politician (1876–1951)

1   Peace is indivisible.

Said on several occasions and at League of Nations, Geneva,
1 July 1936

LIVES OF A BENGAL LANCER
US film 1935. Script by various. Douglass Dumbrille as Mohammed Khan.

2   *Khan:* We have ways of making men talk.

An early example of the film catchphrase, more usually rendered as
'We have ways (and means) of making you talk.'

LOESSER, Frank
US songwriter (1910–69)

3   See What the Boys in the Back Room Will Have.

Title of song, *Destry Rides Again* (1939)

4   Finally found a fellow
He says 'Murder!'—he says!
Every time we kiss he says 'Murder!'—he says!
Is that the language of love?

Song, '"Murder" He Says', *Happy Go Lucky* (1943)
Murder He Says became the title of a film (US, 1945).

5   Yes, time heals all things,
So I needn't cling to this fear,
It's merely that Spring
Will be a little late this year.

Song, 'Spring Will Be a Little Late This Year', *Christmas Holiday* (1944)

6   I'd like to get you on a slow boat to China
All to myself alone.

Song, 'On a Slow Boat to China' (1948)

7   How To Succeed in Business Without Really Trying.

Title of musical (1961)
Taken from Shepherd Meade's non-fiction guidebook of that title.

LOMBARDI, Vince
US football coach (1913–70)

8   □ Winning isn't everything. It's the only thing.

Attrib

Various versions of this oft-repeated statement exist. Lombardi claimed
not to have said it in this form. Henry 'Red' Sanders, a football coach
at Vanderbilt University, does seem to have said it, however, *c*1948.

LONDON, Jack
US writer (1876–1916)

1   The Call of the Wild.
    Title of novel (1903)

THE LONE RANGER
US radio, film and TV Western series, from 1933.

2   Return with us now to those thrilling days of yesteryear . . . the
    Lone Ranger rides again!
    Introductory announcement

3   *Lone Ranger (to horse):* Hi-yo, Silver! (Away!)
    Catchphrase

4   *Tonto:* Him bad man, kemo sabe.
    Stock phrase

LONG, Huey
US demagogue (1893–1935)

5   I looked around at the little fishes present and said, 'I'm the
    Kingfish.'
    Quoted in A. Schlesinger Jr, *The Politics of Upheaval*

6   Every man a king but no man wears a crown.
    Slogan, 1928
    Quoting William Jennings Bryan.

LONGFORD, 7th Earl of
British politician and writer (1905–   )

7   On the whole I would not say that our Press is obscene. I would say
    that it trembles on the brink of obscenity.
    Quoted in the *Observer*, 2 June 1963

8   My own wife, as some people know, had a lot of children—eight, if
    I remember rightly.
    Speech, House of Lords, 1 May 1985

LONGWORTH, Alice Roosevelt
US political hostess (1884–1980)

9   *Embroidered on a cushion at her Washington home:*
    If you haven't anything nice to say about anyone, come and sit by
    me.
    Quoted in the *New York Times*, 25 February 1980

1   *Of Calvin Coolidge:*
    □ Looked as if he had been weaned on a pickle.
    ibid
    She admitted hearing this from someone else at the dentist.

2   *Of Thomas E. Dewey:*
    □ Dewey looks like the bridegroom on the wedding cake.
    ibid
    She admitted to having acquired this from Grace Hodgson Flandrau.

3   *On Dewey's nomination, in 1948:*
    You can't make a soufflé rise twice.
    Attrib

LOOS, Anita
US novelist (1893–1981)

4   Gentlemen Prefer Blondes.

    Title of novel (1925)
    To which a sequel was added: *But Gentlemen Marry Brunettes* (1928).

5   A Girl like I.

    Passim in ibid

6   Kissing your hand may make you feel very good but a diamond and
    safire bracelet lasts forever.

    ibid
    This was the inspiration for the Jule Styne/Leo Robin song 'Diamonds
    Are a Girl's Best Friend' in the 1949 stage musical and 1953 film based
    on the book.

LOTHIAN, 11th Marquess of
British Conservative politician (1882–1940)

7   The only lasting solution is that Europe itself should gradually find
    its way to an internal equilibrium and a limitation of armaments by
    political *appeasement.*
    Letter to *The Times,* 4 May 1934

LOUIS, Joe
US boxer (1914–81)

8   *Before his fight with the quick-moving Billy Conn (whom he beat by a knock-
    out, 19 June 1946):*
    He can run, but he can't hide.

    In *New York Herald Tribune,* 9 June 1946
    Alluded to by President Reagan (1985) in a warning to terrorists: 'You
    can run, but you can't hide'.

LOVE STORY
US film 1970. Script (also novel) by Erich Segal. With Ryan O'Neal as Oliver.

1   *Oliver:* What can you say about a twenty-five-year-old girl who died? That she was beautiful? And brilliant. That she loved Mozart and Bach. And the Beatles. And me.

Soundtrack

2   *Oliver:* Love means never having to say you're sorry.

Soundtrack
In the book it appears as 'Love means not ever . . .'
The graffito 'A vasectomy means never having to say you're sorry' was current before 1974.

LOVELL, James
US astronaut (1928–   )

3   *After an explosion on Apollo XIII had seriously endangered the crew:*
OK, Houston, we have had a problem here . . . Houston, we have a problem.

Radio message, 11 April 1970
It is hard to decipher precisely what was being said and the words have also been attributed to John L. Swigert Jr.

LOW, David
British cartoonist (1891–1963)

4   Very well, alone.

Caption to his cartoon, *Evening Standard*, 18 June 1940
The cartoon showed a British soldier confronting a hostile sea and a sky full of bombers.

LOWELL, Robert
US poet (1917–77)

5   If we see light at the end of the tunnel,
It's the light of the oncoming train.

'Day by Day' (1977)
The idea was probably not original.

LOWRY, L. S.
British painter (1887–1976)

6   A bachelor lives like a king and dies like a beggar.

Attrib

LUDENDORFF, Erich
German General (1865–1937)

1 *On British troops in the First World War:*
   □ Lions led by donkeys.

   Attrib

   In fact, Field Marshal von Falkenhayn in his memoirs records the
   following exchange—Ludendorff: 'The English fight like lions'—
   Hoffman: 'True. But don't we know that they are lions led by donkeys?'
   General Max Hoffman (1869–1927) succeeded Ludendorff as chief of
   the general staff in 1916.

LUTYENS, Sir Edwin
British architect (1869–1944)

2 *Before a Royal Commission:*
   The answer is in the plural and they bounce.

   Attrib

3 This piece of cod passeth all understanding.

   Quoted in R. Lutyens, *Sir Edwin Lutyens* (1942)

LYNCH, Jack
Irish Taoiseach (Head of Government) (1917–)

4 I would not like to leave contraception on the long finger too long.

   Quoted in *Irish Times*, 23 May 1971

McALPINE, Sir Alfred
British civil engineer (1881–1944)

1 Keep Paddy behind the big mixer.

Attrib
Last words.

MacARTHUR, Douglas
US General (1880–1964)

2 The President of the United States ordered me to break through the Japanese lines and proceed from Corregidor to Australia for the purpose, as I understand it, of organizing the American offensive against Japan, a primary object of which is the relief of the Philippines. I came through and I shall return.

Statement, Adelaide, 20 March 1942

3 People of the Philippines, I have returned.

Statement, Leyte, 20 October 1944

4 In war there is no substitute for victory.

Speech to Congress, 19 April 1951

5 *On his dismissal by President Truman:*
The world has turned over many times since I took the oath on the Plain at West Point, and the hopes and dreams have long since vanished. But I still remember the refrain of one of the most popular barrack ballads of that day, which proclaimed, most proudly, that old soldiers never die. They just fade away. And like the old soldier of that ballad, I now close my military career and just fade away—an old soldier who tried to do his duty as God gave him the light to see that duty. Goodbye.

ibid
In fact, the ballad came out of the First World War and is a parody of
the gospel hymn 'Kind Words Can Never Die'.

McCARTHY, Mary
US writer (1912–89)

6 *On Lillian Hellman:*
I once said in an interview that every word she writes is a lie, including 'and' and 'the'.

In the *New York Times*, 16 February 1980

MACAULAY, Rose
British novelist (1881–1958)

1 'Take my camel, dear', said my aunt Dot, as she climbed down from this animal on her return from High Mass.

The Towers of Trebizond (1956)
Opening words.

McAULIFFE, Anthony C.
US General (1898–1975)

2 *When asked to surrender by the Germans at the Battle of Bastogne:*
Nuts!

Message, 23 December 1944
His message may have been worded more explicitly.

MacCARTHY, Sir Desmond
British writer and critic (1877–1952)

3 [Journalists are] more attentive to the minute hand of history than to the hour hand.

Quoted in K. Tynan, *Curtains*

McCARTHY, Senator Joseph
US politician and witch-hunter (1908–57)

4 *Of an alleged Communist sympathizer's stand:*
It makes me sick, sick, sick way down inside.

Quoted in P. Lewis, *The Fifties*

McCARTNEY, Paul
See LENNON, John *and* McCARTNEY, Paul

McCOY, Horace
US writer (1897–1955)

5 They Shoot Horses, Don't They?

Title of novel (1935)

McCRAE, John
Canadian poet (1872–1918)

6 In Flanders fields the poppies blow
Between the crosses, row on row,
That mark our place.

'In Flanders Fields' (1915)

7 If ye break faith with us who die
We shall not sleep, though poppies grow
On Flanders fields.

ibid

211

McCULLOCH, Derek
British broadcaster (1897–1967)

1   Goodbye, children . . . everywhere.

    Stock phrase, *Children's Hour*, BBC radio, from 1930s onwards

McENROE, John
US Wimbledon tennis champion (1959–)

2   *To umpire at Wimbledon:*
    Man, you cannot be serious.

    Remark, June 1981

3   *To umpire at Wimbledon:*
    You guys are the pits of the world.

    Remark, June 1981

McGILL, Donald
British comic postcard artist (1875–1962)

4   □ I've lost my little Willie!

    In fact, this was the caption to a postcard by another artist.

5   'Do you like Kipling?'
    'I don't know, you naughty boy, I've never kippled.'

    Caption to postcard, 1930s

McGOVERN, George
US Democratic politician (1922–)

6   *On his Vice-Presidential running mate:*
    I am one thousand per cent for Tom Eagleton and I have no intention of dropping him from the ticket.

    Attrib, in 1972
    He dropped him shortly afterwards.

McKINNEY, Joyce
US former beauty queen (1950–)

7   *On Mormon ex-lover she had kidnapped:*
    I loved Kirk so much, I would have skied down Mount Everest in the nude with a carnation up my nose.

    In Epsom Magistrates' Court, 6 December 1977

MacLEISH, Archibald
US poet (1892–1982)

1 *On a photograph of the earth as taken from an Apollo spacecraft:*
To see the earth as it truly is, small and blue and beautiful in that eternal silence where it floats, is to see ourselves as riders on the earth together, brothers on that bright loveliness in the eternal cold—brothers who know they are truly brothers.

In the *New York Times*, 25 December 1968

MACLEOD, Iain
British Conservative politician (1913–70)

2 History is too serious to be left to historians.

Quoted in the *Observer*, 16 July 1961

3 *On the method of choosing the Conservative Party leader in the previous year:*
It is some measure of the tightness of the *magic circle* on this occasion that neither the Chancellor of the Exchequer nor the Leader of the House of Commons had any inkling of what was happening.

Article in the *Spectator*, 17 January 1964

4 *On over-protective government:*
The nanny state.

Attrib in *Spectator* articles, 1960s

5 We now have the worst of both worlds—not just inflation on the one side or stagnation on the other side, but both of them together. We have a sort of 'stagflation' situation.

Speech, House of Commons, 17 November 1965

McLUHAN, Marshall
Canadian writer (1911–80)

6 The new electronic interdependence re-creates the world in the image of a global village.

The Gutenberg Galaxy (1962)

7 The medium is the message.

Understanding Media (1964)

8 Television brought the brutality of war into the comfort of the living room. Vietnam was lost in the living rooms of America—not on the battlefields of Vietnam.

Quoted in the Montreal *Gazette*, 16 May 1975
See also **LEARY 199:1.**

MACMILLAN, Harold (later 1st Earl of Stockton)

British Conservative Prime Minister (1894–1986)

1 The Middle Way.

Title of book (1938)

2 *After a summit conference at Geneva:*
There ain't gonna be no war.

Press conference, London, 24 July 1955
Alluding to a *c*1910 music-hall song 'There ain't gonna be no war/So long as we've a king like good King Edward [VII].'

3 *On being a Foreign Secretary:*
Nothing he can say can do very much good, and almost anything he may say may do a great deal of harm. Anything he says that is not obvious is dangerous; whatever is not trite is risky. He is forever poised between the cliché and the indiscretion.

Speech, House of Commons, 27 July 1955

4 *After the resignation of his Chancellor of the Exchequer and others:*
I thought the best thing to do was to settle up these *little local difficulties,* and then turn to the wider vision of the Commonwealth.

Statement, London airport, 7 January 1958

5 Jaw-jaw is better than war-war.

Remark, Canberra, 30 January 1958
See **CHURCHILL 78:3.**

6 Let's be frank about it. Most of our people have never had it so good.

Speech, Bedford, 20 July 1957
'You Never Had It So Good' was a slogan used by the Democrats in the 1952 US Presidential Election.

7 Enough is enough.

Remark to Selwyn Lloyd, Foreign Secretary, Summer 1959
When this was leaked by Macmillan to *The Times* (1 June 1959), the furore caused Lloyd to be retained in the job for a further year.
Compare **DAILY MIRROR 94:2.**

8 □ Exporting is fun.

Speech to businessmen, 1960
He never actually said the words contained in the press advance text.

9 The wind of change is blowing through this continent.

Speech, Parliament, Cape Town, 3 February 1960

1   Power? It's like a Dead Sea fruit; when you achieve it, there's
    nothing there.
    Attrib

2   I do not live among young people fairly widely.
    Speech, House of Commons, 17 June 1963

3   I was determined that no British Government should be brought
    down by the action of two tarts.
    Attrib remark, 13 July 1963
    Alternatively, 'I was not going to have the British Government pulled
    down by the antics of a whore.'

4   *On his resignation as Prime Minister:*
    I hope that it will soon be possible for the customary processes of
    consultation to be carried on within the party about its future
    leadership.
    Statement (read by R. A. Butler) to Conservative Party Conference, 10
    October 1963

5   If people want a sense of purpose they should get it from their
    archbishop. They should certainly not get it from their politicians.
    Quoted in H. Fairlie, *The Life of Politics*

6   *Of Sir Geoffrey Howe:*
    Mogadon Man.
    Attrib

7   After a long life I have come to the conclusion that when all the
    establishment is united, it is always wrong.
    Speech, Carlton Club, October 1982

8   *On the privatization of nationalized industries:*
    [The sale of assets is common with individuals and the state when
    they run into financial difficulties.] First of all the Georgian silver
    goes, and then all that nice furniture that used to be in the saloon.
    Then the Canalettos go.
    Speech to Tory Reform Group, 8 November 1985
    Summarized as 'Selling off the family silver'.

9   Memorial services are the cocktail parties of the geriatric set.
    Quoted in A. Horne, *Macmillan 1957–1986*

MacNEICE, Louis
British poet (1907–63)

10 It's no go the merry-go-round, it's no go the rickshaw,
    All we want is a limousine and a ticket for the peepshow.
    Earth Compels (1937), 'Bagpipe Music'

MAETERLINCK, Maurice

Belgian poet and playwright (1862–1949)

1   The living are just the dead on holiday.

Attrib

MAFFEY, Sir John

British diplomat

2   *As British Ambassador in Dublin, to the Dominions Office in London:*
This temperamental country [Ireland] needs quiet treatment and a patient, consistent policy. But how are you to control Ministerial incursions into your china shop? Phrases make history here.

Letter, 21 May 1945, quoted in R. Fisk, *In Time of War* (1985)

MAGEE, John Gillespie

US/British airforce pilot and poet (1922–41)

3   Oh! I have slipped the surly bonds of earth,
And danced the skies on laughter-silvered wings;
. . . And, while with silent lifting mind I've trod
The high untrespassed sanctity of space,
Put out my hand, and touched the face of God.

'High Flight', *More Poems from the Forces* (1943)
Magee was killed while flying from Britain with the Royal Canadian Air Force.

MAGIC ROUNDABOUT

French TV series devised by Serge Danot. On BBC TV 1965–77. English commentary written and spoken by Eric Thompson.

4   [Boing!] 'It's time for bed,' said Zebedee.

Commentary, *passim*

MAJOR, John

British Conservative Prime Minister (1943–   )

5   *On becoming Chancellor of the Exchequer:*
The harsh truth is that *if the policy isn't hurting, it isn't working.* I know there is a difficult period ahead but the important thing is that we cannot and must not fudge the determination to stop inflation in its tracks.

Speech, Northampton, 27 October 1989

6   *Reacting to an IRA mortar-bomb attack on Downing Street during a Cabinet meeting:*
Gentlemen, I think we had better start again, somewhere else.

Quoted in *The Independent*, 9 February 1991

MALLORY, George Leigh
British mountaineer (1886–1924)

1   *When asked why he wanted to climb Mount Everest:*
Because it is there.

Usual reply during US lecture tour, 1923

MANDELA, Nelson
South African political activisit (1918–   )

2   The struggle is my life.

Attrib
Quoted beneath the bronze bust of the then prisoner, outside the
Royal Festival Hall, London, 1985.

MANDELA, Winnie
South African political activist (1934–   )

3   Together, hand in hand, with our matches and our necklaces, we
shall liberate this country.

Remark, quoted in the *Observer*, 20 April 1986
The 'necklaces' were car tyres filled with petrol.

MANKIEWICZ, Herman J.
US screenwriter (1897–1953)

4   *When a Hollywood agent told him how he had been swimming unscathed in
shark-infested waters:*
I think that's what they call professional courtesy.

Attrib

5   *After vomiting at the table of a fastidious host:*
It's all right, Arthur. The white wine came up with the fish.

Attrib
See also **CITIZEN KANE** *and* **ALL ABOUT EVE.**

MANN, William
British music critic (1924–89)

6   *Reviewing the music of the Beatles:*
The outstanding English composers of 1963 must seem to have
been John Lennon and Paul McCartney . . . the slow sad song about
'That Boy' . . . is expressively unusual for its lugubrious music, but
harmonically it is one of their most interesting, with its chains of
pandiatonic clusters . . . so natural is the Aeolian cadence at the
end of 'Not a Second Time' (the chord progression which ends
Mahler's *Song of the Earth*) . . . autocratic but not by any means
ungrammatical attitude to tonality . . . the quasi-instrumental vocal
duetting . . . the melismas with altered vowels . . .

Article, *The Times*, 27 December 1963

MAN OF LA MANCHA, THE
Musical play, US 1965 (filmed 1972). Lyrics by Joe Darion, music by Mitch Leigh, based on play by Dale Wasserman.

1   To dream the impossible dream,
    To fight the unbeatable foe,
    To bear with unbearable sorrow,
    To run where the brave dare not go.

Song, 'The Impossible Dream'

MANSFIELD, Katherine
New Zealand-born writer (1888–1923)

2   Better far write twaddle or anything, anything, than nothing at all.

Journal 1922 (1927)

MAO ZEDONG (Mao Tse-tung)
Chinese revolutionary and Communist leader (1893–1976)

3   Every Communist must grasp the truth, political power grows out of the barrel of a gun.

In *Quotations from Chairman Mao Tse-tung*, dated 6 November 1938

4   All reactionaries are paper tigers. In appearance, the reactionaries are terrifying, but in reality they are not powerful.

In ibid, from interview, 1946

5   'He who is not afraid of death by a thousand cuts dares to unhorse the emperor'—this is the indomitable spirit needed in our struggle to build socialism and communism.

In ibid

6   We must let a hundred flowers bloom and a hundred schools of thought contend.

Statement, May 1956
Outlining a period of self-criticism which was launched, briefly, in May 1957.

7   The Great Leap Forward.

Name for enforced industrialization, 1958

8   People of the world, unite and defeat the US aggressors and all their running dogs!

Statement, 28 November 1964

1   *To his wife and her colleagues in conspiratorial group:*
     Don't be a gang of four.
     Attrib

2   A fat man should not play the concertina.
     Attrib

MARKS, Leo
British bookseller (1920–   )

3   The life that I have is all that I have,
     And the life that I have is yours.
     The love that I have of the life that I have
     Is yours and yours and yours.
     'Code Poem for the French Resistance'
     The poem was written to be used as the basis for codes used by Special
     Operations Executive agents in the Second World War. Quoted in the
     film *Carve Her Name With Pride* (1958).

MARQUIS, Don
US writer (1878–1937)

4   well archy the world is full of ups and downs but toujours gai is my
     motto.
     archy and mehitabel (1927)

MARSHALL, Arthur
British writer and entertainer (1910–89)

5   It's all part of life's rich pageant.
     'The Games Mistress' (gramophone record), *c*1935
     Suggested as the origin of this phrase.

6   *Of Barbara Cartland:*
     The animated meringue.
     Remark

7   There is nothing like a morning funeral for sharpening the
     appetite for lunch.
     Life's Rich Pageant (1984)

MARSHALL, Thomas R.
US Democratic Vice President (1854–1925)

8   *To the chief clerk of the Senate during a tedious debate, 1917:*
     What this country needs is a really good five cent cigar.
     Quoted in *New York Tribune*, 4 January 1920

MARX, Chico
US film comedian (1886–1961)

1   *When his wife had caught him kissing a chorus girl:*
But I wasn't kissing her. I was whispering in her mouth.
Quoted in G. Marx & R. Anobile, *The Marx Brothers Scrapbook*

MARX, Groucho
US entertainer (1895–1977)

2   *To the Friars Club, Beverly Hills:*
Please accept my resignation. I don't care to belong to any club that will have me as a member.
Quoted in *The Groucho Letters*
Various versions of this statement exist.

3   No, Groucho is not my real name. I'm breaking it in for a friend.
Attrib

4   I eat like a vulture. Unfortunately the resemblance doesn't end there.
Attrib

5   *When excluded from a beach club on racial grounds:*
Since my daughter is only half-Jewish, could she go in the water up to her knees?
Quoted in the *Observer*, 21 August 1977

6   Many years ago I chased a woman for almost two years, only to discover her tastes were exactly like mine: we were both crazy about girls.
Attrib

7   I've been around so long, I knew Doris Day before she was a virgin.
Attrib
See also **LEVANT 204:2.**

8   We in this industry know that behind every successful screenwriter stands a woman. And behind her stands his wife.
Attrib

9   Show me a rose and I'll show you a girl named Sam.
Song, 'Show me a Rose'
Written by Harry Ruby and Bert Kalmar.

10   Hello, I must be going.
Title of song
Written by Harry Ruby and Bert Kalmar.

1   I never forget a face, but I'll make an exception in your case.
     Attrib

2   *On the films of Victor Mature:*
     I never go to movies where the hero's bust is bigger than the
     heroine's.
     Attrib
     Probably regarding Mature's appearance in *Samson and Delilah* (1949).

3   They say a man is as old as the woman he feels. In that case I'm
     eighty-five . . . I want it known here and now that this is what I want
     on my tombstone: Here lies Groucho Marx, and Lies and Lies and
     Lies. P.S. He never kissed an ugly girl.
     The Secret Word is Groucho (1976)
     See also **ANIMAL CRACKERS; THE COCOANUTS; DUCK SOUP.**

MARY, HM Queen
British Royal, wife of George V (1867–1953)

4   *To soldier who had exclaimed 'No more bloody wars for me':*
     No more bloody wars, no more bloody medals.
     Attrib

5   *To Stanley Baldwin on the Abdication (on 17 November 1936):*
     Well, Prime Minister, here's a pretty kettle of fish.
     Quoted in F. Donaldson, *Edward VIII*

MASCHWITZ, Eric
British songwriter (1901–69)

6   The sigh of midnight trains in empty stations . . .
     The smile of Garbo and the scent of roses . . .
     These foolish things
     Remind me of you.
     Song, 'These Foolish Things' (1936)
     Originally published as by 'Holt Marvell', with music by Jack Strachey.

7   A Nightingale Sang in Berkeley Square.
     Title of song, *New Faces* (1940)
     Derived from the title of a Michael Arlen short story 'When the
     Nightingale Sang in Berkeley Square' in *These Charming People* (1923).
     Music by Manning Sherwin.

MASEFIELD, John
British Poet Laureate (1878–1967)

1   I must [go] down to the seas again.

'Sea Fever' (1902)
Although it appears to have been the poet's original intention to omit the word 'go' from this line, it has been included in several editions of his work.

2   Dirty British coaster with a salt-caked smoke-stack
Butting through the Channel in the mad March days.

'Cargoes' (1910)

MASON, Donald
US Navy pilot (1913–   )

3   Sighted sub, sank same.

Radio message, 28 January 1942
On sinking a Japanese submarine in the South Pacific.

MASTERMIND
UK TV general knowledge quiz (BBC), from 1972 onwards. With Magnus Magnusson as chairman.

4   *Magnusson (when time runs out half-way through question):*
I've started so I'll finish.

Stock phrase

5   *Contestant (not knowing answer):*
Pass.

Stock phrase

MATHEW, Sir James
British lawyer (1830–1908)

6   In England, justice is open to all, like the Ritz hotel.

Attrib

MATTHEWS, A. E.
British actor (1869–1960)

7   I always wait for *The Times* each morning. I look at the obituary column, and if I'm not in it, I go to work.

Attrib
His own obituary appeared on 26 July 1960.

MATURE, Victor
US film actor (1915–)

1 *When told he looked as though he had slept in his clothes:*
Don't be ridiculous. I pay someone to do that for me.
Attrib

MAUDLING, Reginald
British Conservative politician (1917–77)

2 *At end of visit to Northern Ireland as Home Secretary:*
I don't think one can speak of defeating the IRA, of eliminating them completely, but it is the design of the security forces to reduce their level of violence to something like an acceptable level.
Statement, 15 December 1971
Remembered, and used against him, as 'acceptable level of violence'.

3 *On being replaced in the Cabinet by a man four years his senior:*
There comes a time in every man's life when he must make way for an older man.
Reported in *The Guardian*, 20 November 1976

MAUGHAM, W. Somerset
British novelist and short-story writer (1874–1965)

4 I stand in the very first row of the second-raters.
The Summing Up (1938)
But untraced in that autobiography.

5 *When a friend said he hated the food in England:*
What rubbish. All you have to do is eat breakfast three times a day.
ibid

6 At a dinner party one should eat wisely but not too well, and talk well but not too wisely.
A Writer's Notebook (1949)

7 I've always been interested in people, but I've never liked them.
Quoted in the *Observer*, 28 August 1949

8 *Of state-aided undergraduates:*
They are scum.
In the *Sunday Times*, 25 December 1955
See also **GIRAUDOUX 138:3; THE LETTER 203:10.**

MAXTON, Jimmy
Independent Labour Party MP (1855–1946)

1 *On a man who had proposed disaffiliation of the ILP from the Labour Party:*
If my friend cannot ride two horses—what's he doing in the bloody circus?

Quoted in G. McAllister, *James Maxton*

MAYS, Willie
US baseball player (1931–   )

2 Say hey!

Characteristic expression

MENCKEN, H. L.
US journalist (1880–1956)

3 Conscience: the inner voice which warns us that somebody may be looking.

A Little Book in C Major (1916)

4 *Standard reply to readers' letters when he was editor of the* American Mercury:
Dear Reader, You may be right.

Attrib

5 *Suggested epitaph:*
If after I depart this vale, you remember me and have thought to please my ghost, forgive some sinner and wink your eye at a homely girl.

The Smart Set, December 1921

6 No one . . . has ever lost money by underestimating the great masses of the plain people.

In the *Chicago Tribune*, 19 September 1926

7 The only really happy people are married women and single men.

Attrib

8 *On President Coolidge:*
Here, indeed, was his one really notable talent. He slept more than any other President, whether by day or by night . . . Nero fiddled, but Coolidge only snored . . . He had no ideas, and he was not a nuisance.

In the *American Mercury*, April 1933

1 Opera in English is, in the main, just about as sensible as baseball in Italian.

Attrib

2 I've made it a rule never to drink by daylight and never to refuse a drink after dark.

Quoted in the *New York Post*, 18 September 1945

3 When women kiss, it always reminds me of prize-fighters shaking hands.

In ibid, 1949

MENZIES, Sir Robert
Australian Liberal Prime Minister (1894–1978)

4 *When accused by a Member of Parliament of harbouring a superiority complex:*
Considering the company I keep in this place, that is hardly surprising.

Quoted in *Time*, 29 May 1978

5 *In answer to heckler who cried, 'I wouldn't vote for you if you were the Archangel Gabriel':*
If I were the Archangel Gabriel, madam, I'm afraid you would not be in my constituency.

Quoted in R. Robinson, *The Wit of Sir Robert Menzies* (1966)

MERCER, Johnny
US lyricist (1909–76)

6 You're just too marvellous,
Too marvellous for words.

Song, 'Too Marvellous for Words', *Ready, Willing and Able* (1937)

7 You're much too much and just too very very
To ever be in Webster's dictionary.

ibid

8 That Old Black Magic (Has Me In Its Spell).

Title of song, *Star Spangled Rhythm* (1942)

9 We're drinking my friend,
To the end of a brief episode;
Make it one for my baby
And one more for the road.

Song, 'One For My Baby', *The Sky's the Limit* (1943)

1   *On seeing a British musical (1975):*
I could eat alphabet soup and *shit* better lyrics.

Attrib

MERCHANT, Vivien
British actress (1929–83)

2   *On her husband, Harold Pinter, when he left her for Lady Antonia Fraser:*
He didn't need to take a change of shoes; he can always wear hers;
she has very big feet you know.

Quoted in the *Observer*, 21 December 1975

MERMAN, Ethel
US entertainer (1908–84)

3   *To Irving Berlin when he wanted to change a song lyric in* **Call Me Madam**
(1950):
Call me Miss Birdseye. This show is frozen.

Quoted in *The Times*, 13 July 1985

MICHAELIS, John H.
US General (1912–85)

4   *To 27th Infantry (Wolfhound) Regiment during the Korean war:*
You're not here to die for your country. You're here to make those
————— die for theirs.

Attrib

MIDLER, Bette
US actress (1944–)

5   *On sex in the age of AIDS:*
These days, you fuck someone, your arm drops off.

Quoted in *The Independent*, 12 November 1988

MIKES, George
Hungarian-born writer in Britain (1912–87)

6   Continental people have a sex life; the English have hot-water
bottles.

How To Be An Alien (1946)

MILLER, Arthur
US playwright (1915–)

7   A good newspaper, I suppose, is a nation talking to itself.

Quoted in the *Observer*, 26 November 1961
See also **THE MISFITS 229:4.**

MILLER, Jonathan
British entertainer, writer and director (1936–   )

1   'Gentlemen, lift the seat' . . . perhaps it's a loyal toast?
    'The Heat-Death of the Universe', *Beyond the Fringe* (1961)

2   I'm not really a Jew; just Jew-ish, not the whole hog, you know.
    'Real Class' in ibid

3   This is Alvar Liddell bringing you news of fresh disasters.
    'The Aftermyth of War' in ibid

MILLER, Max
British comedian (1895–1963)

4   I've got a million of 'em.
    Stock phrase, after delivering joke

5   There'll never be another.
    Catchphrase

6   When I'm dead and gone, the game's finished.
    Catchphrase

MILLIGAN, Spike
Irish entertainer (1918–   )

7   I'm Walking Backwards to Christmas.
    Title of song (1956)

8   The Army works like this: if a man dies when you hang him, keep hanging until he gets used to it.
    Attrib

9   Q. Are you Jewish?
    A. No, a tree fell on me.
    Quoted in *Private Eye*, 1973
    See also **THE GOON SHOW.**

MILNE, A. A.
British writer (1882–1956)

10 They're changing guard at Buckingham Palace—
    Christopher Robin went down with Alice.
    Alice is marrying one of the guard.
    'A soldier's life is terribly hard,'
        Says Alice.
    'Buckingham Palace', *When We Were Very Young* (1924)

1   The King asked
The Queen, and
The Queen asked
The Dairymaid:
'Could we have some butter for
the Royal slice of bread?'

'The King's Breakfast' in ibid

2   Little boy kneels at the foot of the bed,
droops on the little hands, little gold head;
Hush! Hush! Whisper who dares!
Christopher Robin is saying his prayers.

'Vespers' in ibid

3   When Rabbit said, 'Honey or condensed milk with your bread?'
[Pooh] was so excited he said, 'Both,' and then, so as not to seem
greedy, he added, 'But don't bother about the bread, please.'

Winnie-The-Pooh (1926)

4   Time for a little something.

ibid

5   *Pooh:* 'I am a Bear of Very Little Brain, and long words Bother me.'

ibid

6   The more it snows
    (Tiddely pom),
The more it goes
    (Tiddely pom),
The more it goes
    (Tiddely pom)
On snowing.

The House at Pooh Corner (1928)

7   Worraworraworraworraworra. (Tigger)

ibid

MILNER, Alfred 1st Viscount
British imperialist (1854–1925)

8   *On the peers and the Budget:*
If we believe a thing to be bad, and if we have a right to prevent it,
it is our duty to try to prevent it, and to damn the consequences.

Speech, Glasgow, 26 November 1909

MINDER

UK TV drama series (Thames TV), 1979–85. Created by Leon Griffiths. With George Cole as Arthur Daley.

1   *Daley (referring to his wife):*
    'Er indoors.

    Stock phrase

2   *Daley:* A nice little earner.

    Stock phrase

MINOW, Newton N.

US government official (1926–   )

3   *On American TV watched from morn till night:*
    Keep your eyes glued to that set until the station signs off. I can assure you that you will observe a vast wasteland.

    Speech, National Association of Broadcasters, 9 May 1961

THE MISFITS

US film 1961. Script by Arthur Miller (also as novel). With Marilyn Monroe and Clark Gable.

4   *Last words:*
    MM: How do you find your way back in the dark?
    CG: Just head for that big star straight on. The highway's under it. It'll take us right home.

    Soundtrack

MITCHELL, Adrian

British poet and playwright (1932–   )

5   Tell me lies about Vietnam.

    Poem, 'To Whom It May Concern', from play *US* (1966)

6   When I am sad and weary
    When I think all hope has gone
    When I walk along High Holborn
    I think of you with nothing on.

    Poem, 'Celia Celia' (1968)

MITFORD, Nancy

British author (1904–73)

7   She said that all the sights in Rome were called after London cinemas.

    Pigeon Pie (1940)

8   Love in a Cold Climate.

    Title of novel (1949)

1   I love children—especially when they cry, for then someone takes
     them away.
     Attrib
     See also **ROSS 279:2.**

MIZNER, Wilson
US playwright (1876–1933)

2   [Always] be nice to people on your way up, because you'll meet 'em
     on your way down.
     Attrib
     Also ascribed to Jimmy Durante and others.

3   Working for Warner Bros is like fucking a porcupine; it's a
     hundred pricks against one.
     Quoted in D. Niven, *Bring on the Empty Horses*

4   *On Hollywood:*
     A trip through a sewer in a glass-bottomed boat.
     Attrib

5   When you steal from one author, it's plagiarism; if you steal from
     many, it's research.
     Attrib

6   Treat a whore like a lady and a lady like a whore.
     Attrib

MOLA, Emilio
Spanish Nationalist General (1887–1937)

7   *When asked which of his four army columns would capture Madrid from the
     Republicans:*
     The fifth column (*'La quinta columna'*).
     Remark to reporter, October 1936
     Referring to civilian help.

MONKHOUSE, Bob
British comedian (1928–   )

8   Bernie, the bolt!
     Catchphrase, TV show *The Golden Shot*, 1967–75

'MONOLULU, Ras Prince'
Racing tipster in UK (*fl* 1930s/50s)

9   I gotta horse!
     Stock phrase

MONOPOLY
US board game devised by Charles Darrow in 1929

1   GO TO JAIL
MOVE DIRECTLY TO JAIL
DO NOT PASS 'GO'
DO NOT COLLECT £200.

'Chance' card (UK version)

MONROE, Marilyn
US film actress (1926–62)

2   *When asked if she had really posed for a calendar (1947) with nothing on:*
I had the radio on.

Quoted in *Time*, 11 August 1952

3   *On having matzo balls for supper at Arthur Miller's parents:*
Isn't there another part of the matzo you can eat?

Attrib

MONTEFIORE, Hugh
British Anglican clergyman (later Bishop) (1920–)

4   Why did He not marry? Could the answer be that Jesus was not by nature the marrying sort?

At conference, Oxford, 26 July 1967

MONTGOMERY, Bernard (later 1st Viscount Montgomery of Alamein)
British soldier (1887–1976)

5   *Address to officers, when taking command of the Eighth Army, 13 August 1942:*
Here we will stand and fight; there will be no further withdrawal . . . We are going to finish with this chap Rommel once and for all. It will be quite easy. There is no doubt about it. He is definitely a nuisance. Therefore we will hit him a crack and finish with him.

Soundtrack of post-war recording of speech

MONTY PYTHON'S FLYING CIRCUS
British TV comedy series (BBC), 1969–74. Written and performed by Graham Chapman, John Cleese (as Announcer and Praline), Terry Gilliam, Eric Idle (as Norman/Nudge), Terry Jones, and Michael Palin (as Barber).

6   *Announcer:* And now for something completely different.

Catchphrase
In fact, first spoken by Idle not Cleese, 12 October 1969

1   *Norman:* Nudge, nudge, wink, wink. Know what I mean? Say no
    more!
    Catchphrase
    Of prurient character later known as 'Nudge'. The phrases were
    spoken in any order (firstly on 19 October 1969).

2   *Barber:* I'm a lumberjack and I'm OK
    I sleep all night and I work all day.
    Song, 14 December 1969

3   *Praline:* It's not pining, it's passed on. This parrot is no more. It's
    ceased to be. It's expired. It's gone to meet its maker. This is a late
    parrot. It's a stiff. Bereft of life it rests in peace. It would be pushing
    up the daisies if you hadn't nailed it to the perch. It's rung down
    the curtain and joined the choir invisible. It's an ex-parrot.
    'Parrot sketch', 14 December 1969
    From this came the later expression 'dead parrot' for anything one
    wished to describe as undoubtedly moribund.

4   Naughty bits.
    Catchphrase
    Another euphemism for 'private parts', 24 November 1970

5   Always Look on the Bright Side of Life.
    Title of song, in film *Monty Python's Life of Brian* (1979)
    Sung by a group of crucifixion victims.

MORECAMBE, Eric and WISE, Ernie
British entertainers (1926–84) and (1925–   )

6   *Eric:* [Ernie's] Short, fat, hairy legs.
    Catchphrase

7   *Eric:* A touch of hello folks and what about the workers?
    Catchphrase

8   *Eric:* What do you think of the show so far?
    Audience: Rubbish!
    Catchphrase

9   *Eric on Ernie's supposed hair-piece:*
    You can't see the join.
    Catchphrase

10 *Ernie:* This play what I have wrote.
    Catchphrase

MORGAN, J. Pierpoint, Jr.
US banker (1867–1943)

1   *When asked how much a yacht cost in upkeep, by a man who was thinking of buying one:*
If you have to ask the price, you can't afford it.
Attrib

MORGANFIELD, McKinley ('Muddy Waters')
US lyricist and blues singer (1915–83)

2   Got My Mojo Workin'.
Title of song

MORRIS, Desmond
British zoologist and anthropologist (1928–   )

3   The Naked Ape.
Title of book (1967)

4   The city is not a concrete jungle, it is a human zoo.
The Human Zoo (1969)

MORRIS, James (later Jan Morris)
British writer (1926–   )

5   There's romance for you! There's the lust and dark wine of Venice! No wonder George Eliot's husband fell into the Grand Canal.
Venice (1960)
Closing words.

6   DEDICATED GRATEFULLY TO THE WARDEN AND FELLOWS OF ST ANTONY'S COLLEGE, OXFORD. EXCEPT ONE.
The Oxford Book of Oxford (1978)

MORRISON, Herbert (later Lord Morrison of Lambeth)
British Labour politician (1888–1965)

7   *Calling for a voluntary labour force as Minister of Supply in wartime:*
Go to it.
Radio broadcast, 22 May 1940

MORRISON, Herbert
US broadcaster (1905–89)

8   *On the* **Hindenburg** *airship disaster:*
It is in smoke and flames now! Oh, the humanity!
Radio commentary, Lakehurst, New Jersey, 1937

MORTIMER, John
British lawyer, playwright and novelist (1923–   )

1   No brilliance is needed in the law. Nothing but common sense, and relatively clean finger-nails.

A Voyage Round My Father (1970)

2   In the beginning was the Word. It's about the only sentence on which I find myself in total agreement with God.

Quoted in the *Observer*, 1 July 1984

3   □ The shelf life of the modern hardback writer is somewhere between the milk and the yoghurt.

Quoted in the *Observer*, 28 June 1987
In fact he was quoting the US humorous columnist Calvin Trillin (*b*1935).

MORTON, Rogers
US government official (1914–79)

4   *Refusing any last-ditch attempts to rescue President Ford's re-election campaign, 1976:*
I'm not going to do anything to rearrange the furniture on the deck of the *Titanic*.

Quoted in *The Times*, 13 May 1976
Rogers was Ford's campaign manager.

Earl MOUNTBATTEN of Burma
British Royal, military commander and Viceroy (1900–79)

5   Edwina and I spent all our married lives getting into other people's beds.

Remark quoted in P. Ziegler, *Mountbatten*

6   In my experience, I have always found that you cannot have an efficient ship unless you have a happy ship, and you cannot have a happy ship unless you have an efficient ship. That is the way I intend to start this commission, and that is the way I intend to go on—with a happy and efficient ship.

Initial address to crew of *HMS Kelly*, 1939
Adopted *verbatim* by Noël Coward in the script of the film *In Which We Serve*.

7   The nuclear arms race has no military purpose. Wars cannot be fought with nuclear weapons . . . The world now stands on the brink of the final abyss. Let us all resolve to take all possible practical steps to ensure that we do not, through our own folly, go over the edge.

Speech, Strasbourg, 1979

1   I can't think of a more wonderful thanksgiving for the life I have
     had than that everyone should be jolly at my funeral.

     TV interview, shown after his assassination in August 1979

MRS DALE'S DIARY

UK radio soap opera (BBC), 1948–69 (latterly *The Dales*). With Ellis Powell and
Jessie Matthews as Mrs Dale.

2   *Mrs Dale (on her husband):*
     I'm worried about Jim.

     Stock phrase

MUGGERIDGE, Kitty

British writer and wife of Malcolm M.

3   *Of David Frost:*
     He rose without trace.

     Attrib remark, *c*1965

MUGGERIDGE, Malcolm

British writer and broadcaster (1903–90)

4   Twilight of empire . . . a phrase which occurred to me long ago.

     Diaries (entry for 21 December 1947)

5   *On Queen Elizabeth II:*
     Frumpish and banal.

     Magazine article, October 1957

6   The orgasm has replaced the Cross as the focus of longing and the
     image of fulfilment.

     'Down with Sex', *Tread Softly For You Tread on My Jokes* (1966)

7   *On Evelyn Waugh:*
     He looked, I decided, like a letter delivered to the wrong address.

     'My Fair Gentleman', in ibid

8   *On Anthony Eden:*
     He was not only a bore; he bored for England.

     'Boring for England', in ibid

9   *On **Punch** (which he had once edited):*
     Very much like the Church of England. It is doctrinally
     inexplicable but it goes on.

     Attrib

1 I have had my [TV] aerials removed—it's the moral equivalent of a prostate operation.

Quoted in the *Radio Times*, April 1981

2 Sex on the brain is the wrong place to have it.

Attrib

MUIR, Frank
British writer and broadcaster (1920–)

3 *Of Joan Bakewell:*
The thinking man's crumpet.

Attrib

MURROW, Edward R.
US broadcaster (1908–65)

4 This . . . is . . . London.

Standard beginning to his wartime reports, 1940s

5 Goodnight . . . and good luck.

Stock phrase

6 He [Churchill] mobilized the English language and sent it into battle to steady his fellow countrymen and hearten those Europeans upon whom the long dark night of tyranny had descended.

Broadcast, 30 November 1954
See **KENNEDY 184:3.**
See also **ANONYMOUS SAYINGS 12:4.**

MUSSOLINI, Benito
Italian fascist leader (1883–1945)

7 Italy has need of a blood bath.

Letter to Bruno Buozzi, 1913

8 It is blood which moves the wheels of history.

Speech, Parma, 13 December 1914

9 I will make the trains run on time and create order out of chaos.

Untraced remark, 1920s
Mussolini is quoted in a biography by Giorgio Pini (1939) as having exhorted a station-master to let trains leave on time. The improvement was being commented on by 1925.

10 This Berlin–Rome connection is not so much a diaphragm as an axis, around which can revolve all those states of Europe with a will towards collaboration and peace.

Speech, Milan, 1 November 1936

1   We have buried the putrid corpse of liberty.
     Attrib

2   *On Hitler:*
     That garrulous monk.
     Quoted in W. Churchill, *The Second World War*, Vol.1 (1948)

MUSSOLINI, Vittorio
Italian airforce pilot and son of Benito

3   *On a bombing raid in Abyssinia:*
     I dropped an aerial torpedo right in the centre, and the group
     opened up like a flowering rose. It was most entertaining.
     Voli sulle Ambe (1937)

NABOKOV, Vladimir
Russian-born novelist (1899–1977)

1   Lolita, light of my life, fire of my loins. My sin, my soul.

Lolita (1955)
Opening words.

THE NAKED CITY
US film 1948. Script by Malvin Wald and Albert Matz.

2   *Last lines:*
Narrator: There are eight million stories in the naked city. This has been one of them.

Soundtrack
Also used in TV series of the same name.

NASH, Ogden
US poet (1902–71)

3   Candy
Is dandy
But liquor
Is quicker.

'Reflection on Ice-Breaking', *Hard Lines* (1931)

4   I think that I shall never see
A billboard lovely as a tree.
Perhaps unless the billboards fall,
I'll never see a tree at all.

'Song of the Open Road', *Happy Days* (1933)
Compare **KILMER 187:5.**

NATHAN, George Jean
US theatre critic (1882–1958)

5   The test of a real comedian is whether you laugh at him before he opens his mouth.

In *American Mercury,* September 1929

NAUGHTON, Bill
British playwright (1910–92)

6   It seems to me if they ain't got you one way then they've got you another. So what's it all about, that's what I keep asking myself, what's it all about?

Alfie (1966), film script of his stage and radio play
The phrase 'What's it all about, Alfie?' was popularized by Burt
Bacharach and Hal David's title song, sung by Cilla Black on the British
release of the film and by Cher in the US.

THE NAVY LARK

UK radio comedy series (BBC), 1960s/70s. Script by Lawrie Wyman. With Leslie Phillips and Jon Pertwee.

1   *LP:* Left hand down a bit.
     JP: Left hand down a bit, it is, sir.

Stock phrase, when docking ship or similar

NETWORK

US film 1976. Script by Paddy Chayevsky. With Peter Finch as Howard Beale.

2   *Beale:* I want you to get up out of your chairs. I want you to get up right now and go to the window, open it and stick your head out and tell, I'm as mad as hell, and I'm not going to take this anymore!

Soundtrack

Last section also used by US politician Howard Jarvis as a slogan for his tax-pegging campaign in California, 1978.

NEVINS, Allan

US writer and teacher (1890–1971)

3   The former allies had blundered in the past by offering Germany too little and offering even that too late, until finally Nazi Germany had become a menace to all mankind.

Article in *Current History*, May 1935

NICHOLLS, Janice

British clerk/telephonist (1946–   )

4   *When judging new record releases:*
     I'll give it foive.

Stock phrase, TV show, *Thank Your Lucky Stars*, c1963

NICHOLSON, Vivian

British football pools winner (1936–   )

5   *On winning £152,000 in September 1961:*
     I'm going to spend, spend, spend, that's what I'm going to do.

Recounted in V. Nicholson & S. Smith, *Spend, Spend, Spend*

NICOLSON, Sir Harold

British writer and politician (1886–1968)

6   The gift of broadcasting is, without question, the lowest human capacity to which any man could attain.

Quoted in the *Observer*, 5 January 1947

NIGHTINGALE, Florence
British nurse (1820–1910)

1 *When given the Order of Merit in 1907:*
Too kind, too kind.

Quoted in E. Cook, *Life of Florence Nightingale* (1913)

NIVEN, David
British actor (1909–83)

2 I have a face that is a cross between two pounds of halibut and an explosion in an old-clothes closet. If it isn't mobile, it's dead.

Attrib

3 You know where you are with Errol Flynn. He *always* lets you down.

Attrib

NIXON, Richard M.
US Republican President (1913–)

4 *On 'Checkers', a dog given to his daughters:*
Regardless of what they say about it, we are going to keep it.

TV address, 23 September 1952
He was defending himself, when running as Vice Presidential candidate, against charges that he had a secret fund.

5 I don't believe I ought to quit because I am not a quitter.

ibid

6 *To the press, on losing a California Governorship election:*
Just think about how much you're going to be missing. You won't have Nixon to kick around any more, because, gentlemen, this is my last press conference.

Remark, 7 November 1962

7 I have a secret plan to end the [Vietnam] war.

Attrib remark, 1968

8 And this certainly has to be the most historic phone call ever made.

Telephone call to astronauts on moon, 20 July 1969

9 *On USS **Hornet** welcoming astronauts home:*
This is the greatest week in the history of the world since the Creation.

24 July 1969

10 *On a plan for Vietnam peace:*
And so, tonight—to you, the great silent majority of my fellow Americans—I ask for your support.

Broadcast address, 3 November 1969

1   I don't give a shit about the lira.
     In conversation, 23 June 1972, revealed in tape transcript

2   I feel it could be cut off at the pass . . . the obstruction of justice.
     In conversation, 21 March 1973, revealed in tape transcript

3   *On the Watergate cover-up:*
     I don't give a shit what happens. I want you all to stonewall it, let
     them plead the Fifth Amendment, cover-up or anything else, if it'll
     save it, save the plan.
     In conversation, 22 March 1973, revealed in tape transcript

4   There can be no whitewash at the White House.
     Speech, 17 April 1973

5   *On a charge of tax avoidance:*
     People have got to know whether or not their President is a crook.
     Well, I am not a crook. I've earned everything I have got.
     Press conference, 17 November 1973

6   *To General Alexander Haig on 7 August 1974:*
     You fellows, in your business, you have a way of handling problems
     like this. Somebody leaves a pistol in the drawer. I don't have a
     pistol.
     Quoted in R. Woodward & C. Bernstein, *The Final Days*

7   I have never been a quitter. To leave office before my term is
     completed is abhorrent to every instinct in my body. But as
     president I must put the interests of America first . . . Therefore, I
     shall resign the presidency, effective at noon tomorrow.
     Broadcast, 8 August 1974

8   This country needs good farmers, good businessmen, good
     plumbers . . .
     Farewell address to White House staff, 9 August 1974

9   When the President does it, that means it is not illegal.
     TV interview with D. Frost, 19 May 1977

10   I brought myself down. I gave them a sword and they stuck it in and
     they twisted it with relish. And I guess if I'd been in their position
     I'd have done the same thing.
     ibid

NORTHCLIFFE, 1st Viscount

British newspaper proprietor (1865–1922)

1 News is what someone, somewhere doesn't want published . . . all the rest is advertising.

Attrib

NOVELLO, Ivor

British composer and actor (1893–1951)

2 Keep the Home Fires Burning.

Title of song (written to words by Lena Guilbert Ford) (1915)
Originally entitled 'Till the Boys Come Home'.

3 And Her Mother Came Too.

Title of song, 'A to Z' (1922)
Written to words by Dion Titheradge
See also **TARZAN THE APE MAN 317:4.**

NOW VOYAGER

US film 1942. Based on the novel by Olive Higgins Prouty. With Bette Davis as Charlotte Vale.

4 *Charlotte:* Let's not ask for the moon—we have the stars.

Soundtrack
Closing words.

OATES, Capt. Lawrence 'Titus'
British explorer (1880–1912)

1   *Leaving companions in tent on return from South Pole, 16 March 1912:*
I am just going outside, and I may be some time.

Quoted in R. F. Scott, *Scott's Last Expedition*

O'CASEY, Sean
Irish playwright (1884–1964)

2   The whole worl' is in a state o' chassis.

Juno and the Paycock (1924)

3   *On P. G. Wodehouse:*
English literature's performing flea.

Quoted in P. G. Wodehouse, *Performing Flea* (1953)

O'CONNOR, Edwin
US writer (1918–68)

4   The Last Hurrah.

Title of novel (1956)

OLIVIER, Sir Laurence (later Lord Olivier)
British actor (1907–89)

5   *To Dustin Hoffman during the filming of **Marathon Man** (c1975)—
Hoffman having stayed up for three nights in order to portray a sleepless
character:*
Dear boy, why not try acting?

Attrib

6   Success smells like Brighton.

Quoted in *Peter Hall's Diaries* (1983)

O'MALLEY, Frank Ward
US writer (1875–1932)

7   Life is just one damned thing after another.

Attrib

O'NEILL, Eugene
US playwright (1888–1953)

8   A Long Day's Journey Into Night.

Title of play (1940–1)

9   The Iceman Cometh.

Title of play (1946)

O'NEILL, Terence (later Lord O'Neill of the Maine)

Ulster Unionist politician (1914–1990)

1 Ours is called a Christian country. We could have enriched our politics with our Christianity, but far too often we have debased our Christianity with our politics.

Attrib

ONE MILLION YEARS BC

UK film 1966.

2 The characters and incidents portrayed and the names used herein are fictitious and any similarity to the names, character or history of any person is entirely accidental and unintentional.

Caption on film
Standard disclaimer—at the start of a film in which the dialogue consists entirely of cavemen's grunts.

OPPENHEIMER, J. Robert

US physicist (1904–67)

3 *Quoting Vishnu from the **Gita**, at explosion of first atomic bomb, New Mexico, 16 July 1945:*
I am become death, the destroyer of worlds.

Attrib

ORCZY, Baroness

Hungarian-born novelist (1865–1947)

4 We seek him here, we seek him there,
Those Frenchies seek him everywhere.
Is he in heaven?—Is he in hell?
That demmed, elusive Pimpernel?

The Scarlet Pimpernel (1905)

ORTON, Joe

British playwright (1933–67)

5 ☐ Prick Up Your Ears

Title for unmade film
Suggested by his friend and murderer Kenneth Halliwell, used by John Lahr for biography of Orton (1978) and by Alan Bennett for film about Orton and Halliwell (1987).

6 You were born with your legs apart. They'll send you to the grave in a Y-shaped coffin.

What the Butler Saw (1967)

'ORWELL, George'

British novelist and journalist (1903–50)

1 There can hardly be a town in the South of England where you could throw a brick without hitting the niece of a bishop.
The Road to Wigan Pier (1937)

2 I'm fat, but I'm thin inside. Has it ever struck you that there's a thin man inside every fat man, just as they say there's a statue inside every block of stone?
Coming Up for Air (1939)
See also **CONNOLLY 82:4; WHITEHORN 345:3.**

3 *On the BBC:*
Its atmosphere is something halfway between a girls' school and a lunatic asylum.
Diary, 14 March 1942

4 [Attlee] reminds me of nothing so much as a recently dead fish before it has had time to stiffen.
Diary, 19 May 1942

5 *Reviewing a book by Edmund Blunden:*
Mr Blunden is no more able to resist a quotation than some people are to refuse a drink.
In the *Manchester Evening News*, 20 April 1944

6 Four legs good, two legs bad.
Animal Farm (1945)

7 All animals are equal, but some are more equal than others.
ibid

8 Comrade Napoleon is always right.
ibid

9 It was a bright cold day in April, and the clocks were striking thirteen.
Nineteen Eighty-Four (1949)

10 BIG BROTHER IS WATCHING YOU.
ibid

1 WAR IS PEACE. FREEDOM IS SLAVERY. IGNORANCE IS STRENGTH.

ibid

2 If you want a picture of the future, imagine a boot stamping on a human face—for ever.

ibid

OSBORNE, Charles
Australian-born writer and arts administrator (1927–)

3 *At (British) Arts Council press conference:*
If a third of all the novelists and maybe two-thirds of all the poets now writing dropped dead suddenly the loss to literature would not be great.

Quoted in the *Observer*, 3 November 1985
Compare **WEST 343:7.**

OSBORNE, John
British playwright (1929–)

4 Oh heavens, how I long for just a little ordinary enthusiasm. Just enthusiasm, that's all. I want to hear a warm, thrilling voice cry out Hallelujah! *(He bangs his breast theatrically)* Hallelujah! I'm alive!

Look Back in Anger (1956)

5 They spend their time mostly looking forward to the past.

ibid

6 There aren't any good brave causes left.

ibid

7 This is a letter of hate. It is for you my countrymen. I mean those men of my country who have defiled it . . . There is murder in my brain and I carry a knife in my heart for every one of you. Macmillan, and you, Gaitskell, you particularly . . . Till then, damn you, England. You're rotting now, and quite soon you'll disappear.

'A Letter To My Fellow Countrymen' in *Tribune*, August 1961
Written from the south of France.

8 Don't clap too hard—it's a very old building.

The Entertainer (1957)
But an old music-hall joke.

9 She's not going to walk in here . . . and turn it into a Golden Sanitary Towel Award Presentation.

Hotel in Amsterdam (1968)

OWEN, Dr David (later Lord Owen)

British Labour, then Social Democrat, politician (1938–)

1   We are fed up with fudging and mudging, with mush and slush.

> Speech, Labour Party Conference, Blackpool, 2 October 1980
> Later it became an obsession of the Liberal and Social Democrat
> parties to avoid the same accusation.

OWEN, Wilfred

British poet (1893–1918)

2   Above all, this book is not concerned with Poetry. The subject of it
     is War, and the pity of War. The Poetry is the pity.

> 'Preface', *Poems* (1920)

3   Move him into the sun—
     Gently its touch awoke him once.

> 'Futility' in ibid

OXFORD UNION SOCIETY

4   That this House will in no circumstances fight for its King and
     Country.

> Motion debated 9 February 1933
> It was carried by 275 votes to 153.

PACKARD, Vance
US writer (1914–)

1 The Hidden Persuaders.

Title of book, 1957

PAINE, Albert Bigelow
US writer (1861–1937)

2 The Great White Way.

Title of novel (1901)
Later used as a name for Broadway.

PALMER, Tony
British critic and film-maker (1935–)

3 *Reviewing the Beatles' 'White Album':*
If there is still any doubt that Lennon and McCartney are the greatest songwriters since Schubert . . .

Article in the *Observer*, November 1968

PARKER, Dorothy
US writer (1893–1967)

4 Guns aren't lawful;
Nooses give;
Gas smells awful;
You might as well live.

'Resumé', *Enough Rope* (1927)

5 Men seldom make passes
At girls who wear glasses.

'News Item' in ibid

6 *On A. A. Milne's* **The House at Pooh Corner** *in her column 'Constant Reader':*
Tonstant Weader fwowed up.

In the *New Yorker*, 20 October 1928

7 *When told that she was 'very outspoken':*
Outspoken by whom?

Attrib

8 Scratch an actor and you'll find an actress.

Attrib

9 *In reply to comment, 'Anyway, she's always very nice to her inferiors':*
Where does she find them?

Quoted in the *Lyttelton Hart-Davis Letters*

1   *When told that Calvin Coolidge had died:*
    How can they tell?
    Attrib remark, 1933

2   Go to the Martin Beck Theatre and watch Katharine Hepburn run
    the whole gamut of emotions from A to B.
    Reviewing *The Lake* (1933)

3   One more drink and I'd be under the host.
    Quoted in J. Keats, *You Might As Well As Live*

4   Brevity is the soul of lingerie—as the Petticoat said to the Chemise.
    In ibid

5   *Suggested epitaphs:*
    This is on me. Excuse my dust. If you can read this you are standing
    too close.
    In ibid

6   You know, that woman speaks eighteen languages? And she can't
    say 'no' in any of them.
    In ibid

7   *When a man asked to be excused to go to the men's room:*
    He really needs to telephone, but he's too embarrassed to say so.
    In ibid

8   Tell him I've been too fucking busy—or vice versa.
    In ibid

9   *When Clare Booth Luce, going through a swing-door with her, said, 'Age
    before beauty':*
    Pearls before swine.
    In ibid
    Luce denied the exchange had ever taken place.

10 *When someone said, 'They're ducking for apples' at a Hallowe'en party:*
    There, but for a typographical error, is the story of my life.
    In ibid

11 *On her requirements for an apartment:*
    [Enough space] to lay a hat—and a few friends.
    In ibid

12 *On naming her canary 'Onan':*
    Because he spills his seed on the ground.
    In ibid

1   *Telegram to Mrs Robert Sherwood, when delivered of a baby:*
    DEAR MARY, WE ALL KNEW YOU HAD IT IN YOU.
    In ibid

2   *When pregnant herself:*
    It serves me right for putting all my eggs in one bastard.
    In ibid

3   *Challenged to compose a sentence including the word 'horticulture':*
    You can lead a whore to culture but you can't make her think.
    In ibid

4   If all the young girls at the Yale Prom were laid end to end, I
    wouldn't be at all surprised.
    Attrib

5   Oh, life is a glorious cycle of song,
    A medley of extemporanea;
    And love is a thing that can never go wrong
    And I am Marie of Roumania.
    'Comment', *Not So Deep as a Well* (1937)
    See also **TYNAN 332:6.**

PARKER, Johnny
British naval lieutenant

6   *On helping to free British seamen held captive on the German ship* **Altmark***:*
    The Navy's here!
    Quoted in *The Times*, 19 February 1940
    Precisely who said the words is in doubt, but Parker has emerged as the
    most likely person—and he claimed that he did.

PARKINSON, C. Northcote
British author and historian (1909–)

7   It is a commonplace observation that work expands so as to fill the
    time available for its completion.
    In the *Economist*, 19 November 1955
    Later known as 'Parkinson's Law'.

8   The Law of Triviality . . . means that the time spent on any item on
    the agenda will be in inverse proportion to the sum involved.
    Parkinson's Law (1958)

PATERSON, A. B. 'Banjo'
Australian writer (1864–1941)

1 Oh! there once was a swagman camped in a Billabong,
　　Under the shade of a Coolabah tree;
　And he sang as he looked at his old billy boiling,
　　'Who'll come a-waltzing Matilda with me?'

Song, 'Waltzing Matilda'
Written in 1894, the song was first published in 1903.

PATTON, George S., Jr
US General (1884–1945)

2 It is foolish and wrong to mourn the men who died. Rather we should thank God that such men lived.

Speech, Boston, Mass., 7 June 1945

PAUL, Leslie
British social philosopher (1905–85)

3 Angry Young Man.

Title of autobiographical book (1951)
Use of the phrase to describe a group of writers in the fifties can be traced to publicity material for John Osborne's play *Look Back in Anger*, first produced at the Royal Court Theatre, London, May 1956.

PEALE, Norman Vincent
US clergyman and writer (1898–　)

4 The Power of Positive Thinking.

Title of book (1952)

PEARSON, Hesketh
British biographer (1887–1964)

5 A widely-read man never quotes accurately . . . Misquotation is the pride and privilege of the learned.

Common Misquotations (1937)

6 Misquotations are the only quotations that are never misquoted.

ibid

THE PEOPLE
London Sunday newspaper

7 Our reporter made an excuse and left.

Quoted in *The Times*, 17 October 1981
Standard exit line after a reporter had set up a compromising situation—e.g. provoking prostitutes or pimps to reveal their game. From the 1920s onwards?

PERELMAN, S. J.
US writer (1904–79)

1 I've got Bright's disease and he's got mine.

Judge, 16 November 1929

2 [Movie scriptwriting] is no worse than playing the piano in a call house.

Caption to cartoon in *Strictly from Hunger* (1937)

PERKINS, Carl
US singer/songwriter (1932–)

3 It's a-one for the money
Two for the show
Three to get ready
Now go, cat, go,
But don't you step on my blue suede shoes.

Song, 'Blue Suede Shoes' (1956)

PERKINS, Frances
US politician (1882–1965)

4 □ Call me madam.

Discussed in G. Martin, *Madam Secretary—Frances Perkins* (1976)
Said to have been her reply when asked—as the first woman to hold US Cabinet rank—how she wished to be addressed. In fact, a man's words to the effect that 'Madam Secretary' would be in order were put into her mouth.

PÉTAIN, Henri Philippe
French soldier and politician (1856–1951)

5 *Defending Verdun:*
□ They shall not pass.

Attrib, 26 February 1916
Although associated with Pétain, 'The Hero of Verdun', this slogan appears to have been said first by General Robert Nivelle (1856–1924) in the form *'Vous ne les laisserez pas passer'*.
See also **IBARRURI 169:1.**

PETER, Dr Laurence J.
Canadian writer (1919–90)

6 In a hierarchy every employee tends to rise to his level of incompetence.

The Peter Principle—Why Things Always Go Wrong (with R. Hull) (1969)

7 The noblest of all dogs is the hot-dog; it feeds the hand that bites it.

Quotations for Our Time (1977)

PHILIP, HRH the Prince
Greek-born British Royal (1921–   )

1   The *Daily Express* is a bloody awful newspaper.

Remark, press reception, Rio de Janeiro, 1962
In 1975, he said, 'the reasons for my remark no longer exist'.

2   Just at this moment we are suffering a national defeat comparable to any lost military campaign, and what is more it is self-inflicted . . . I think it is about time we pulled our finger out.

Speech to businessmen, 17 October 1961

3   Dentopedology is the science of opening your mouth and putting your foot in it. I've been practising it for years.

Attrib

PICASSO, Pablo
Spanish artist (1881–1973)

4   *On painting:*
Je ne cherche pas, je trouve ('I do not seek, I find').

Attrib

PICKLES, Wilfred
British broadcaster (1904–78)

5   Welcome to a spot of homely fun, presenting the people to the people . . . with Mabel at the table and Harry Hudson at the piano.

Introductory material, *Have A Go*, BBC radio, 1946–67

6   Are yer courtin'?

Stock question to young participants in ibid

7   'Ave you ever 'ad any embarrassing moments?

Stock question in ibid

8   Give 'im/'er the money, Barney.

Stock remark to winners in ibid
Barney Colehan (*d*1991) was the producer of the show.

9   What's on the table, Mabel?

Stock remark to his wife, presiding over the prizes in ibid

PINTER, Harold
British playwright (1930–   )

1   *(Pause.)*

    Characteristic stage direction

2   If only I could get down to Sidcup! I've been waiting for the
    weather to break. He's got my papers, this man I left them with, it's
    got it all down there, I could prove everything.

    The Caretaker (1960)

3   *Asked what his plays were about:*
    The weasel under the cocktail cabinet.

    Quoted in J. Russell Taylor, *Anger and After*

4   I tend to believe that cricket is the greatest thing that God ever
    created on earth . . . certainly greater than sex, although sex isn't
    too bad either.

    Interview in the *Observer*, 5 October 1980

PIRSIG, Robert M.
US writer (1929–   )

5   Zen and the Art of Motorcycle Maintenance.

    Title of book (1974)

PITKIN, William B.
US professor in journalism (1878–1953)

6   Life Begins at Forty.

    Title of book (1932)

PLATT, Ken
British comedian (1922–   )

7   *Of a person:*
    Daft as a brush.

    Catchphrase, from 1940s onwards
    Adapted from the northern saying, 'Soft as a brush'.

8   I won't take me coat off—I'm not stopping.

    Catchphrase, from 1951 onwards

PLAY TITLES

1 Another Country (Julian Mitchell)

From the second verse of 'I vow to thee my country' by Sir C. A. Spring-Rice (*q.v.*): 'There is another country . . . ' i.e. heaven (though the play refers to the Soviet Union).

2 Cat On a Hot Tin Roof (Tennessee Williams)

From the US expression, to be 'as nervous as a cat on a hot tin roof'.

3 Conduct Unbecoming (Barry England)

From British military regulations of the 19th century: 'conduct unbecoming the character of an officer and a gentleman' (whence also the final phrase).

4 Fings Ain't Wot They Used T'be (Lionel Bart)

After song, 'Things Ain't What They Used To Be', by Mercer Ellington and Ted Persons (1939).

5 Journey's End (R. C. Sherriff)

Not from Shakespeare or Dryden, but from a book Sherriff omitted to name in his autobiography.

6 The Long and the Short and Tall (Willis Hall)

From the song 'Bless 'em All' (by Jimmy Hughes and Frank Lake, 1940)—or rather its parody, 'Sod 'em All.'

7 My Fair Lady (Lerner and Loewe)

From the nursery rhyme 'London Bridge is Broken/Falling Down'. Also said to resemble the Cockney pronunciation of 'Mayfair Lady'.

8 No Sex Please We're British (Anthony Marriott & Alastair Foot)

Title of long-running comedy in the West End (1971–87).

9 Oh! Calcutta! (revue devised by Kenneth Tynan)

From the French expression, *'Oh, quel cul t'as'* ('what a lovely arse you've got'), possibly late 19th century.

10 A Patriot for Me (John Osborne)

When a servant of the Habsburg Empire was being recommended as a sterling patriot to Franz II, he asked, 'But is he a patriot for me?'

11 Speed-the-Plow (David Mamet)

From the pre-1500 expression, 'God speed the plough'—when wishing luck in any venture.

1 Stop the World, I Want To Get Off (Anthony Newley and Leslie Bricusse)

From a graffito.

2 Who's Afraid of Virginia Woolf? (Edward Albee)

From a graffito seen in Greenwich Village.

PLOMER, William
British writer and poet (1903–73)

3 Patriotism is the last refuge of the sculptor.

Attrib

POPEYE
US strip and film cartoon series, 1933–50

4 I yam what I yam and that's all that I yam.

Stock phrase
Original character created by Elzie Crisler.

PORTER, Cole
US composer and lyricist (1891–1964)

5 And when they ask us, how dangerous it was,
We never will tell them, we never will tell them:
How we fought in some café
With wild women night and day,
'Twas the wonderfulest war you ever knew.'

'War Song' included in the *Complete Lyrics of Cole Porter* Usually ascribed to Anon., this parody of the Jerome Kern/ Herbert Reynolds song 'They Didn't Believe Me' is now believed to have originated with Porter during the First World War.

6 Birds do it, bees do it
Even educated fleas do it
Let's do it, let's fall in love.

Song, 'Let's Do It, Let's Fall in Love', *Paris* (1928)

7 Goldfish in the privacy of bowls do it.

ibid

8 Night and day you are the one.

Song, 'Night and Day', *Gay Divorce* (1932)

9 Miss Otis regrets she's unable to lunch today.

Song, 'Miss Otis Regrets', *Hi Diddle Diddle* (1934)

10 Anything Goes.

Title of song and musical (1934)

1   I get no kick from champagne.
Mere alcohol doesn't thrill me at all,
So tell me why should it be true
That I get a kick out of you?

Song, 'I Get a Kick Out of You' in ibid

2   You're the Top!

Title of song in ibid

3   When they begin the beguine.

'Begin the Beguine', *Jubilee* (1935)

4   A trip to the moon on gossamer wings.

'Just One of Those Things' in ibid

5   So goodbye, dear, and amen.

ibid

6   It was great fun,
But it was just one of those things.

ibid

7   I've Got You Under My Skin.

Title of song, *Born to Dance* (1936)

8   While the crowds in all the night clubs punish the parquet.

Song, 'Down in the Depths', *Red, Hot and Blue* (1936)

9   It's delightful, it's delicious, it's de-lovely.

Song, 'It's De-Lovely', in ibid

10   My Heart Belongs to Daddy.

Title of song, *Leave It To Me* (1938)

11   Ev'ry Time We Say Goodbye (I Die A Little).

Title of song, *Seven Lively Arts* (1944)

12   There's no love song finer
But how strange
The change
From major to minor.

ibid

13   Another Op'nin, Another Show.

Song title, *Kiss Me Kate* (1948)

1   He may have hair upon his chest
    But, sister, so has Lassie.
    'I Hate Men' in ibid

2   Brush Up Your Shakespeare.
    Title of song in ibid

3   Always True to You in my Fashion.
    Title of song in ibid
    Derived from 'I have been faithful to thee, Cynara! in my fashion'—
    Ernest Dowson, *Non Sum Qualis Eram* (1896).

4   Paris Loves Lovers.
    Title of song, *Silk Stockings* (1955)

5   Who Wants to Be a Millionaire?
    Title of song, *High Society* (1956)

PORTER, Peter
Australian-born poet (1929–   )

6   In Australia
    Inter alia,
    Mediocrities
    Think they're Socrates.
    Unpublished clerihew.

POTTER, Beatrix
British author and artist (1866–1943)

7   You may go into the fields or down the lane, but don't go into Mr
    McGregor's garden: your Father had an accident there; he was put
    in a pie by Mrs McGregor.
    The Tale of Peter Rabbit (1902)

POTTER, Gillie
British entertainer (1887–1975)

8   Good evening, England. This is Gillie Potter speaking to you in
    English.
    Greeting in radio broadcasts, 1940s/50s

POTTER, Stephen
British writer (1900–69)

1 *Defining 'One-Upmanship':*
How to be one up—how to make the other man feel that
something has gone wrong, however slightly.
Lifemanship (1950)

2 *A blocking phrase for conversation:*
'Yes, but not in the South', with slight adjustments will do for any
argument about any place, if not about any person.
ibid

3 *How to promote a Cockburn '97, clearly past its best:*
Talk of the 'imperial decay' of your invalid port. 'Its gracious
withdrawal from perfection, keeping a hint of former majesty,
withal, as it hovers between oblivion and the divine *Untergang* of
infinite recession.'
One-Upmanship (1952)

POWELL, Colin
US General (1937–)

4 *As Chairman of the US Joint Chiefs of Staff, on allied strategy for defeating
the Iraqi army in the Gulf War:*
First we are going to cut it off, then we are going to kill it.
Quoted in *The Independent*, 26 January 1991

POWELL, Enoch
British Conservative, then Ulster Unionist, politician (1912–)

5 *On the prospect for race relations in Britain:*
As I look ahead, I am filled with foreboding. Like the Roman, I
seem to see 'the River Tiber foaming with much blood.'
Speech, Birmingham, 20 April 1968
Alluding to Virgil, *Aeneid,* Bk. VI: *'Thybrim multo spumantem sanguine
cerno.'*

6 All political lives, unless they are cut off in mid-stream at a happy
juncture, end in failure, because that is the nature of politics and of
human affairs.
Joseph Chamberlain (1977)

7 Milk is rendered immortal in cheese.
Attrib
Anticipated by Clifton Fadiman (*b*1904) in *Any Number Can Play* (1957):
'Cheese, milk's leap toward immortality.'

POWELL, Jane
US film actress (1929–)

1 A celebrity is one who works all his life to become well-known and then goes through back streets wearing dark glasses so he won't be recognized.

Attrib

POWELL, Sandy
British entertainer (1900–82)

2 Can you hear me, mother?

Catchphrase, from mid-1930s

PRIESTLEY, J. B.
British novelist and playwright (1894–1984)

3 Let the People Sing.

Title of novel (1939)

4 *On the 'little holiday steamers' used in the rescue from Dunkirk:*
[They] made an excursion to hell and came back glorious.

'Postscript to the News', BBC radio, 5 June 1940

5 [Admass] . . . this is my name for the whole system of an increasing productivity . . . plus high-pressure advertising and salesmanship, plus mass communication, and the creation of the mass mind, the mass man.

Journey Down a Rainbow (with J. Hawkes) (1955)

6 God can stand being told by Professor Ayer and Marghanita Laski that he doesn't exist.

Quoted in the *Listener,* 1 July 1965

7 I have always been a grumbler. I am designed for the part—sagging face, weighty underlip, rumbling, resonant voice. Money couldn't buy a better grumbling outfit.

Quoted in the *Guardian,* 15 August 1984

THE PRISONER
British TV series, 1967. Written by George Markstein et al. With Patrick Magoohan as Political Prisoner Number Six.

8 *Number Six:* I'm not a number, I'm a free man.

Stock phrase

PRIVATE EYE

British satirical magazine (founded 1962)

1 Tired and emotional.

>   Euphemism for 'drunk' derived from spoof Foreign Office memo, dating from 1966–68, when George Brown was Foreign Secretary.

2 Shock, horror, probe, sensation.

>   Stock sensational newspaper headline.

3 (Cont. page 94)

>   Standard way of finishing an article.

4 Phew! What a scorcher.

>   Stock popular newspaper weather headline.

5 This one will run and run.

>   Stock quote from theatre critic—originated by Fergus Cashin in the *Sun*.

6 Talking about Uganda.

>   This euphemism was first used (9 March 1973) to denote sexual intercourse at a party between a woman and a Ugandan diplomat. It is said to have been coined by James Fenton, the poet and critic. Later, 'Ugandan practices', 'Ugandan discussions' or 'discussing Ugandan affairs' were also employed.

7 Pass the sick-bag, Alice.

>   In parodies of newspaper style of Sir John Junor from *c*1979. Junor confirmed (1985) that he had used the phrase once.

8 I think we should be told.

>   ibid
>   Junor denied (1985) that he had ever used the phrase.

9 Shome mishtake (here) shurely?

>   Alluding to speech style of William (later Lord) Deedes, newspaper editor.

10 I wonder if, by any chance, they are related?

>   Stock remark about lookalikes.

11 Takes out onion.

>   Stock phrase to denote phoney emotion, from *c*1984.

THE PRIVATE LIFE OF HENRY VIII

UK film 1934. Script by Lajos Biro and Frederick Lonsdale. With Charles Laughton as Henry VIII.

1 *Before getting into bed with one of his brides:*
The things I've done for England . . .
Soundtrack

PROFUMO, John

British Conservative politician (1915–)

2 There was no impropriety whatsoever in my acquaintanceship with Miss [Christine] Keeler.
Speech, House of Commons, 22 March 1963
It later became clear there had been.

3 I shall not hesitate to issue writs for libel and slander if scandalous allegations are made or repeated outside the House.
ibid

PROUST, Marcel

French novelist (1871–1922)

4 I raised to my lips a spoonful of the tea in which I had soaked a morsel of the cake . . . suddenly the memory returns. The taste was of the little crumb of madeleine which on Sunday mornings at Combray . . . my aunt Leonie used to give me, dipping it first in her own cup of real or of lime-flower tea.
'Du côté de chez Swann', *A la recherche du temps perdu* (1913)
In the C. K. Scott Moncrieff translation.
See also **TELEGRAMS AND CABLES 318:1.**

PROVERBS

(of probable 20th century origin)

5 All publicity is good publicity.
Origin unknown, although Brendan Behan (*d*1964) has been quoted as saying, 'There's no such thing as bad publicity except your own obituary.')

6 Bed is the poor man's opera.
Translated from the Italian.

7 The best things in life are free.
From the title of a song (1927) by Buddy De Sylva and Lew Brown, to music by Ray Henderson.

8 Better the cold blast of winter than the hot breath of a pursuing elephant.
Suggested Chinese origin.

1   The camera cannot/does not lie.

A saying well-established by the second half of the century.

2   Do not remove a fly from your friend's forehead with a hatchet.

Suggested Chinese origin.

3   Don't read it—measure it.

Of publicity.

4   Every man likes the smell of his own farts.

Quoted in *Faber Book of Aphorisms* (ed. Auden & Kronenberger)
Described as of Icelandic origin. *See also* **AUDEN 18:6.**

5   Garbage in, garbage out.

Computerese, current by 1964, meaning 'If it's not right going in, it won't come out right.' Usually shortened to 'GIGO'.

6   If you're not part of the solution, you're part of the problem.

A saying used on several occasions, in various forms, by Eldridge Cleaver in 1968, but possibly not coined by him.

7   It takes two to tango.

From the song with this title by Al Hoffman and Dick Manning (1952).

8   Life's a bitch, and then you die.

Source untraced; probably US.

9   One does not insult the river god while crossing the river.

Suggested Chinese origin.

10 One picture is worth ten thousand words.

Created by Frederick R. Barnard for *Printer's Ink*, 8 December 1921, but misleadingly ascribed to Chinese origin.

11 The opera ain't/isn't over till the fat lady sings.

Quoted in the *Washington Post*, 13 June 1978
Dan Cook, a Texan journalist, is said to have invented this saying in 1975.

12 The trees are tall, but they do not reach up to the sky.

A favourite of Winston Churchill's—in 1953 he attributed it to Goethe (perhaps wrongly).

13 What a difference a day makes.

After the song 'What a Difference a Day Made' (1934) translated by Stanley Adams from the Spanish lyric *'Cuando Vuelva a Tu Lado'* by Maria Grever.
See also **LANCE 193:6.**

PRYDE, James
British artist (1866–1941)

1   *At the unveiling of an unlifelike statue of Nurse Edith Cavell:*
My god, they've shot the wrong person!

Attrib

PUDNEY, John
British poet (1909–77)

2   Do not despair
For Johnny head-in-air;
He sleeps as sound
As Johnny underground.

'For Johnny' (1945)
Lines used in film *The Way to the Stars.*

PUNCH
British humorous weekly

3   Look here, Steward, if this is coffee, I want tea; but if this is tea, then I wish for coffee.

Caption to cartoon by G. D. Armour, vol. cxxiii, 23 July 1902

4   *Mr Binks:* One of my ancestors fell at Waterloo.
Lady Clare: Ah? Which platform?

Caption to cartoon by F. H. Townsend, vol. cxxix, 1 November 1905

5   *Vicar's wife (sympathizingly):* Now that you can't get about, and are not able to read, how do you manage to occupy the time?
Old Man: Well, mum, sometimes I sits and thinks; and then again I just sits.

Caption to cartoon by Gunning-King, vol. cxxxi, 24 October 1906

PUZO, Mario
US novelist (1920–   )

6   He's a businessman. I'll make him an offer he can't refuse.

The Godfather (1969)

7   A lawyer with his briefcase can steal more than a thousand men with guns.

ibid

PYM, Barbara

British novelist (1928–80)

1 *On having a novel rejected:*

Perhaps in retirement . . . a quieter, narrower kind of life can be worked out and adopted. Bounded by English literature and the Anglican Church and small pleasures like sewing and choosing dress material for this uncertain summer.

Diary entry for 6 March 1972

QUAYLE, Dan

US Republican Vice President (1947–   )

1   *As head of the Space Council:*
Space is almost infinite. As a matter of fact, we think it *is* infinite.

Remark, quoted in *The Guardian*, 8 March 1989

2   *On the Nazi Holocaust:*
It was an obscene period in our nation's history . . . No, not in our nation's but in World War II. We all lived in this century; I didn't live in this century but in this century's history.

ibid

RALEIGH, Sir Walter
British academic (1861–1922)

1 I wish I loved the Human Race;
I wish I loved its silly face;
I wish I liked the way it walks;
I wish I liked the way it talks;
And when I'm introduced to one
I wish I thought *What Jolly Fun!*

'Wishes of an Elderly Man', *Laughter from a Cloud* (1923)

RAMBO: FIRST BLOOD: PART TWO
US film 1985. With Sylvester Stallone as Rambo.

2 *Rambo (a hunk bringing home American prisoners left behind in the Vietnam War):*
Do we get to win this time?

Soundtrack

RANDOLPH, David
3 *On Wagner's **Parsifal**:*
The kind of opera that starts at six o'clock and after it has been going three hours, you look at your watch and it says 6.20.

Quoted in *The Frank Muir Book*

RANSOME, Arthur
British novelist and journalist (1884–1967)

4 BETTER DROWNED THAN DUFFERS IF NOT DUFFERS WON'T DROWN.

Swallows and Amazons (1930)

RAPHAEL, Frederic
British writer (1931–)

5 He glanced with disdain at the big centre table where the famous faces of the Cambridge theatre were eating a loud meal. 'So this is the city of dreaming spires,' Sheila said. 'Theoretically speaking that's Oxford,' Adam said. 'This is the city of perspiring dreams.'

The Glittering Prizes (1976)
See also **DARLING 95:2.**

RATTIGAN, Terence (later Sir Terence)
British playwright (1911–77)

1 French Without Tears.

Title of play (1937)

2 She has ideas above her station . . . How would you say that in French? . . . you can't say **au-dessus de sa gare.** It isn't that sort of station.

ibid

3 A nice, respectable, middle-class, middle-aged maiden lady, with time on her hands and the money to help her pass it . . . Let us call her Aunt Edna . . . Aunt Edna is universal, and to those who may feel that all the problems of the modern theatre might be solved by her liquidation, let me add that . . . she is also immortal.

Preface, *Collected Plays*, Vol. II (1953)

RATUSHINSKAYA, Irina
Ukrainian poet (1954–)

4 Grey Is the Colour of Hope.

Title of book (1988)
Referring to the colour of her uniform as the inmate of a Soviet labour camp.

RAYMOND, Ernest
British author (1888–1974)

5 Tell England, ye who pass this monument,
We died for her, and here we rest content.

Tell England (1922)
Inscription on grave at Gallipoli, echoing one by the Greek poet Simonides.

RAY'S A LAUGH
UK radio comedy series (BBC), from 1949 to 1960. Written by Ted Ray and others. With Ted Ray as Ivy, Bob Pearson as Mrs Hoskin, Graham Stark as Tommy Trafford, etc.

6 *Mrs Hoskin:* Ee, it was agony, Ivy.

Catchphrase

7 *Ivy:* He's loo-vely, Mrs Hoskin, he's loo-oo-vely!

Catchphrase

8 *Tommy Trafford:* If you haven't been to Manchester, you haven't lived.

Catchphrase

READ, Al
British comedian (1909–87)

1 Cheeky monkey!
Catchphrase, 1950s radio shows

2 Right, monkey!
Catchphrase, 1950s

REAGAN, Ronald
US film actor, Republican Governor and President (1911–)

3 Sex is best in the afternoon after coming out of the shower.
Attrib

4 *To President Carter during 1980 election:*
There you go again!
TV debate, 29 October 1980

5 You can tell a lot about a fellow's character by the way he eats jelly beans.
Quoted in the *Daily Mail*, 22 January 1981

6 *To surgeons, as he entered the operating room after attempted assassination, 30 March 1981:*
Please tell me you're Republicans.
Quoted in *Time*, 13 April 1981

7 *When told by an aide that the Government was running normally, on the same occasion:*
What makes you think I'd be happy about that?
In ibid

8 In your discussions of the nuclear freeze proposals, I urge you to beware the temptation of pride—the temptation blithely to declare yourselves above it all and label both sides equally at fault, to ignore the facts of history and the aggressive impulses of an evil empire [the Soviet Union].
Speech, Florida, 8 March 1983

9 *During microphone test prior to radio broadcast:*
My fellow Americans, I am pleased to tell you that I have signed legislation to outlaw Russia for ever. We begin bombing in five minutes.
Audio recording, 13 August 1984

1   *On his challenger, Walter Mondale, during 1984 election:*
I will not make age an issue of this campaign. I am not going to exploit for political purposes my opponent's youth and inexperience.

TV debate, 22 October 1984

2   A shining city on a hill.

Quoted in *Time*, 5 November 1984

Evocation of the US as a land of security and success, frequently used
in speeches during 1984 re-election campaign, but also as early as
1976. Possibly derived from the Puritan, John Winthrop (1588–1649):
'We shall be as a city upon a hill, the eyes of all people are upon us.'

3   *In victory speech on re-election:*
This is not the end of anything, this is the beginning of everything.

Quoted in *The Times*, 8 November 1984

4   *On the same occasion, and during the preceding campaign:*
You ain't seen nothing yet!

Quoted in the *Daily Express*, 8 November 1984
Compare **JOLSON 178:3.**

5   *To the American Business Conference:*
I have my veto pen drawn and ready for any tax increase that Congress might even think of sending up. And I have only one thing to say to the tax increasers. Go ahead—make my day.

Quoted in *Time*, 25 March 1985

The last sentence was originally spoken by Clint Eastwood to a gunman
he was holding at bay in the film *Sudden Impact* (1983). It reappeared
in 1984 in a parody of the *New York Post* put together by editors, most of
them anti-Reagan, who imagined the President starting a nuclear war
by throwing down that dare to the Kremlin.

6   *After hi-jack of US plane by Shi'ite Muslims:*
We are not going to tolerate these attacks from outlaw states run by the strangest collection of misfits, Looney Tunes and squalid criminals since the advent of the Third Reich.

Speech, 8 July 1985

7   It's true hard work never killed anybody, but I figure, why take the chance?

Speech, 28 March 1987

8   Once you begin a great movement, there's no telling where it will end. We meant to change a nation, and instead, we changed a world.

Farewell Address to the Nation, Washington DC, 11 January 1989
See also **BRIDGES AT TOKO-RI 48:6; DEMPSEY 99:4; KING'S ROW
188:4; LOUIS 207:8.**

REED, Henry
British poet and playwright (1914–)

1   *In parody of T. S. Eliot:*
As we get older we do not get any younger.
Seasons return, and today I am fifty-five,
And this time last year I was fifty-four,
And this time next year I shall be sixty-two.

'Chard Whitlow', *A Map of Verona* (1946)

2   Today we have naming of parts. Yesterday,
We had daily cleaning. And tomorrow morning
We shall have what to do after firing. But today,
Today we have naming of parts.

'Lessons of the War' in ibid

REED, John
US writer (1887–1920)

3   Ten Days that Shook the World.

Title of book (on Russian Revolution) (1919)
Also used as the alternative, English, title of Sergei Eisenstein's 1927
film *October*.

REED, Rex
US critic (1938–)

4   Cannes is where you lie on the beach and stare at the stars—or vice
versa.

Attrib

REICH, Charles
US author (1928–)

5   The extraordinary thing about this new consciousness [an anti-
urban counter-culture] is that it has emerged out of the wasteland
of the Corporate State. For one who thought the world was
irretrievably encased in metal and plastic and sterile stone, it seems
a remarkable greening of America.

The Greening of America (1971)

REID, Beryl
British actress (1918–)

6   As the art mistress said to the gardener . . .

Catchphrase as 'Monica' in *Educating Archie,* BBC radio, 1950s

7   Jolly hockey-sticks.

Catchphrase in ibid

1   Good evening, each!

    Catchphrase as 'Marlene' in ibid

REITH, John (later Lord Reith)
British broadcasting administrator (1889–1971)

2   It was in fact the combination of public service motive, sense of moral obligation, assured finance and the brute force of monopoly which enabled the BBC to make of broadcasting what no other country has made of it.

    Into the Wind (1949)

3   I was inordinately ambitious, I suppose, to be *fully stretched* . . . inordinately ambitious to be of service.

    Lord Reith Looks Back, BBC TV (1967)

4   I hear you.

    ibid
    Using a Scots expression meaning that a remark is not worth considering or is untrue.

5   *On the best form of government:*
    Despotism tempered by assassination.

    ibid
    Alluding to a Russian remark quoted by Count Münster, the German statesman (1766–1839).

REMARQUE, Erich Maria
German novelist (1897–1970)

6   All Quiet on the Western Front.

    English translation of book title, 1929
    Remarque's original title was *Im Westen Nichts Neues* ('No News in the West'). The translation echoes the title of 'All Quiet Along the Potomac', an American song derived from a poem about the Civil War.

REPINGTON, Lieut-Col. Charles A'Court
British soldier and journalist (1858–1925)

7   I saw Major Johnstone, who is here to lay the bases of an American History. We discussed the right name of the war. I said that we called it now *The War*, but that this could not last. The Napoleonic War was *The Great War*. To call it *The German War* was too much flattery for the Boche. I suggested *The World War* as a shade better title, and finally we mutually agreed to call it *The First World War* in order to prevent the millennium folk from forgetting that the history of the world was the history of war.

    Diary entry for 10 September 1918, published in *The First World War 1914–18* (1920)

THE RETURN OF SHERLOCK HOLMES

UK film 1929. With Clive Brook as Holmes and H. Reeves-Smith as Watson.

1   *Watson:* Amazing, Holmes.
    Holmes: Elementary, my dear Watson, elementary.

    Nowhere in the writings of Sir Arthur Conan Doyle *(q.v.)* does the
    great detective say this phrase. These were the last lines of dialogue of
    the first sound film version.

REUBEN, David

US doctor and author (1933–)

2   Everything You Always Wanted To Know About Sex But Were
    Afraid To Ask.

    Title of book (1970)

REUTHER, Walter

US labor leader (1907–70)

3   *On how to recognize a Communist:*
    If it walks like a duck, and quacks like a duck, then it just may be a
    duck.

    Attrib
    Has also been attributed, rather curiously, to Cardinal Cushing.

RHODES, Cecil

British-born colonialist (1853–1902)

4   [Being an Englishman was] the greatest prize in the lottery of life.

    Recounted in Sir A. Weston Jarvis, *Jottings from an Active Life* (1928)

5   *Near to his death:*
    So little done, so much to do.

    Attrib
    Echoing Tennyson, 'So many worlds, so much to do,/ So little done,
    such things to be'—*In memoriam A. H. H.* (1850).

6   *Last words:*
    Turn me over, Jack.

    Attrib

RIBBLESDALE, Lord

British aristocrat (1854–1925)

7   It [is] gentlemanly to get one's quotations very slightly wrong. In
    that way one unprigs oneself and allows the company to correct
    one.

    Recounted in Lady D. Cooper, *The Light of Common Day*

RICE, Grantland
US sports journalist and poet (1880–1954)

1   For when the One Great Scorer comes
    To write against your name,
    He marks—not that you won or lost—
    But how you played the game.

    'Alumnus Football' (1941)

RICE, Tim
British lyricist (1944–)

2   Jesus Christ Superstar!

    Title of musical (with music by A. Lloyd Webber) (1970)
    Based on a 1960s Las Vegas billing, 'Tom Jones—Superstar' . . .

3   *Herod to Christ:*
    Prove to me that you're no fool,
    Walk across my swimming pool.

    Song, 'King Herod's Song' in ibid

4   Don't Cry for Me, Argentina.

    Title of song, *Evita* (1976)

RICE-DAVIES, Mandy
British woman (1944–)

5   *When told that Lord Astor had denied her allegations of some amorous*
    involvement with her:
    Well, he would, wouldn't he?

    Magistrates Court hearing, London, 28 June 1963

RICHARD, Keith see JAGGER, Mick and RICHARD, Keith

'RICHARDS, Frank'
British writer (1875–1961)

6   *The cries of 'Billy Bunter':*
    Yarooh! . . . I say you fellows! . . . You beast!

    Passim in Billy Bunter stories (1908–40)

7   The rottenfulness is terrific!

    Passim in ibid
    Said by Hurree Jamset Ram, the basic formula was 'the —— fulness is
    terrific'.

RIPLEY, Robert L.
US strip creator and illustrator (1893–1949)

1   Believe It or Not.

> Title of syndicated newspaper feature, from 1918 popularizing a phrase already in existence.

RIVERS, Joan
US comedienne (1937–   )

2   Can we talk?

> Stock phrase

THE ROAD TO MOROCCO
US film 1942. With Bob Hope and Bing Crosby.

3   Like Webster's Dictionary
    We're Morocco bound.

> Song, 'Road to Morocco'
> Written by Johnny Burke, to music by Jimmy van Heusen.

ROBERTS, Tommy Rhys, QC
Welsh lawyer (1910–75)

4   Lloyd George knew my father.

> Sung to the tune of 'Onward Christian Soldiers', this was his party piece at legal dinners, from the 1940s on. His father had once shared a legal practice with Lloyd George. This is but one suggested source for the popular song.

ROBEY, Sir George
British comedian (1869–1954)

5   The Prime Minister of Mirth.

> Bill matter

6   Desist!

> Catchphrase

ROBIN, Leo
US songwriter (1899–1985)

7   Thanks for the Memory.

> Title of song, *The Big Broadcast of 1938*. Written with Ralph Rainger.
> *See also* **LOOS 207:6.**

ROBINSON, Rt Revd John
British Anglican bishop (1919–83)

1   *On D. H. Lawrence's* **Lady Chatterley's Lover**:
    What I think is clear is that what Lawrence is trying to do is to
    portray the sex relationship as something essentially sacred . . . as in
    a real sense an act of holy communion.

    Evidence in *Regina v. Penguin Books Ltd*, 27 October 1960

ROBSON, Bobby
British football manager (1933–   )

2   The first ninety minutes are the most important.

    Quoted as title of TV documentary, 1983

ROCKEFELLER, Nelson
US Republican politician and Vice President (1908–79)

3   The brotherhood of man under the fatherhood of God.

    Slogan, quoted in *Time*, 1 March 1982
    The words came originally from a saying of his father, John D.
    Rockefeller Jr (1874–1960)—'These are the principles upon which
    alone a new world recognizing the brotherhood of man and the
    fatherhood of God can be established.' Rendered by others with the
    acronym 'BOMFOG'.

ROCKNE, Knute
US football coach (1888–1931)

4   Show me a good and gracious loser and I'll show you a failure.

    Attrib 1920s
    See also **KNUTE ROCKNE 191:3.**

ROGERS, Will
US humorist (1879–1935)

5   I never met a man I didn't like.

    Frequent saying, by 1926
    More specifically, 'I joked about every prominent man of my time, but
    I never met a man I dident [*sic*] like.' Also as suggested epitaph.

6   Dear Mr Coolidge: Well all I know is just what I read in the papers.

    The Letters of a Self-Made Diplomat to His President (1927)

7   *On the Venus de Milo:*
    See what'll happen if you don't stop biting your finger-nails.

    Quoted in B. Cerf, *Shake Well Before Using*

ROHE, Ludwig Mies van der
German-born architect (1886–1969)

1   Less is more.

Quoted in the *New York Herald Tribune*, 1969
The phrase had earlier been used by Robert Browning in a different
artistic context in 'Andrea del Sarto', *Men and Women* (1864).

2   God is in the details.

Quoted in ibid, but said earlier, possibly by Flaubert.

ROONEY, Mickey
US film actor (1920–   )

3   *In films with Judy Garland, 1930s/40s:*
Let's put on a show! . . . Let's do the show right here in the barn!

Attrib stock phrase

4   Had I been brighter, the ladies been gentler, the Scotch been
weaker, had the gods been kinder, had the dice been hotter, this
could have been a one-sentence story: Once upon a time I lived
happily ever after.

Attrib, in 1965

ROOSEVELT, Franklin D.
US Democratic President (1882–1945)

5   I pledge you, I pledge myself to a New Deal for the American
people.

Speech to the Democratic Convention, 2 July 1932

6   First of all, let me assert my belief that the only thing we have to
fear is fear itself—nameless, unreasoning, unjustified terror which
paralyses needed efforts to convert retreat into advance.

Inaugural address, Washington, 4 March 1933

7   There is a mysterious cycle in human events. To some generations
much is given. Of other generations much is expected. This
generation of Americans has a *rendezvous with destiny*.

Speech, Democratic convention, 1936

8   A radical is a man with both feet firmly planted in the air.

Radio broadcast, 26 October 1939

9   I have told you once and I will tell you again—your boys are not
going to be sent into any foreign wars.

Election speech, Boston, Mass., 30 October 1940

1   And who voted against the appropriations for an adequate national defense? MARTIN, BARTON and FISH.

Election speeches, 1940

2   We must be the great arsenal of democracy.

Radio 'fireside chat', 29 December 1940

3   *On the Japanese attack at Pearl Harbor:*
Yesterday, December 7 1941, a date which will live in infamy, the United States of America was suddenly and deliberately attacked by naval and air forces of the Empire of Japan.

Speech to Congress, 8 December 1941

ROOSEVELT, Theodore
US Republican President (1858–1919)

4   I am as strong as a bull moose and you can use me to the limit.

Letter to Mark Hanna, 27 June 1900.
When standing as Vice President. He later tried to make a Presidential comeback as a 'Bull Moose' candidate in 1912.

5   There is a homely adage which runs, 'Speak softly and carry a big stick—and you will go far.' If the American nation will speak softly and yet build and keep at a pitch of the highest training a thoroughly efficient navy, the Monroe Doctrine will go far.

Speech (as Vice President), Minnesota State Fair, 2 September 1901

6   *On Maxwell House coffee:*
Good . . . to the last drop.

Attrib remark
Visiting Joel Cheek, the perfector of the blend, 1907. The line has been used as the brand's slogan for many years.

7   The *lunatic fringe* in all reform movements.

Autobiography (1913)

ROSE, Billy
US impresario and songwriter (1899–1966)

8   Does the Spearmint Lose Its Flavour on the Bedpost Overnight?

Title of song, 1924
Usually credited to Marty Bloom and Ernest Breuer 'with assistance from' Rose. 'Chewing-gum' substituted for 'Spearmint' when the song was revived in Britain in 1959.
See also **HARBURG 153:4.**

ROSEBERY, 5th Earl of
British Liberal Prime Minister (1847–1929)

1 *On breaking away from his Liberal Party colleagues:*
  For the present, at any rate, I must proceed alone. I must plough
  my own furrow alone, but before I get to the end of that furrow it is
  possible that I may not find myself alone.

  Speech, 19 July 1901

ROSS, Alan S. C.
British academic (1907–)

2 U and Non-U. An Essay in Sociological Linguistics.

  Title of essay in *Noblesse Oblige* (ed. Nancy Mitford, 1956)
  Ross had first used 'U' to denote 'upper class' verbal usage and 'Non-
  U' to denote incorrect, non-upper class usage, in a 1954 article.

ROSS, Harold
US editor of the *New Yorker* (1892–1951)

3 Who he?

  Quoted in J. Thurber, *The Years With Ross*
  Customary query on finding a name he did not know in an article.

4 *Upon founding the **New Yorker** in 1925:*
  The *New Yorker* will not be edited for the old lady from Dubuque.

  Remark
  Later she became known as 'the little old lady from Dubuque.'

ROTH, Philip
US novelist (1933–)

5 So (said the doctor). Now vee may perhaps to begin. Yes?

  Portnoy's Complaint (1969)
  Last words.

'ROTTEN, Johnny'
British pop singer (1957–)

6 Love is two minutes fifty-two seconds of squishing [*or* squelching]
  noises. It shows your mind isn't clicking right.

  Attrib remark, in 1978
  In 1983 Rotten was quoted by the *Daily Mirror* as saying that it had
  become more like five minutes as he had acquired a new technique.

ROUND THE HORNE

UK radio comedy series (BBC), 1964–9. Script by Marty Feldman and Barry Took. With Kenneth Horne, Betty Marsden as Lady Beatrice Counterblast and Kenneth Williams as Sandy.

1   *Sandy:* That's yer actual French.

Catchphrase

2   *Counterblast:* Many, many times!

Catchphrase

ROWAN AND MARTIN'S LAUGH-IN
see *LAUGH-IN*

ROWLAND, Helen
US columnist and writer (1875–1950)

3   A bachelor never quite gets over the idea that he is a thing of beauty and a boy forever.

A Guide to Men (1922)

ROWLAND, Richard
US film executive (?1881–1947)

4   *When the United Artists film company was established in 1919:*
The lunatics have taken over the asylum.

Attrib

See also **STALLINGS 311:5** *and* **GEORGE 135:5.**

ROYDEN, Maude
British social reformer and preacher (1876–1956)

5   The Church [of England] should go forward along the path of progress and be no longer satisfied only to represent the Conservative Party at prayer.

Speech, London, 16 July 1917
Possibly quoting an established expression (sometimes 'Tory Party at prayer'), though no evidence has been found connecting it with Benjamin Disraeli.

RUBIN, Jerry
US 'yippie' leader (1938–   )

6   □ Don't trust anyone over thirty.

Quoted in S.B. Flexner, *Listening to America*
Actually first uttered by Jack Weinberg at Berkeley in 1964 during a free speech demonstration.

RUNCIE, Most Revd Robert (later Lord Runcie)

British Archbishop of Canterbury (1921–)

1 *On discussions with the Prince and Princess of Wales prior to marrying them:*
   My advice was delicately poised between the cliché and the indiscretion.

   Quoted in *The Times*, 14 July 1981
   See also **MACMILLAN 214:3.**

RUNCIE, Rosalind

Wife of the above (1932–)

2 Too much religion makes me go pop.

   Quoted in M. Duggan, *Runcie: The Making of an Archbishop*

RUNYON, Damon

US writer (1884–1946)

3 Strictly a Hurrah Henry.

   'Tight Shoes'
   Jim Godbolt adapted this to 'Hooray Henry' in 1951 to describe a sub-species of British upper-class twit.

4 The race is not always to the swift nor the battle to the strong, but that's the way to bet.

   Attrib
   Alluding to Ecclesiastes 9:11.

RUSK, Dean

US Democratic politician (1909–)

5 *In conversation with journalist during Cuban Missile Crisis, 24 October 1962:*
   We're eyeball to eyeball and I think the other fellow just blinked.

   Quoted in W. Safire, *Political Dictionary*

RUSSELL, Bertrand (3rd Earl Russell)

British philosopher and mathematician (1872–1970)

6 Drunkenness is temporary suicide: the happiness that it brings is merely negative, a momentary cessation of unhappiness.

   The Conquest of Happiness (1930)

1   Three passions, simple but overwhelmingly strong, have governed
    my life: the longing for love, the search for knowledge, and
    unbearable pity for the suffering of mankind . . . I have sought love,
    first, because it brings ecstasy—ecstasy so great that I would often
    have sacrificed all the rest of life for a few hours of this joy. I have
    sought it, next, because it relieves loneliness—that terrible
    loneliness in which one shivering consciousness looks over the rim
    of the world into the cold unfathomable lifeless abyss. I have sought
    it, finally, because in the union of love I have seen, in a mystic
    miniature, the prefiguring vision of the heaven that saints and
    poets have imagined. This is what I sought, and though it might
    seem too good for human life, this is what—at last—I have found.

    'What I have lived for', Prologue to Vol. 1, *The Autobiography of Bertrand
    Russell* (1967)

2   I have never but once succeeded in making [George Moore] tell a
    lie, that was by a subterfuge. 'Moore,' I said, 'do you *always* speak
    the truth?' 'No,' he replied. I believe this to be the only lie he had
    ever told.

    ibid

SABATINI, Rafael
Italian-born novelist (1875–1950)

1   Born with the gift of laughter and a sense that the world was mad.
Scaramouche (1921)

SACKS, Oliver
British-born neurologist in the US (1933–)

2   The Man Who Mistook His Wife For A Hat.
Title of book (1985)

SACKVILLE-WEST, Vita
British novelist and poet (1892–1962)

3   They rustle, they brustle, they crackle, and if you can crush beech nuts under foot at the same time, so much the better. But beech nuts aren't essential. The essential is that you should tramp through very dry, very crisp, brown leaves—a thick drift of them in the Autumn woods, shuffling through them, kicking them up . . . walking in fact 'through leaves'.
Broadcast talk, 1950
Explaining a family expression 'through leaves' to express pure happiness as shown by young children shuffling through drifts of dry Autumn leaves.

SAHL, Mort
US satirist (1926–)

4   *During viewing of lengthy film,* **Exodus***:*
Let my people go!
As told on LP album 'The New Frontier' (1961)
Another version is that Sahl, invited by the director, Otto Preminger, to a preview, stood up after three hours and said, 'Otto—let my people go!'

'SAKI' (H. H. Munro)
British short-story writer (1870–1916)

5   The cook was a good cook, as cooks go; and as cooks go she went.
'Reginald on Besetting Sins', *Reginald* (1904)

6   Waldo is one of those people who would be enormously improved by death.
'The Feast of Nemesis', *Beasts and Super-Beasts* (1914)

7   *Last words:*
Put that bloody cigarette out!
Quoted in A. J. Langguth, *Life of Saki*
Said by Corporal Munro to one of his men who had lit up. He was killed by a German sniper.

SALINGER, J. D.

US novelist (1919–)

1　If you really want to hear about it, the first thing you'll probably want to know is where I was born and what my lousy childhood was like, and how my parents were occupied and all before they had me, and all that David Copperfield kind of crap.

The Catcher in the Rye (1951)
Opening words.

SALISBURY, 5th Marquess of

British Conservative politician (1893–1972)

2　*On Iain Macleod:*
The present Colonial Secretary has been too clever by half. I believe he is a very fine bridge player. It is not considered immoral, or even bad form to outwit one's opponent at bridge. It almost seems to me as if the Colonial secretary, when he abandoned the sphere of bridge for the sphere of politics, brought his bridge technique with him.

Speech, House of Lords, 7 March 1961

SANDBURG, Carl

US poet (1878–1967)

3　Sometime they'll give a war and nobody will come.

The People, Yes (1936)
Charlotte Keyes (1914–) wrote an article in *McCall's* (October 1966) which was given the title 'Suppose They Gave a War, and No One Came?' A US film (1969) was called *Suppose They Gave a War and Nobody Came?*

4　Slang is a language that rolls up its sleeves, spits on its hands and goes to work.

In the *New York Times*, 13 February 1959

SARONY, Leslie

British entertainer and writer (1897–1985)

5　(S)he sits among the cabbages and peas.

Song, 'Mucking About the Garden', (1920s)
Using the pen name, 'Q. Cumber'. Similar song also associated with Marie Lloyd.

6　Ain't It Grand To be Bloomin' Well Dead?

Title of song

SARTRE, Jean-Paul
French philosopher and writer (1905–80)

1 *L'Enfer, c'est les Autres* ('Hell is other people').

Huis clos (1944)

SAVILE, Jimmy (later Sir James)
British entertainer (1926–)

2 As it happens.

Stock phrase

3 How's about that, then, guys and gals?

Stock phrase

SAYERS, Dorothy L.
British detective novelist (1893–1957)

4 *Lord Peter Wimsey proposing to Harriet Vane:*
Placetne, magistra? ('Does it please you, mistress?')

Gaudy Night (1936)
She replies *'Placet'* ('It pleases').

SCHACHT, Hjalmar
German banker (1877–1970)

5 I wouldn't believe Hitler was dead, even if he told me so himself.

Attrib remark, on 8 May 1945

SCHOENBERG, Arnold
German composer (1874–1951)

6 *When told his violin concerto needed a soloist with six fingers:*
Very well, I can wait.

Attrib

SCHROEDER, Patricia
US Democratic politician (1940–)

7 [Ronald Reagan is] perfecting the Teflon-coated presidency because nothing sticks to him.

Speech, US House of Representatives, August 1983

SCHULTZ, Charles M.
US cartoonist and creator of 'Peanuts' strip (1922–   )

1   Good grief, Charlie Brown!

Stock phrase
The behaviour of 'Charlie Brown' frequently elicits this exclamation
from other characters.

2   It Was a Dark and Stormy Night . . .

Title of book
Derived from a children's 'circular' story-telling game.

3   Happiness is a warm puppy.

From strip *c*1957
Also the title of a book, 1962. This gave rise to numerous other
'Happiness is . . . ' slogans.

SCHUMACHER, E. F.
German-born British economist (1911–77)

4   Small is Beautiful. A study of economics as if people mattered.

Title of book (1973)

SCOTT, C. P.
British newspaper editor (1846–1932)

5   Comment is free, but facts are sacred.

Manchester Guardian, 5 May 1921
In a signed editorial marking the paper's centenary.

6   Television? No good will come of this device. The word is half
Greek and half Latin.

Attrib

SCOTT, Captain R. F.
British explorer (1868–1912)

7   *On the South Pole:*
Great God! This is an awful place and terrible enough for us to
have laboured without the reward of priority.

Scott's Last Expedition: Journals (1913)

8   *Message to the public:*
Had we lived, I should have had a tale to tell of the hardihood,
endurance, and courage of my companions which would have
stirred the hearts of every Englishman. These rough notes and our
dead bodies must tell the tale.

ibid

1   *Last entry:*
    For God's sake look after our people.

    ibid, 29 March 1912

SELFRIDGE, H. Gordon
US store owner (?1856–1947)

2   There are — shopping days to Christmas.

    Quoted in A. H. Williams, *No Name On The Door*

3   Complete satisfaction or money cheerfully refunded.

    Slogan in ibid

4   The customer is always right.

    Slogan in ibid
    César Ritz (*d*1918) was being quoted by 1908 as saying, 'The customer is never wrong.'

5   'Business as usual' must be the order of the day.

    Speech, 26 August 1914
    In the context of the early days of the First World War, the traditional store-keeper's slogan (as might be used after a fire, or similar) was first used by H. E. Morgan, an associate of Selfridge's. Winston Churchill also took up the cry.

6   This famous store needs no name on the door.

    Slogan
    His Oxford Street, London, store opened in 1909.

SELLAR, W. C. and YEATMAN, R. J.
British humorists (1898–1951) and (1897–1968)

7   1066 and All That.

    Title of book (1930)

8   [The Roman Conquest was, however,] a Good Thing .

    Passim in ibid

9   *Honi soie qui mal y pense* ('Honey, your silk stocking's hanging down').

    ibid

10 Shortly after this the cruel Queen, Broody Mary, died and a post-mortem examination revealed the word 'CALLOUS' engraved on her heart.

    ibid

1   [Gladstone] spent his declining years trying to guess the answer to the Irish Question; unfortunately, whenever he was getting warm, the Irish secretly changed the question.

   ibid

2   Do not on any account attempt to write on both sides of the paper at once.

   ibid

SELLERS, Peter
British actor (1925–80)

3   *As Indian:*
   Goodness, gracious me.

   Recording of song, 'Goodness Gracious me' (1960)
   The song, written by Herbert Kretzmer to music by Dave Lee, was recorded with Sophia Loren and based on characters in the film of Shaw's *The Millionairess.*

4   *Of Britt Ekland:*
   A professional girlfriend and an amateur actress.
   Attrib

SERVICE, Robert W.
Canadian poet (1874–1958)

5   Ah! the clock is always slow;
   It is later than you think.
   'Spring'

6   And watching his luck was his light-o'-love, the lady that's known as Lou.
   'The Shooting of Dan McGrew' (1917)
   Written with Cuthbert Clarke.

SEYLER, Athene (later Dame Athene)
British actress (1889–1990)

7   *Of Hannen Swaffer, journalist:*
   Whenever I see his fingernails, I thank God I don't have to look at his feet.
   Remark, quoted in B. Forbes, *Ned's Girl*

SHANKLY, Bill
British football manager (1914–81)

8   Some people think football is a matter of life and death. I don't like that attitude. I can assure them it is much more serious than that.
   Attrib remark, 1973

SHAW, George Bernard
Irish playwright and critic (1856–1950)

1 *On the song, 'The Red Flag':*
The funeral march of a fried eel.

Quoted in W. S. Churchill, *Great Contemporaries*

2 *On Lord Rosebery:*
A man who never missed an occasion to let slip an opportunity.

Attrib

3 □ The question of who are the best people to take charge of children is a very difficult one; but it is quite certain that parents are the very worst.

Quoting William Morris
Compare **BELL 31:2.**

4 England and America are two countries separated by the same language.

Quoted in ibid
But in *Readers' Digest* by 1942. Compare O. Wilde *The Canterville Ghost* (1887): 'We have really everything in common with America nowadays except, of course, language.'

5 Hell is full of musical amateurs: music is the brandy of the damned.

Man and Superman (1903)

6 Titles distinguish the mediocre, embarrass the superior, and are disgraced by the inferior.

ibid

7 There are two tragedies in life. One is to lose your heart's desire. The other is to gain it.

ibid

8 Do not do unto others as you would they should do unto you. Their tastes may not be the same.

ibid 'Maxims for Revolutionists'

9 The golden rule is that there are no golden rules.

ibid

10 He who can does. He who cannot, teaches.

ibid

11 Marriage is popular because it combines the maximum of temptation with the maximum of opportunity.

ibid

1   I am a Millionaire. That is my religion.
    Major Barbara (1907)

2   Wot prawce Selvytion nah? [What price salvation now?]
    ibid

3   Assassination is the extreme form of censorship.
    The Shewing-Up of Blanco Posnett (1909)

4   He's a gentleman: look at his boots.
    Pygmalion (1914)

5   Remember that you are a human being with a soul and the divine
    gift of articulate speech: that your native language is the language
    of Shakespeare and Milton and the Bible; and don't sit there
    crooning like a bilious pigeon.
    ibid

6   I shall make a duchess of this draggletailed guttersnipe.
    ibid

7   My aunt died of influenza: so they said . . . But it's my belief (as
    how) they done the old woman in.
    ibid
    The words 'as how' were inserted by Mrs Patrick Campbell in her
    performances as Eliza. Also incorporated in the 1938 film.

8   *Freddy:* Are you walking across the Park, Miss Doolittle? If so—
    Liza: Walk! Not bloody likely. *(Sensation).* I am going in a taxi.
    ibid

9   Where the devil are my slippers, Eliza?
    ibid
    Last words of the 1938 film version (and of the musical adaptation *My
    Fair Lady*—in the order 'Eliza, where the devil are my slippers?'—but
    not in Shaw's text (not even the updated one of 1941 incorporating
    extra material for the film). However, the lines 'I wonder where the
    devil my slippers are?' and 'What the devil have I done with my
    slippers?' do occur in the fourth act.

10 The new slang, you do it ever so well.
    Pygmalion (1938 film version)

11 The rain in Spain stays mainly in the plains.
    ibid

12 In Hampshire, Hereford and Hertford,
    Hurricanes hardly ever happen.
    ibid

1   *The Serpent:* You see things; and you say 'Why?' But I dream things that never were; and I say 'Why not?'

Back to Methuselah (1921)
Quoted by John F. Kennedy and Robert F. Kennedy many times—to the extent that it is sometimes ascribed to them.

2   *To Helen Keller:*
I wish all Americans were as blind as you.

Quoted in H. Pearson, *Bernard Shaw*
Sometimes misquoted as 'All Americans are deaf, dumb, and blind.'

3   *To a Swiss woman who had written, 'You have the greatest brain in the world and I have the most beautiful body; so we ought to produce the most perfect child':*
Yes, but fancy if it were born with my beauty and your brains?

Quoted in ibid

4   *To Alfred Hitchcock who had said, 'One look at you, Mr Shaw, and I know there's famine in the land':*
One look at you, Mr Hitchcock, and I know who caused it.

Quoted in B. Patch, *Thirty Years with GBS*

5   *When Samuel Goldwyn asked him if he would sell the film rights to his plays:*
The trouble is, Mr Goldwyn, that you are only interested in art and I am only interested in money.

Quoted in P. French, *The Movie Moguls*

6   *On dancing:*
A perpendicular expression of a horizontal desire.

Quoted in the *New Statesman*, 23 March 1962

7   With the single exception of Homer, there is no eminent writer, not even Sir Walter Scott, whom I can despise so entirely as I despise Shakespeare when I measure my mind against his . . . It would positively be a relief to me to dig him up and throw stones at him.

Dramatic Opinions and Essays, Vol. 2 (1907)
Quoting a view stated 1895–8.

8   Youth is a wonderful thing; what a crime to waste it on children.

Quoted in the *Treasury of Humorous Quotations* (1951)
Unverified.
See also **CAMPBELL 57:7; CHESTERTON 69:5; CHURCHILL 72:2; FRASER 128:1; LENIN 201:2.**

SHAWCROSS, Sir Hartley (later Lord Shawcross)
British Labour Attorney-General (1902–   )

1   □ We are the masters now.

Speech, House of Commons, 2 April 1946
In fact, he said: 'We are the masters at the moment, and not only at the moment, but for a very long time to come.'

SHINWELL, Emanuel (later Lord Shinwell)
British Labour politician (1884–1986)

2   We know that you, the organized workers of the country, are our friends . . . As for the rest, they do not matter a tinker's curse.

ETU Conference, Margate, 7 May 1947

SHUBERT, Lee
US impresario (1875–1953)

3   *On costume drama:*
Audiences don't like plays where people write letters with feathers.

Attrib

Also ascribed to Max Gordon, Broadway producer, and to a Missouri cinema owner about costume epics, mid-1930s.

SHULTZ, George
US Republican politician (1920–   )

4   *Objecting to Government meddling, as Labor Secretary:*
Don't just do something, stand there.

Speech, 1970, quoted in W. Safire, *Political Dictionary*

5   *As Secretary of State, after signing of missile treaty:*
'Trust but verify' is really an ancient saying in the United States, but in a different guise. Remember the storekeeper who was a little leery of credit, and he had a sign in his store that said, IN GOD WE TRUST—ALL OTHERS CASH. This [the verification procedures] is the cash.'

Reported in *Time*, 14 December 1987
Comparing Russian and American proverbial expressions.

SIBELIUS, Jean
Finnish composer (1865–1957)

6   Pay no attention to what the critics say. No statue has ever been put up to a critic.

Attrib, by 1937

SICKERT, Walter
British painter (1860–1942)

1   *To Denton Welch:*
    Come again when you can't stay so long.

    Quoted in D. Welch, 'Sickert at St Peter's', *Horizon*, Vol. vi No. 32 (1942)

SILLITOE, Alan
British writer (1928–   )

2   The Loneliness of the Long Distance Runner.

    Title of novel (1959)

SIMENON, Georges
Belgian novelist (1903–89)

3   I have made love to ten thousand women.

    Interview with *Die Tat*, Zurich, February 1977
    Later his wife said, 'The true figure is no more than twelve hundred.'

SIMON, Carly
US singer/songwriter (1945–   )

4   You're so vain, you probably think this song is about you.

    Song, 'You're So Vain' (1972)

SIMON, Neil
US playwright (1927–   )

5   The Odd Couple.

    Title of play (1965)

6   New York . . . is not Mecca. It just smells like it.

    California Suite (1976)

SIMON, Paul
US singer/songwriter (1941–   )

7   Like a bridge over troubled water,
    I will ease your mind.

    Song, 'Bridge Over Troubled Water' (1970)

8   The words of the prophet are written
    On the subway halls and tenement walls.

    Song, 'Sound of Silence' (1970)

9   Still Crazy After All These Years.

    Song and album title (1975)

'SIMPLE, Peter' (Michael Wharton)
British columnist (1913–)

1   Rentacrowd Ltd, the enterprising firm which supplies crowds for all occasions and has done so much to keep progressive causes in the public eye.

    In 'The Way of the World', the *Daily Telegraph*, 1962 and *passim* thereafter

SIMPSONS, THE
US TV cartoon series, 1990–.

2   *Bart Simpson:* Eat my shorts!

    Catchphrase

3   *Bart:* I'm Bart Simpson—who the hell are you?

    Catchphrase

4   *Bart:* Underachiever and proud of it.

    Catchphrase

SIMS, George R.
British writer (1847–1922)

5   It is Christmas Day in the Workhouse.

    The Dagonet and Other Poems (1903)

SITWELL, Dame Edith
British poetess (1887–1964)

6   The fire was furry as a bear.

    'Dark Song', *Façade* (1922)

7   Still falls the Rain—
    Dark as the world of man, black as our loss—
    Blind as the nineteen hundred and forty nails
    Upon the cross.

    Still Falls the Rain (1940)

8   *On novelist Ethel Mannin:*
    I do not want Miss Mannin's feelings to be hurt by the fact that I have never heard of her . . . At the moment I am debarred from the pleasure of putting her in her place by the fact that she has not got one.

    Quoted in J. Pearson, *Façades*
    Used subsequently about various other targets.

1   *On Virginia Woolf:*
    I enjoyed talking to her, but thought *nothing* of her writing. I considered her 'a beautiful little knitter'.

    Letter to G. Singleton, 11 July 1955

SITWELL, Sir Osbert
British writer (1892–1969)

2   Educated: in the holidays from Eton.

    Entry in *Who's Who* (1929)

SKELTON, Noel
British Conservative politician (1880–1935)

3   To state as clearly as may be what means lie ready to develop a property-owning democracy, to bring the industrial and economic status of the wage-earner abreast of his political and educational, to make democracy stable and four-square . . .

    Article in the *Spectator*, 19 May 1923
    The phrase 'property-owning democracy' was later popularized by Anthony Eden and Winston Churchill (1946).

SLOGANS

(in alphabetical order)

4   All human life is there.

    Advertising slogan for the *News of the World*, 1958–9. A quotation from Henry James.

5   All power to the soviets.

    Workers in Petrograd, 1917.

6   Any time, any place, anywhere.

    Martini ads., UK, 1970s.

7   At sixty miles an hour the loudest noise in this new Rolls-Royce comes from the electric clock.

    Rolls-Royce advertisements, US, from 1958. From a car test by the Technical Editor of the *Motor*.

8   Avoid 'five o'clock shadow'.

    Slogan for Gem Razors and Blades, US, from the 1930s on.

9   B.O. ('Body odour')

    Lifebuoy soap advertisements, US, from 1933.

10 Balfour must go.

    An early such slogan (*c*1905)—followed later by 'Eden Must Go' (1956) and 'Marples Must Go' (1962/3).

1   Ban the bomb.

Slogan of nuclear disarmament campaigners, initially in the US, from *c*1953.

2   Beanz means Heinz.

Heinz Baked Beans advertisements, UK, from 1960s.

3   Berlin by Christmas.

Anti-German slogan, in Britain, 1914.

4   Better red than dead.

Slogan of the British nuclear disarmament movement, from *c*1958.

5   The big one.

Circus slogan, dating from 1907 amalgamation of Ringling Brothers Circus with Barnum and Bailey.

6   Black is beautiful.

US civil rights slogan, from *c*1962 (when used by Stokely Carmichael).

7   Black power.

US civil rights slogan (used by Stokely Carmichael in 1966).

8   [Is it true . . .] blondes have more fun?

Clairol (hair colouring) advertisements, in US, from 1957.

9   Blow some my way.

Chesterfield cigarette advertisements, US, from 1926.

10 Bombs away with Curt Lemay.

Peace chant, US (1967).

11 Britain can take it.

British war-time slogan, 1940.

12 Burn, baby, burn!

Black extremist slogan, US, 1965.

13 Burn your bra!

Feminist slogan from US, *c*1970.

14 Can *you* tell Stork from butter?

Slogan for Stork margarine, UK, *c*1956.

15 Careless talk costs lives.

British war-time security slogan, from mid-1940.

1   Clunk, click, *every* trip.

Car seat-belt advertisements, UK, from 1971.

2   Come on, Aussie, come on.

Australian slogan, from song by Alan Johnston and Alan Stuart Morris, 1978.

3   Coughs and sneezes spread diseases.

UK war-time health slogan, from *c*1942.

4   Daddy, what did *you* do in the Great War?

Daughter to father in First World War recruiting poster.
This became the catchphrase, 'What did you do in the Great War, Daddy?'

5   Desperation, Pacification, Expectation, Acclamation, Realization.

UK advertisements for Fry's chocolate, from 1920s on.

6   Does she . . . or doesn't she? Only her hairdresser knows for sure.

Clairol (hair colour) advertisements, US, from 1955.

7   Don't ask a man to drink and drive.

UK road safety slogan, from 1964.

8   Don't forget the fruit gums, mum.

UK advertisements for Rowntree's Fruit Gums, 1958–61.

9   Drinka pinta milka day.

Slogan for the National Milk Publicity Council of England and Wales, 1958.

10 Dull it isn't.

UK recruiting advertisements for Metropolitan police, 1972.

11 The East is red.

Chinese communist slogan, in song, from 1960s.

12 *Ein Reich, ein Volk, ein Führer* ('One realm, one people, one leader').

German Nazi slogan, from 1934.

13 *Enosis* ('Union').

Call for unification of Cyprus with mainland Greece, from 1952.

14 Even your best friends won't tell you.

Advertisements for mouthwash, probably Listerine.

1 Export or die.

UK slogan, 1940s.

2 The eyes and ears of the world.

Paramount News (cinema newsreel), UK, 1927–57.

3 The family that prays together stays together.

Devised by Al Scalpone for the Roman Catholic Rosary Crusade in the US (1947).

4 Food shot from guns.

Slogan for Quaker Puffed Wheat and Puffed Rice, originally in the US, from the early 1900s.

5 Go for gold.

Olympic slogan, from 1980, especially in the US.

6 Go for it.

Widely used in business from the early 1980s—also by Jane Fonda in aerobics ('Go for it, go for the burn').

7 Go to work on an egg.

Slogan for British Egg Marketing Board, 1958.

8 Gone for a Burton.

Slogan possibly used to promote a Bass beer in the UK, in the 1930s, giving rise to the Second World War expression meaning to have gone missing, presumed dead. No evidence of its use as a slogan survives.

9 Guinness is good for you.

Guinness beer, UK, from 1929.

10 Gung ho.

Chinese for 'Work together', adopted by US Marines under General Carlson during the Second World War.

11 Hang the Kaiser!

Slogan promoted by Northcliffe newspapers and others at the time of the Versailles Peace Conference, 1919.

12 Hearts and minds.

US Government slogan of sorts—meaning what had to be won—in the Vietnam War.

13 Heineken refreshes the parts other beers cannot reach.

Heineken lager advertisements, UK, from 1975.

14 Hell no, we won't go!

US anti-war chant, 1965.

1 Hey, hey, L. B. J., how many kids did you kill today?

Anti-President Johnson chant during Vietnam War, c1966.

2 I bet *he* drinks Carling Black Label.

UK, by 1990.

3 I like Ike.

Republican slogan, supporting Dwight D. Eisenhower's bid for the US
Presidency, from 1947.

4 I love New York.

Slogan, originally for the New York State Department of Commerce,
from 1977.

5 ***Illegitimi(s) non carborundum.*** ('Don't let the bastards grind you
down').

Cod Latin phrase used by US General 'Vinegar Joe' Silwell as his motto
during the Second World War, although he did not devise it.
'Carborundum' is the trade name for silicon carbide, used in grinding.

6 I'm backing Britain.

Campaign slogan, UK, 1968.

7 I'm only here for the beer.

Slogan for Double Diamond beer, in the UK, from 1971.

8 Is your journey really necessary?

British war-time travel slogan, from 1939.

9 It beats . . . as it sweeps . . . as it cleans.

Slogan for Hoover carpet sweepers, originally in the US, from 1919.

10 I thought . . . until I discovered Smirnoff.

Slogan for Smirnoff vodka in the UK, from 1970–5.

11 It's fingerlickin' good.

Advertisements for Kentucky Fried Chicken, originally US, by 1958.

12 It's so bracing.

Advertisements for Skegness, UK holiday resort, with jolly fisherman
symbol, from 1909.

13 I was a seven stone weakling.

Line from Charles Atlas body-building advertising—originally in the
US—from 1920s on.

14 Keep on truckin'.

Slogan of cartoon character devised by Robert Crumb and generally
popular from late 1960s.

1 Labour isn't working.

British Conservative Party slogan 1978/9, on poster showing dole queue.

2 Let's get America moving again.

Slogan used by John F. Kennedy in US Presidential Election, 1960.

3 Life's better with the Conservatives . . . don't let Labour ruin it.

British Conservative Party slogan, 1959.

4 LS/MFT ('Lucky Strike Means Finer Tobacco').

Lucky Strike cigarette advertisements, US, from 1940s?

5 Make do and mend.

UK war-time slogan, 1940s, based on Royal Navy expression for free time devoted especially to mending clothes.

6 Make love, not war.

'Peacenik'/'Flower Power' slogan from mid-1960s. Also attrib. to G. Legman (sic), sexologist, of the Kinsey Institute.

7 The man you love to hate.

Referring to the actor, Erich von Stroheim, for his role in the film *The Heart of Humanity* (1918).

8 Mean! Moody! Magnificent!

Advertisement, US, for Jane Russell film *The Outlaw* (1943).

9 Nation shall speak peace unto nation.

First motto of the BBC (1927), suggested by Dr Montague Rendall, and echoing Micah 4:3: 'Nation shall not lift up a sword against nation.'

10 Never again.

Slogan of the Jewish Defence League, from 1960s. Referring to the 'Holocaust' of the Second World War—though it had been used generally about wars before this.

11 Never knowingly undersold.

Sales policy of John Lewis Partnership, UK, from 1920s on.

12 Nice one, Cyril.

Line from TV advertisements for Wonderloaf bread, in the UK, 1972. Later taken up by supporters of footballer, Cyril Knowles.

13 Ninepence for fourpence.

Promoting contributory national insurance, in the UK, c1908, principally by David Lloyd George.

1   No more war.

Recurrent slogan during the century.

2   Nothing over sixpence.

Slogan for Woolworth stores in UK, from after 1909.

3   Often a bridesmaid, but never a bride.

US advertisements for Listerine mouthwash, from 1923 on. The song 'Why Am I Always the Bridesmaid, Never the Blushing Bride' was written in 1917 by Lily Morris, Charles Collins and Fred W. Leigh.

4   Out of the closets and into the streets.

Slogan for US Gay Liberation Front, from *c*1969.

5   Power to the people.

Slogan of the US Black Panther movement, 1969—later taken up by others.

6   Put a tiger in your tank.

Slogan for Esso petroleum, worldwide, from *c*1964. Possibly inspired by the song '(I Want to Put a) Tiger in Your Tank' (by W. Dixon).

7   Safety first.

British Conservative Party slogan, General Election, 1929—but earlier road safety use.

8   Save water—bath with a friend.

Semi-official slogan, UK, from mid-1970s.

9   Say it with flowers.

Slogan originally devised for the Society of American Florists, 1917.

10   Second front now.

Demand for invasion of the European mainland (with Soviet help), current 1942–3.

11   Snap . . . crackle . . . pop!

Line from Kellogg's Rice Krispies advertising, originally in the US, from *c*1928.

12   Someone, somewhere, wants a letter from you.

UK Post Office slogan, 1960s.

13   Stop me and buy one.

Slogan for vendors of T. Walls & Sons ice cream, UK, from 1923.

14   Strength through joy *(Kraft durch Freude)*.

A German Labour Front slogan, coined *c*1933 by Robert Ley, also used as the name of a Nazi organization which provided regimented leisure.

1 That'll do nicely, sir.

UK advertisements for American Express credit card, 1970s.

2 That's a h**l of a way to run a railroad!

Advertising for Boston & Maine railroad (in the 1930s). Derived from cartoon in a US magazine (c1932) showing two trains about to collide. A signalman comments: 'Tch-tch—what a way to run a railroad!'

3 Thirteen wasted years (of Tory misrule).

Unofficial Labour Party slogan, UK, prior to 1964 General Election.

4 Today . . ., tomorrow the world!

Probable origin is in 'Heute Presse der Nationalsozialitsen, Morgen Presse der Nation' ('Today the press of the Nazis, tomorrow the press of the nation'), slogan for the National Socialist Press in Germany, in the early 1930s.

5 Top people take The Times.

Slogan for the London paper, from 1957.

6 Try it, you'll like it.

Waiter encouraging customer to indulge himself, in Alka-Seltzer advertisements, US, from 1971.

7 Votes for women.

Slogan of the Women's Social and Political Union (suffragettes), in UK, from October 1905.

8 Walls have ears.

British war-time security slogan, early 1940s, employing an established phrase.

9 The weekend starts here.

UK TV pop show, Ready, Steady, Go!, from 1963.

10 We never closed.

Windmill Theatre, London, referring to the period of the Blitz in the Second World War.

11 We shall overcome.

From a song with a long history, revived 1946, becoming the civil rights anthem of the 1960s.

12 We want eight and we won't wait.

Popular cry in UK, 1908, for building of more Dreadnought battleships.

1   When You Got It, Flaunt It.

Line from advertising for US Braniff airline, c1969. Probably taken from the film *The Producers* (1967), where the line is spoken to the owner of a large limousine.

2   Where's the Beef?

Wendy Hamburgers, US, 1984. And used by Walter Mondale in the same year to describe what he saw as a lack of substance in the policies of his rival for the Democratic Presidential nomination, Gary Hart.

3   Which twin has the Toni?

Headline from advertising for Toni home perms, originally US, from early 1950s.

4   Who dares, wins.

Motto of UK Special Air Services regiment, from 1940s on.

5   Wot, no Watneys?

Beer slogan 1940s/50s derived from Second World War graffiti bewailing shortages in the UK—e.g. 'Wot no beer/char/cake?' etc.

6   Would you be more careful if it was you that got pregnant?

Family planning campaign for Health Education Council, 1970. On poster of 'pregnant' man.

7   Yesterday's men.

Labour Party election slogan (referring to Conservative leaders), 1970.

8   You don't have to be Jewish . . .

Used to promote Levy's rye bread, US, from 1967—but a show with this title had run on Broadway in 1965.

9   You'll wonder where the yellow went
When you brush your teeth with Pepsodent.

Pepsodent toothpaste advertisements, US, from 1950s.

10   You too can have a body like mine.

Slogan for Charles Atlas body-building courses—originally in the US—from 1920s on.

11   Your country needs you!

Advertisement on cover of *London Opinion*, 5 September 1914, and subsequently used on recruiting posters.

12   Your king and country need you.

Advertisement in newspapers, 5 August 1914.

13   You're never alone with a Strand.

Notably unsuccessful slogan for Strand cigarettes, UK, 1960.

1   You've come a long way baby.

    Virginia Slims cigarette advertisements, US, from 1968.

2   You want the best seats, we have them.

    Keith Prowse ticket agency, UK, from 1925.

SMITH, Alfred E.
US politician (1873–1944)

3   *Referring to Hearst press support for a rival:*
    The kiss of death.

    Speech, 25 October 1926

4   *On the folly of attacking Government benefit programmes:*
    Nobody shoots at Santa Claus.

    Campaign speeches, 1936
    First said of the New Deal, 1933.

5   No matter how thin you slice it, it's still baloney.

    ibid

SMITH, Bessie
US blues singer (1894–1937)

6   When my bed is empty,
    Makes me feel awful mean and blue.
    My springs are getting rusty,
    Living single like I do.

    Song, 'Empty Bed Blues' (*c*1928)

SMITH, Cyril (later Sir Cyril)
British Liberal politician (1928–)

7   If the fence is strong enough I'll sit on it.

    Quoted in the *Observer*, 15 September 1974

SMITH, Edward
British sea captain (18??–1912)

8   *Reputed last words before going down with the **Titanic**:*
    Be British, boys, be British.

    Attrib

SMITH, F. E. (later 1st Earl of Birkenhead)
British lawyer and Liberal politician (1872–1930)

1   *To Mr Justice Darling who had asked who George Robey was:*
    Mr George Robey is the Darling of the music-halls, m'lud.

    Quoted in W. Churchill, *Great Contemporaries*

2   *When Labour MP, J. H. Thomas complained he "ad a 'eadache':*
    Try taking a couple of aspirates.

    Attrib

3   *To judge who complained that he was no wiser at the end than when he had started hearing one of Smith's cases:*
    Possibly not, My Lord, but far better informed.

    Quoted in Birkenhead, *Life of F. E. Smith*

4   *On Winston Churchill:*
    Winston has devoted the best years of his life to preparing his impromptu speeches.

    Attrib

5   The world continues to offer glittering prizes to those who have stout hearts and sharp swords.

    Rectorial Address, Glasgow University, 7 November 1923

SMITH, Ian
Rhodesian Prime Minister (1919–   )

6   We have the happiest Africans in the world.

    Quoted in the *Observer*, 28 November 1971

7   Let me say again, I don't believe in black majority rule ever in Rhodesia. Not in a thousand years.

    Radio broadcast, 20 March 1976
    It came about in 1979.

SMITH, Logan Pearsall
US writer (1865–1946)

8   People say that life is the thing, but I prefer reading.

    Afterthoughts (1931)

9   A best-seller is the gilded tomb of a mediocre talent.

    ibid

10 Thank heavens, the sun has gone in, and I don't have to go out and enjoy it.

    Last Words (1933)
    Not his dying words, as sometimes asserted.

SMITH, Stevie
British poetess (1902–71)

1 Not Waving, But Drowning.

Title of poem (1957)

SNAGGE, John
British broadcaster (1904–)

2 I don't know who's ahead—it's either Oxford or Cambridge.

Radio commentary on Oxford and Cambridge University Boat Race, 1949

SNOW, C. P. (later Lord Snow)
British novelist and scientist (1905–80)

3 The official world, the corridors of power, the dilemmas of conscience and egotism—she disliked them all.

Homecomings (1956)
Snow later used 'Corridors of Power' as the title of a novel (1964).

4 The Two Cultures and the Scientific Revolution.

Title of Rede Lecture, Cambridge (1959)
'The two cultures' had been used earlier as the title of an article in the *New Statesman* (6 October 1956) and became a way of describing the lack of understanding between the camps of science and literature/religion.

SNOWDEN, Philip (later Viscount Snowden)
British socialist politician (1864–1937)

5 I hope you have read the election programme of the Labour Party. It is the most fantastic and impracticable programme ever put before the electors . . . This is not Socialism. It is Bolshevism run mad.

Radio election broadcast, 17 October 1931
Snowden, who had been Chancellor of the Exchequer in the 1929 Labour Government, was now supporting the National Government.

SOME LIKE IT HOT
US film 1959. Script by Billy Wilder and I. A. L. Diamond. With Joe E. Brown.

6 *Last line:*
JEB (to Jack Lemmon, in drag, who has confessed that he is not a woman):
Nobody's perfect.

Soundtrack

SOMOZA, Anastasio
Nicaraguan dictator (1925–80)

7 Indeed, you won the elections, but I won the count.

Quoted in *The Guardian*, 17 June 1977

SONG TITLES

1 Another little drink wouldn't do us any harm.

By Clifford Grey to music by Nat D. Ayer, included in the show *The Bing Boys are Here* (1916)

2 (If you want to know the time) Ask a p'liceman (1901).

By E. W. Rogers (1864–1913) with A. E. Durandeau.

3 C'mon, baby, light my fire (1967).

By Jim Morrison (1943–71) and others.

4 Don't go down in the mine, Dad (1910).

Words by Robert Donnelly, music by Will Geddes. Usually quoted as 'Don't go down the mine, Daddy'.

5 Down in the Forest (Something Stirred).

Words by H. Simpson, music by Sir Landon Ronald.

6 I Don't Like Mondays.

Written and performed by Bob Geldof and the Boom Town Rats (1979), this song takes its title from the reply given by Brenda Spencer, a San Diego schoolgirl, who killed and wounded several people, when asked why she had done it.

7 Into Each Life Some Rain Must Fall (1944).

Written by Roberts/Fisher. Quoting from Longfellow's 'The Rainy Day' (1841–6).

8 I Took My Harp To a Party (But Nobody Asked Me to Play) (1933).

A Desmond Carter-Noel Gay composition.

9 Life is just a bowl of cherries (1931).

By Lew Brown to music by Ray Henderson, in the musical *Scandals of 1931*.

10 Mighty Lak' a Rose (1901).

By Frank L. Stanton, to music by Ethelbert Nevin.

11 Naughty, but nice.

There is more than one song incorporating this phrase, starting with 'It's naughty, but it's nice', a US song of the 1890s (Minnie Schultz sang it). It was used as a film title in 1939. There followed a Johnny Mercer/Harry Warren composition for *Belle of New York* in 1952.

12 *Non, je ne regrette rien.* ('*No, I don't regret anything*')

Lyrics by Michael Vaucaire, to music by Charles Dumont. Popularized by Edith Piaf (1915–63).

13 Open the door, Richard! (1947)

Words by 'Dusty' Fletcher and John Mason.

1   Pennies from Heaven (1937).

Written by Johnny Burke. Music by Arthur Johnston.

2   Praise the Lord, and pass the ammunition (1942).

Used as the title of a song by Frank Loesser, this is supposed to have been said originally by an American naval chaplain during the Japanese attack on Pearl Harbor. The names of Howell M. Forgy (1908–83) and W. H. Maguire (1890–1953) are those of possible perpetrators. In fact, the phrase dates from the American Civil War.

3   See you later, alligator (1956).

Written by Robert Guidry.

4   Sex & Drugs & Rock & Roll (1977).

Ian Dury and Chaz Jankel wrote the song whose title almost became a youth slogan.

5   She's a Bird in a Gilded Cage.

Written by J. Lamb (1870–1928).

6   There'll always be an England (1939).

By Ross Parker and Hughie Charles.

7   To Know Him Is To Love Him (1958)

By Phil Spector, who took the title from his father's gravestone. The phrase, referring to Christ, also appears in a religious chorus, current in 1928.

8   *(Mais apart ça, Madame la Marquise) Tout va très bien* (*'But apart from that, Madam, everything's all right?'*) (1936).

By Paul Misraki (1908–   ).

9   When You're All Dressed Up and No Place to Go (1912)

Written by Silvio Hein (1879–1928) and Benjamin Burt (1882–1950).

10   Where have all the flowers gone? (1961)

By Pete Seeger (1919–   ).

11   A Whiter Shade of Pale.

Written by Garry Brooker/Keith Reid and recorded by Procol Harum (1967).

SOUTHERN, Terry
US novelist (1924–)

1 *Last lines:*
While the hopeless ecstasy of his huge pent-up spasm began . . .
sweet Candy's melodious voice rang out through the temple in
truly mixed feelings: 'GOOD GRIEF—IT'S DADDY!'
Candy (1958).
Written with Mason Hoffenberg and originally published as by
'Maxwell Kenton'.

2 She says, 'Listen, who do I have to fuck to get *off* this picture?
Blue Movie (1970)
Also attributed to Shirley Wood of NBC TV in the 1960s as 'Who do
you have to fuck to get out of show business?' But, more likely, it
originated with some anonymous Hollywood starlet of the 1930s.

SPARK, Muriel
British novelist (1918–)

3 I am putting old heads on young shoulders . . . and all my pupils
are the *crème de la crème.*
The Prime of Miss Jean Brodie (1961)

4 Give me a girl at an impressionable age, and she is mine for life.
ibid
Compare the old Jesuit saying: 'Give us a child until it is seven and it is
ours for life.'

SPENCER, Sir Stanley
British painter (1891–1959)

5 Painting is saying 'Ta' to God.
Quoted in letter to the *Observer* from his daughter Shirin, 7 February
1988

SPENDER, Stephen (later Sir Stephen)
British poet (1909–)

6 I think continually of those who were truly great . . .
The names of those who in their lives fought for life,
Who wore at their hearts the fire's centre.
Born of the sun, they travelled a short while towards the sun
And left the vivid air signed with their honour.
'I Think Continually of Those Who Were Truly Great' (1930–3)

SPOONER, Revd William
British academic (1844–1930)

1   *To Oxford undergraduate after the First World War:*
    Was it you or your brother who was killed in the war?
    Attrib

2   Through a dark glassly . . .
    Attrib by James Laver, in conversation with the author (1969)
    The word 'spoonerism' had already been coined by 1900 and most of
    the famous examples must have occurred by that date.

3   *To Sir Julian Huxley:*
    It is no further from the north coast of Spitsbergen to the North
    Pole than it is from Land's End to John of Gaunt.
    Quoted in W. Hayter, *Spooner*

4   Poor soul—very sad; her late husband, you know, a very sad
    death—eaten by missionaries—poor soul.
    In ibid

SPRING, Howard
British novelist (1889–1965)

5   The author of this novel and all the characters mentioned in it are
    completely fictitious. There is no such city as Manchester.
    Shabby Tiger (1934)

SPRING-RICE, Sir Cecil
British diplomat and poet (1859–1918)

6   I vow to thee, my country—all earthly things above—
    Entire and whole and perfect, the service of my love.
    'I Vow to Thee, My Country' (1918)

7   And there's another country, I've heard of long ago—
    Most dear to them that love her, most great to them that know.
    ibid

8   And her ways are ways of gentleness and all her paths are Peace.
    ibid

SQUIRE, Sir John
British poet, essayist and critic (1884–1958)

9   I'm not so think as you drunk I am.
    'Ballade of Soporific Absorption' (1931)

STAGE DOOR

US film 1937. Script by Morrie Ryskind and Anthony Veiller, based on a play by Edna Ferber and George S. Kaufman. With Katharine Hepburn.

1   *KH (in a play within the film):* The Calla lilies are in bloom again. Such a strange flower, suitable to any occasion. I carried them on my wedding day, and now I place them here in memory of something that has died.

   Soundtrack

STALIN, Joseph

Soviet Communist leader (1879–1953)

2   *Pierre Laval, French Foreign minister, asked Stalin in 1935, 'Can't you do something to encourage religion and the Catholics in Russia? It would help me so much with the Pope'. Stalin replied:*
   Oho! The Pope! How many divisions has he got?

   Quoted in W.S. Churchill, *The Second World War*

3   He who is not with us is against us.

   Attrib
   Alluding to Jesus Christ (Luke 11:23). Josef Kadar (1912–89), the
   Hungarian leader, was wont to say, 'He who is not against us is with us.'

4   Gaiety is the most outstanding feature of the Soviet Union.

   Attrib

STALLINGS, Laurence

US writer (1894–1968)

5   Hollywood—a place where the inmates are in charge of the asylum.

   Attrib
   See also **ROWLAND 280:4** *and* **GEORGE 135:5.**

STANTON, Colonel Charles E.

US soldier (1859–1933)

6   *On the arrival of the American Expeditionary Force in France:*
   Here and now, in the presence of the illustrious dead, we pledge our hearts and our honour in carrying this war to a successful issue. Lafayette, we are here!

   Speech at tomb of Lafayette, Paris, 4 July 1917
   General Pershing may have originated the phrase, though—according
   to *Bartlett*—he disclaimed having said 'anything so splendid'.

STARTREK

US TV science fiction series, 1966–9, created by Gene Roddenberry (1921–91).
With William Shatner as Captain Kirk.

1   Space—the final frontier. These are the voyages of the starship
Enterprise. It's five year mission: to explore strange new worlds, to
seek out new life and new civilizations, to boldly go where no man
has gone before.

Introductory statement

2   □ *Kirk (to Lt. Commander 'Scotty' Scott, chief engineer):*
Beam me up, Scotty.

Catchphrase
'Beam us up, Mr Scott' appears to be the nearest thing actually spoken
in the series.

STAR WARS

US film 1977. Script by George Lucas.

3   May the Force be with you.

Repeated phrase

STEEL, David (later Sir David)
British Liberal politician (1938–   )

4   I have the good fortune to be the first Liberal leader for over half a
century who is able to say to you at the end of our annual assembly:
go back to your constituencies and prepare for government.

Speech, Liberal Party Assembly, Llandudno, 18 September 1981

STEFFENS, Lincoln
US journalist (1866–1936)

5   *After a visit to the Soviet Union in 1919:*
I have seen the future and it works.

Autobiography (1931)
It is said that Steffens had been rehearsing this formula even before he
went to the Soviet Union. Initially he said, 'I have been over into the
future, and it works.'

STEIN, Gertrude
US poetess (1874–1946)

6   Rose is a rose is a rose is a rose.

'Sacred Emily' (1913)
Frequently this is misquoted as 'A rose is . . . ' It may refer to Sir Francis
Rose, an English painter.

7   *Last words:*
What *is* the answer? . . . In that case, what is the question?

Quoted in D. Sutherland, *G.S., a Biography of her Work*
There is more than one version of what she said.

STEINBECK, John
US writer (1902–68)

1   A man got to do what he got to do.

> *The Grapes of Wrath* (1939)
> The earliest appearance traced of 'A man's gotta do what a man's gotta do', though maybe not original to Steinbeck.

2   *On critics:*
    Unless the bastards have the courage to give you unqualified praise, I say ignore them.

> Quoted in J.K. Galbraith, *A Life in Our Times*

STEPTOE AND SON
UK TV comedy series (BBC), from 1964–73. Script by Alan Simpson and Ray Galton. With Harry S. Corbett as the Younger Steptoe.

3   *Younger Steptoe (to father):*
    You dirty old man.

> Stock phrase

STEVENSON, Adlai
US Democratic politician (1900–65)

4   Eggheads of the world unite; you have nothing to lose but your yolks.

> Attrib
> 'Egghead' as a synonym for 'intellectual' was popularized by the columnist Joseph Alsop during the 1952 US Presidential campaign.

5   I suppose flattery hurts no one—that is, if he doesn't inhale.

> *Meet the Press*, TV broadcast, 29 March 1952

6   Someone asked me as I came down the street, how I felt, and I was reminded of a story that a fellow townsman used to tell—Abraham Lincoln. They asked him how he felt once after an unsuccessful election. He felt like a little boy who had stubbed his toe in the dark. He said that he was too old to cry, but it hurt too much to laugh.

> Speech, conceding defeat, 5 November 1952

7   A politician is a statesman who approaches every question with an open mouth.

> Attrib
> Also ascribed to Arthur Goldberg, on diplomats.

8   *Of the Republican Party:*
    [Needs to be] dragged kicking and screaming into the twentieth century.

> Quoted in K. Tynan, *Curtains*

1   I will make a bargain with the Republicans. If they will stop telling lies about the Democrats, we will stop telling the truth about them.

Campaign remark, 10 September 1952

Apparently this was originated by Senator Chauncey Depew about the Democrats earlier in the century.

STEVENSON, Sir Melford
British judge (1902–87)

2   *On living in Manchester, to the husband in a divorce case:*
A totally incomprehensible choice for any free human being to make.

Quoted in the *Daily Telegraph*, 11 April 1979

STOCKWOOD, Mervyn
British Anglican Bishop (1913–)

3   A psychiatrist is a man who goes to the *Folies-Bergère* and looks at the audience.

Quoted in the *Observer*, 15 October 1961

STONE, Irving
US author (1903–89)

4   The Agony and the Ecstasy.

Title of novel, 1961

STOPPARD, Tom
British playwright (1937–)

5   *In answer to journalists' clichéd question 'Where do you get your ideas from?':*
If I knew, I'd go there.

Attrib

Joyce Grenfell in *Joyce Grenfell Requests the Pleasure* (1976) stated that this was her reply to the question, 'Where do you get the ideas for your monologues?'

STORY, Jack Trevor
British novelist (1917–)

6   Live Now, Pay Later.

Title of screenplay (1962)

STRACHEY, Lytton
British biographer (1880–1932)

7   *When appearing before military tribunal as a conscientious objector in the First World War, he was asked what he would do if he saw a German soldier trying to rape his sister. He replied:*
I would try to get between them.

Quoted in R. Graves, *Goodbye To All That*

SULLIVAN, 'Big Tim'
US trade union leader

1   I don't care what the papers say about me as long as they spell my
     name right.

> Quoted in W. Safire, *Political Dictionary*

THE SUN
London newspaper

2   Page 3 girl.

> Stock phrase
> Name for (usually) topless model appearing on page three of the
> newspaper, from within one year of the paper's re-launch under
> Rupert Murdoch's ownership on 17 November 1969.

3   WINTER OF DISCONTENT. Lest we forget . . . the *Sun* recalls the
     long, cold months of industrial chaos that brought Britain to its
     knees.

> Headline to feature, 30 April 1979
> Probably the first major use of this phrase to characterize the industrial
> unrest of the winter of 1978/9. Alluding to Shakespeare, *King Richard
> III*, (I.i.1).

4   GOTCHA!

> Headline, 4 May 1982 (first edition only)
> On the sinking of the Argentine cruiser *General Belgrano* during the
> Falklands war.

5   FREDDIE STARR ATE MY HAMSTER—Comic put a live pet in
     sandwich, says beauty.

> Headline, 13 March 1986
> *See also* **CALLAGHAN 57.3.**

SUNDAY SPORT
London newspaper

6   WORLD WAR II BOMBER FOUND ON THE MOON.

> Headline, *c*1987

SUNSET BOULEVARD
US film 1950. Script by Charles Brackett, Billy Wilder and D. M. Marshman.
With Gloria Swanson as Norma Desmond and William Holden as Joe Gillis.

7   *Joe:* You used to be big in pictures.
     Norma: I *am* big. It's the pictures that got small.

> Soundtrack

SVEVO, Italo
Italian novelist (1861–1928)

1　There are three things I always forget. Names, faces, and—the third I can't remember.

Attrib

SWAFFER, Hannen
British journalist (1879–1962)

2　Freedom of the press in Britain is freedom to print such of the proprietor's prejudices as the advertisers don't object to.

In conversation with Tom Driberg, c1928

SYLVESTER, Victor
British ballroom orchestra conductor (1902–78)

3　Slow, slow, quick, quick, slow [quickstep tempo].

Stock phrase

TAKE IT FROM HERE

UK radio comedy series (BBC), from 1948 on. Script by Frank Muir and Denis Norden. With Jimmy Edwards, Dick Bentley and June Whitfield.

1   *Edwards:* Black mark, Bentley!

Catchphrase

2   *Edwards:* Gently, Bentley!

Catchphrase

3   *Eth (Whitfield):* Oh, Ron . . .
    Ron (Bentley): Yes, Eth?

Catchphrase in 'The Glums' sketches

TARZAN THE APE MAN

US film 1932. Script by Ivor Novello. With Johnny Weissmuller as Tarzan.

4   □ Me Tarzan, you Jane.

In fact he says simply 'Tarzan . . . Jane'. The line does not occur in the original novel by Edgar Rice Burroughs.

TEBBIT, Norman (later Lord Tebbit)

British Conservative politician (1931–)

5   *Of his father who had grown up in the 1930s:*
    He didn't riot. He got on his bike and looked for work and he kept looking till he found it.

Speech, Conservative Party Conference, 15 October 1981
A recipe for dealing with unemployment, popularly rendered as 'get on yer bike' echoing the expression 'on your bike', meaning 'go away'.

TELEGRAMS AND CABLES

6   HAVE STRONG SUSPICIONS THAT CRIPPEN LONDON CELLAR MURDERER AND ACCOMPLICE ARE AMONGST SALOON PASSENGERS MOUSTACHE TAKEN OFF GROWING BEARD ACCOMPLICE DRESSED AS BOY VOICE MANNER AND BUILD UNDOUBTEDLY A GIRL BOTH TRAVELLING AS MR AND MASTER ROBINSON.

From Captain Kendall to Scotland Yard, 22 July 1910
This was the first time a wireless telegraphy message from a ship at sea led to the arrest of criminals.

7   *Magazine editor to Cary Grant's agent:* HOW OLD CARY GRANT?
    Grant: OLD CARY GRANT FINE. HOW YOU?

Probably apocryphal.

8   WINSTON'S BACK.

Signal to all ships of the Royal Navy from the Admiralty when Winston Churchill was reappointed First Lord, 3 September 1939.

1 VERY SORRY CAN'T COME. LIE FOLLOWS BY POST.

Lord Charles Beresford (1846–1919) to the Prince of Wales after
receiving a dinner invitation at short notice. The same joke occurs in
Marcel Proust, *Le Temps retrouvé* (1927), as *'Impossible venir, mensonge
suit.'*

2 TO HELL WITH YOU. OFFENSIVE LETTER FOLLOWS.

To Sir Alec Douglas-Home.

3 SPREAD ALARM AND DESPONDENCY.

Wireless message to Vladimir Peniakoff, *c*18 May 1942, (using phrase
from the Army Acts).
See also **BENCHLEY 32:4, CHESTERTON 69:2, COWARD 87:1, 88:6; PARKER
250:1; WILDER 346:4.**

TELEVISION PROGRAMME TITLES

4 The Last of the Summer Wine.

This was writer Roy Clarke's provisional title for the BBC series
(1974–). It stuck, however, and it is not a quotation, though 'last of the
wine' is an established expression.

5 Mission Impossible.

Series (1966–72) to do with government agents and investigators in the
Impossible Missions Force. The title proved a useful phrase in other
situations.

6 Murder, She Wrote.

US series (from mid-1980s) featuring Angela Lansbury as a crime
writer. Originally, this title was given to a 1961 film of Agatha Christie's
story *4.50 from Paddington.* In turn, the title echoes that of the song,
'Murder, He Says' (*see* **LOESSER 205:4**), which was also the title of a
film in 1945.

7 The Name of the Game.

This US series (1968–71) grew out of the TV movie *Fame is the Name of
the Game* (1966) and helped launch a cliché phrase of the late 1960s.

8 Not So Much a Programme, More a Way of Life.

A usage (1964) which spawned many a 'Not so much a . . . ' variation.

9 Only Fools and Horses.

From an old Cockney expression, 'Only fools and horses work.'

10 Only in America.

This short series (1980) concerned immigration to the US—indeed
this was the 'immigrants' testament', an exclamation used especially by
those of Jewish stock. It is short for 'only in America could this happen
. . .'

1   Softly, Softly.

'Softly, softly, catchee monkee' has been described as a Negro proverb. More particularly, in this case, the title was taken from the saying's use as motto of the Lancashire Constabulary Training School—which inspired the BBC series (1966–76).

2   Some Mothers Do 'ave 'Em.

An old northern English expression, popularized in the 1950s and 60s by the comedian Jimmy Clitheroe (1916–73). In his radio shows he would say, 'Don't some mothers 'ave 'em?'

3   thirtysomething.

Written as such, this title (1987–91) proved a handy tag for a certain age group and its concerns.

4   Who Pays the Ferryman?

Not a quotation but an allusion to the Greek legend of Charon who demanded a fee to ferry the dead across the River Styx.
See also **THAT WAS THE WEEK THAT WAS 322:7.**

THATCHER, Margaret (later Baroness Thatcher)
British Conservative Prime Minister (1925–   )

5   No woman in my time will be Prime Minister or Chancellor or Foreign Secretary—not the top jobs. Anyway, I wouldn't want to be Prime Minister. You have to give yourself 100%.

Interview, the *Sunday Telegraph*, 26 October 1969

6   *When Secretary of State for Education:*
I do not think there will be a woman Prime Minister in my lifetime . . . I would not wish to be Prime Minister, dear. I have not enough experience for that job. The only full ministerial position I've held is Minister of Education and Science. Before you could even *think* of being Prime Minister, you'd need to have done a good deal more jobs than that.

Interviewed on *Val Meets the VIPS*, BBC TV, 1973

7   I owe nothing to Women's Lib.

Attrib in the *Observer*, 1 December 1974

1 Ladies and gentlemen, I stand before you tonight in my green chiffon evening gown, my face softly made up, my fair hair gently waved . . . the Iron Lady of the Western World. Me? A cold war warrior? Well, yes—if that is how they wish to interpret my defence of values, and freedoms fundamental to our way of life.

Speech, 31 January 1976
On 19 January, she had said: 'The Russians are bent on world dominance . . . the Russians put guns before butter.' A week later, the Soviet Defence Ministry newspaper *Red Star*, in an article signed by Captain Y. Gavrilov, had accused this 'Iron Lady' of seeking to revive the Cold War. The article wrongly suggested that she was already known by this nickname in the UK at the time. On the other hand, Marjorie Proops had already referred to her as the 'Iron Maiden' in the *Daily Mirror* on 5 February 1975.

2 There are a few times when I get home at night and everything has got on top of me when I shed a few tears, silently, alone.

Interview, *Woman's World*, September 1978

3 Let us make this a country safe to work in. Let us make this a country safe to walk in. Let us make it a country safe to grow up in. Let us make it a country safe to grow old in. And [the message of the 'other' Britain] says, above all, may this land of ours, which we love so much, find dignity and greatness and peace again.

Political broadcast, 30 April 1979
The final sentence contains an unattributed quotation. *See* **COWARD 87:7.**

4 *On becoming Prime Minister:*
I would just like to remember some words of St Francis of Assisi which I think are really just particularly apt at the moment— 'Where there is discord, may we bring harmony; where there is error may we bring truth; where there is doubt, may we bring faith; and where there is despair, may we bring hope.'

Outside 10 Downing Street, 4 May 1979
Actually, there is some doubt as to whether St Francis had anything to do with the prayer at all. A former Bishop of Ripon writing to the *Church Times* suggested the prayer was of French origin and probably no older than the 19th century.

5 There is no easy popularity in that [harsh economic measures already set in train by the Government] but I believe people accept there is no alternative.

Speech, Conservative Women's Conference, 21 May 1980
And on several occasions thereafter.

1   To those waiting with bated breath for that favourite media
    catchphrase, the U-turn, I have only one thing to say. You turn if
    you want to. The *lady's not for turning.*
    Speech, Conservative Party Conference, 11 October 1980

2   Failure? Do you remember what Queen Victoria once said?
    'Failure?—the possibilities do not exist.'
    TV news interview, at start of Falklands war, 5 April 1982

3   *On the recapture of South Georgia, to newsmen outside 10 Downing Street:*
    Just rejoice at that news and congratulate our forces and the
    Marines. Goodnight. Rejoice!
    TV news coverage, 25 April 1982
    Usually rendered as, 'Rejoice! Rejoice!'

4   *Victorian values* . . . those were the values when our country became
    great, not only internationally but at home.
    During TV interview with Brian Walden, 17 January 1983
    Walden fed her the phrase.

5   We had to fight the enemy without in the Falklands. We always have
    to be aware of the *enemy within* which is more difficult to fight and
    more dangerous to liberty.
    Speech to 1922 Committee, 19 July 1984

6   *On her feelings after she had escaped death in the IRA bomb explosion at
    Brighton:*
    In church on Sunday morning—it was a lovely morning and we
    haven't had many lovely days—the sun was coming through a
    stained-glass window and falling on some flowers, falling right
    across the church. It just occurred to me that this was the day I was
    meant not to see.
    TV interview, 14 October 1984

7   I like Mr Gorbachev, we can do business together.
    Remark, TV news, 17 December 1984

8   We must try to find ways to starve the terrorists of the *oxygen of
    publicity* on which they depend.
    Speech to American Bar Association meeting in London, 15 July 1985

9   *To reporters, on the question of local unemployment:*
    Stop being moaning minnies.
    Remark, Tyneside, 11 September 1985

10 *On reviewing candidates for appointments:*
    Is he one of us?
    Attrib, 1980s

1   *On her future as Prime Minister:*
    Yes, I hope to go on and on.
    BBC interview with John Cole, 11 May 1987
    Possibly repeating an earlier remark.

2   *To broadcasting executives:*
    Broadcasting is the last bastion of restrictive practices in British
    industry.
    Remark, 20 September 1987

3   We have not successfully rolled back the frontiers of the state in
    Britain, only to see them re-imposed at a European level, with a
    European super-state exercising a new dominance from Brussels.
    Speech, Bruges, 20 September 1988

4   We have become a grandmother.
    Remark to newsmen, 3 March 1989

5   *On being forced out of office:*
    It's a funny old world.
    Remark to the Cabinet, 22 November 1990

6   Home is where you come to when you have nothing better to do.
    Interview, *Vanity Fair*, May 1991
    The meaning of this observation was disputed. She was addressing the
    comment to her children . . . meaning their home was always there.

THAT WAS THE WEEK THAT WAS
UK TV satire series (BBC), 1962–3. Title also used in the US.

7   That Was the Week That Was.
    Title
    Said to have been suggested by the actor John Bird (*b*1936) in
    imitation of the 'That's Shell—That Was' advertisements of the early
    1930s. Often abbreviated to 'TW3'.

8   Well, it was satire, wasn't it? . . . You can say bum, you can say po,
    you can say anything . . . Well, he said it! The thin one! He said
    bum one night. I heard him! Satire!
    Sketch, 'Close Down' (by Keith Waterhouse and Willis Hall)
    See also **FROST 129:3.**

THEROUX, Paul
US writer (1941–   )

9   Ever since childhood, when I lived within earshot of the Boston and
    Maine, I have seldom heard a train go by and not wished I was on
    it.
    The Great Railway Bazaar (1975)

THE THING

US film 1951, (known in the UK as *The Thing From Another World*)

1   *Last speech:*
    I bring you warning—to every one listening to the sound of my
    voice. Tell the world, tell this to everyone wherever they are: *watch
    the skies*, watch everywhere, keep looking—*watch the skies!*

    Soundtrack
    The key phrase was later used to promote the film *Close Encounters of the
    Third Kind* (1977) and was the original title of that film.

THE THIRD MAN

UK film 1949. Script by Graham Greene and Carol Reed. With Orson Welles as
Harry Lime.

2   *Harry Lime:* You know what the fellow said—in Italy, for thirty years
    under the Borgias, they had warfare, terror, murder and
    bloodshed, but they produced Michelangelo, Leonardo da Vinci
    and the Renaissance. In Switzerland, they had brotherly love; they
    had five hundred years of democracy and peace—and what did that
    produce? The cuckoo clock.

    Soundtrack
    Welles contributed this part of the script, as Graham Greene
    confirmed to the author (1978). Welles suggested that the lines came
    originally from 'an old Hungarian play'.

THOMAS, Dylan
British poet (1914–53)

3   And Death Shall Have no Dominion.

    Title of poem (1943)
    Compare Romans 6:9: 'Christ being raised from the dead dieth no
    more, death hath no more dominion over him.'

4   Time held me green and dying
    Though I sang in my chains like the sea.

    'Fern Hill' (1946)

5   Do not go gentle into that good night.
    Rage, rage against the dying of the light.

    'Do Not Go Gentle Into That Good Night' (1951)

6   It is spring, moonless night in the small town, starless and bible-
    black.

    Under Milk Wood (1954)

7   Will you take this woman Matti Richards . . . to be your awful
    wedded wife?

    ibid

1   Oh, isn't life a terrible thing, thank God?
    ibid

2   It's organ organ all the time with him . . . Up every night until
    midnight playing the organ . . . I'm a martyr to music.
    ibid

3   Praise the Lord! We are a musical nation.
    ibid

4   The land of my fathers—my fathers can have it.
    Quoted in J. Ackerman, *Dylan Thomas*

5   Someone's boring me. I think it's me.
    Quoted in R. Heppenstall, *Four Absentees* (1960)

6   An alcoholic is someone you don't like who drinks as much as you
    do.
    Quoted in C. Fitzgibbon, *Life of Dylan Thomas* (1965)

7   *When asked, 'Why did you come to the US?':*
    To continue my lifelong search for naked women in wet
    mackintoshes.
    Attrib

8   *Boast to a girlfriend towards the end of his life:*
    I've had eighteen straight whiskies. I think that's the record . . .
    After thirty-nine years, this is all I've done.
    Attrib
    He had probably only had four or five.

THOMAS, Edward
British poet (1878–1917)

9   Yes; I remember Adlestrop —
    The name, because one afternoon
    Of heat the express-train drew up there
    Unwontedly. It was late June.
    'Adlestrop', *Poems* (1917)

THOMAS, George (later Viscount Tonypandy)
British Labour politician (1909–   )

1   *As Speaker of the House of Commons:*
Order, order!

Stock phrase
The traditional cry became very much his own when radio broadcasts
of proceedings in parliament began on 3 April 1978.

2   He who commands must be a bridge (*'Bid ben, bid bont'*)

Motto, on assuming peerage
From the *Mabinogion*, ancient Welsh folk stories.

THOMAS, Gwyn
British writer (1913–81)

3   There are still parts of Wales where the only concession to gaiety is
a striped shroud.

Article in *Punch*, 18 June 1958

4   She was a blonde—with a brunette past.

Broadcast, BBC2 TV *Line-Up*, 25 October 1969

THOMAS, Irene
British broadcaster (1920–   )

5   No matter how you have searched, there will always be one
teaspoon left at the bottom of the washing-up water.

The Bandsman's Daughter (1979)

THOMPSON, Hunter S.
US writer (1939–   )

6   Fear and Loathing in Las Vegas.

Title of book (1972)
After articles in *Rolling Stone*, 11/25 November 1971.

THOMPSON, William Hale 'Big Bill'
US politician and Mayor of Chicago (1867–1944)

7   *On what he would do if King George V were ever to set foot in Chicago:*
□ I'd punch him in the snoot.

No direct quotation exists of whatever it was he said when running for
a third term in 1927—'poke in the snoot', 'bust in the snoot' are other
reported versions—but his Anglophobia was not in question.

THOMSON, Roy (later Lord Thomson)
Canadian-born industrialist (1894–1976)

1 *To a neighbour in Edinburgh just after the opening of Scottish Television (a commercial TV company he had founded) in August 1957:*
You know, it's just like having a licence to print your own money.
Quoted in R. Braddon, *Roy Thomson*

2 Editorial is what keeps the ads apart.
Attrib

THORPE, Jeremy
British Liberal politician (1929–   )

3 *On the 'Night of the Long Knives', when Harold Macmillan sacked half his Cabinet, 1962:*
Greater love hath no man than this, that he lay down his friends for his life.
Remark, 13 July 1962
Alluding to St John 15:13.

4 *After a General Election which resulted in no party having a clear majority:*
Looking around the House, one realizes that we are all minorities now.
Speech, House of Commons, 6 March 1974
Alluding to 'We are all socialists nowadays'—a remark often attributed to King Edward VII as Prince of Wales in 1895, but in fact said before that date by Sir William Harcourt (1827–1904), the Liberal politician.

5 *To Norman Scott:*
Bunnies *can* (and *will*) go to France.
Private letter, 13 February 1961 (pub. 1976)
Scott later alleged they had had a homosexual relationship. Thorpe was acquitted in 1979 of plotting to murder him.

THURBER, James
US cartoonist and writer (1894–1961)

6 All right, have it your way—you heard a seal bark.
Caption to cartoon 'The Seal in the Bedroom' (1932)

7 The Secret Life of Walter Mitty.
Title of short story (1932)

8 Early to rise and early to bed makes a male healthy and wealthy and dead.
'The Shrike and the Chipmunks', *Fables for Our Time* (1940)

1   It's a Naive Domestic Burgundy without Any Breeding, But I Think
     You'll be amused by its Presumption.

     Caption to cartoon in *Men, Women and Dogs* (1943)

2   Well, if I Called the Wrong Number, Why Did You Answer the
     Phone?

     ibid

TILL DEATH US DO PART

UK TV comedy series (BBC), 1964–74. Script by Johnny Speight. With Warren
Mitchell as Alf Garnett.

3   *Alf (to his wife):*
     You silly (old) moo!

     Catchphrase

TIME

US news magazine

4   World War II began last week at 5.20 a.m. (Polish time) Friday,
     September 1, when a German bombing plane dropped a projectile
     on Puck, fishing village and air base in the armpit of the Hel
     Peninsula.

     September 1939
     Others, more cautiously, were only talking of 'the war in Europe' at
     this time.

TIMES, THE

London newspaper

5   *On the accession of King Edward VII:*
     We shall not pretend that there is nothing in his long career which
     those who respect and admire him would wish otherwise.

     Leading article, 23 January 1901

6   □ Small earthquake in Chile. Not many dead.

     Quoted in C. Cockburn, *I Claud*
     Cockburn claimed to have won a competition for dullness among sub-
     editors with this headline in the 1930s. However, an exhaustive search
     has failed to find it in the paper.

7   IT *IS* A MORAL ISSUE

     Title of leading article about the Profumo affair, 11 June 1963

1   At social gatherings he was liable to engage in heated and noisy
     arguments which could ruin a dinner party, and made him the
     dread of hostesses on both sides of the Atlantic. The tendency was
     exacerbated by an always generous, and occasionally excessive
     alcoholic intake.
     Obituary of Randolph Churchill, 7 June 1968
     Said to have been written by Malcolm Muggeridge.

2   Lord George-Brown drunk is a better man than the Prime Minister
     [Harold Wilson] sober.
     Leading article, 6 March 1976

3   WHO BREAKS A BUTTERFLY ON A WHEEL?
     Headline on leading article, 1 July 1967
     Alluding to Alexander Pope's *Epistle to Dr Arbuthnot* (1735). The
     editorial was about the prison term given to Mick Jagger on drugs
     charges.

TIMES LITERARY SUPPLEMENT, THE
London journal

4   *Reviewing Kenneth Grahame's* The Wind in the Willows *(1908):*
     As a contribution to natural history, the work is negligible.
     Quoted in P. Green, *The Life of Kenneth Grahame*

TO BE OR NOT TO BE
US film, 1942. Script by Edwin Justis Mayer. With Jack Benny as Joseph Tura,
Sig Rumann as Colonel Ehrhardt.

5   *Ehrhardt (to Tura, in disguise):*
     What he [Tura] did to Shakespeare, we are doing now to Poland.
     Soundtrack

6   *Tura (disguised as Ehrhardt):*
     So, they call me Concentration Camp Ehrhardt?!
     Soundtrack

TO HAVE AND HAVE NOT
US film 1945. Script by Jules Furthman and William Faulkner from the novel by
Ernest Hemingway. With Lauren Bacall as Slim and Humphrey Bogart as Steve.

7   *Slim:* You know you don't have to act with me, Steve. You don't have
     to say anything, and you don't have to do anything. Not a thing.
     Oh, maybe just whistle. You know how to whistle, don't you, Steve?
     You just put your lips together and blow.
     Soundtrack

TOLKIEN, J. R. R.
British novelist and academic (1892–1973)

1   In a hole in the ground there lived a hobbit.

The Hobbit (1937)

2   Nearly all marriages, even happy ones, are mistakes: in the sense that almost certainly (in a more perfect world, or even with a little more care in this very imperfect one) both partners might have found more suitable mates. But the real soul-mate is the one you are actually married to.

Letter to Michael Tolkien, 6–8 March 1941

TOLSTOY, Count Leo
Russian novelist (1828–1910)

3   *To Anton Chekhov:*
Shakespeare's plays are bad enough, but yours are even worse.

Remark, quoted in A. N. Wilson, *Tolstoy* (1988)

TOMALIN, Nicholas
British journalist (1931–73)

4   The only qualities essential for real success in journalism are rat-like cunning, a plausible manner, and a little literary ability.

Article in the *Sunday Times Magazine*, 26 October 1969

TO TELL THE TRUTH
US TV panel game, 1956–66. Also produced elsewhere.

5   *Host:* Will the real [person's name], please stand up!

Stock phrase
The panel tried to guess which two of three challengers were impostors.

TOYNBEE, Arnold
British historian (1889–1975)

6   *Pressing for a greater British voice in UNO, 1947:*
No annihilation without representation.

Attrib

7   America is a large, friendly dog in a very small room. Every time it wags its tail it knocks over a chair.

Attrib

TOYTOWN

UK radio children's drama series (BBC), 1940s/50s. Scripts from books by S. Hulme-Beaman. With Ralph de Rohan as Mr Grouser and Derek McCulloch as Larry the Lamb.

1   *Mr Growser:* It is disgraceful—it ought not to be allowed.

    Stock phrase

2   *Larry (bleating):* Larry the La-a-a-a-mb!

    Stock phrase

TREE, Sir Herbert Beerbohm

British actor-manager (1853–1917)

3   Sir, I have tested your machine [a gramophone]. It adds new terror to life and makes death a long-felt want.

    Quoted in H. Pearson, *Beerbohm Tree*

4   *Pointing at stamp in middle of sheet, at Post Office:*
    I'll have that one, please.

    In ibid

5   *To man struggling under the weight of a grandfather clock:*
    My poor fellow, why not carry a watch?

    In ibid

6   My nose bleeds for you.

    In ibid

7   *Of Israel Zangwill:*
    He is an old bore; even the grave yawns for him.

    In ibid

8   A committee should consist of three men, two of whom are absent.

    In ibid

9   *To unsuitable actresses:*
    Ladies, just a little more virginity, if you don't mind.

    Quoted in A. Woollcott, *Shouts and Murmurs* (1923)

TRINDER, Tommy

British comedian (1909–89)

10   You lucky people!

    Catchphrase

TROTSKY, Leon
Russian revolutionary (1879–1940)

1   *To his Menshevik opponents:*
Go where you belong from now on—the dustbin of history.
History of the Russian Revolution (1933)

TROUP, Bobby
US songwriter (1919–)

2   If you ever plan to motor west,
Travel my way, take the highway, that's the best,
Get your kicks on Route 66.
Song, 'Route 66' (1946)

TRUMAN, Harry S.
US Democratic President (1884–1972)

3   *To journalists, on succeeding F. D. Roosevelt:*
I don't know whether you fellows ever had a load of hay fall on you,
but when they told me yesterday what had happened, I felt like the
moon, the stars, and all the planets had fallen on me.
Remark, 1945

4   *On the Hiroshima atom bomb:*
This is the greatest thing in history.
Remark, 6 August 1945

5   *To Omar Bradley of General MacArthur:*
The son of a bitch isn't going to resign on me, I want him fired.
Attrib
Truman was about to sack MacArthur from his command of UN forces
in Korea, 1951, for insubordination.

6   If you can't stand the heat, get out of the kitchen.
Quoted *Time*, 28 April 1952
Possibly a cleaned-up version of an earthier expression, referring to
another room in the house.

7   The buck stops here.
Motto
Displayed on his desk in the Oval Office.

8   It's a recession when your neighbour loses his job: it's a depression
when you lose yours.
Quoted in the *Observer*, 13 April 1958

'TWAIN, Mark'
US writer (1835–1910)

1 Golf is a good walk spoiled.

Attrib

2 Always do right. This will gratify some people, and astonish the rest.

Talk to young people, Brooklyn, 16 February 1901

3 *Quoting Disraeli:*
There are lies, damn lies—and statistics.

Autobiography (1924)

THE TWO RONNIES
UK TV comedy series (BBC), from 1970s on. With Ronnie Barker and Ronnie Corbett.

4 *Corbett:* It's goodnight from me . . .
Barker: And it's goodnight from him.

Stock closing routine

2001: A SPACE ODYSSEY
UK film 1968. Script by Stanley Kubrick and Arthur C. Clarke. With Keir Dullea as Dave Bowman.

5 *Stranded astronaut Dave, to computer:* Open the pod-bay doors, Hal!

Soundtrack

TYNAN, Kenneth
British critic (1927–80)

6 □ Verlaine was always chasing Rimbauds.

In fact, as a schoolboy critic, he took this from Dorothy Parker.

7 *On Noël Coward (1953):*
Forty years ago he was Slightly in Peter Pan, and you might say that he has been wholly in Peter Pan ever since.

Curtains (1961)

8 Even the youngest of us will know, in fifty years' time, exactly what we mean by 'a very Noël Coward sort of person'.

ibid

9 *On Greta Garbo (1953):*
What, when drunk, one sees in other women, one sees in Garbo sober.

ibid

1   *Joining the New Yorker as drama critic, 1958:*
They say the *New Yorker* is the bland leading the bland. I don't know
if I'm bland enough.

Quoted in K. Tynan, *The Life of Kenneth Tynan*

2   *In answer to a question whether he would allow 'a play to be put on at the
National Theatre in which, for instance, sexual intercourse took place on the
stage?':*
I think so certainly . . . I doubt if there are any rational people to
whom the word 'fuck' would be particularly diabolical, revolting or
totally forbidden. I think that anything that can be printed or said
can also be seen.

Interviewed on *BBC3* programme, BBC TV, 13 November 1965
This was the first time the f-word had been spoken, noticeably, in a
British broadcast.

3   *High definition performance* . . . supreme professional polish, hard-
edged technical skill, the effortless precision without which no
artistic enterprise—however strongly we may sympathize with its
aims or ideas—can inscribe itself on our memory . . . the hypnotic
saving grace of high and low art alike, the common denominator
that unites tragedy, ballroom dancing, conversation and cricket.

Article in the *Observer*, 7 April 1968

4   I do not see the EEC as a great love affair. It is more like nine
middle-aged couples with failing marriages meeting at a Brussels
hotel for a group grope.

Quoted in the *Observer*, 11 May 1975

UNITED NATIONS UNIVERSAL DECLARATION OF HUMAN RIGHTS

1 All human beings are born free and equal in dignity and rights.

Adopted 10 December 1948

UPTON, Ralph R.

2 *Notice at US railway crossings, 1912:*
Stop; look; listen.

Quoted in R. Hyman, *Dictionary of Famous Quotations*

USTINOV, Peter (later Sir Peter)

British actor and writer (1921–)

3 A diplomat these days is nothing but a head-waiter who's allowed to sit down occasionally.

Romanoff and Juliet (1956)

VALENTI, Jack
US film executive and Presidential aide (1921–)

1 I sleep each night a little better, a little more confidently, because Lyndon Johnson is my President. For I know he lives and thinks and works to make sure that for all America and, indeed, the growing body of the free world, the morning shall always come.
Speech, Boston, 28 June 1965

VARIETY
US show business newspaper

2 *On the Wall Street crash:*
WALL ST. LAYS AN EGG
Headline, 30 October 1929

3 STICKS NIX HICKS PIX.
Headline, 17 July 1935
Meaning that cinema-goers in rural areas were not attracted to films with bucolic themes.

4 EGGHEAD WEDS HOURGLASS.
Headline, 1956
On marriage of playwright Arthur Miller to Marilyn Monroe.

VAUGHAN, Norman
British comedian (1927–)

5 Dodgy!
Catchphrase, from 1960s

6 Swingin'!
Catchphrase, from 1960s

7 A touch of the . . .
Stock format phrase

VICTORIA, HM Queen
British Royal (1819–1901)

8 *Last word:*
Bertie!
Attrib
Referring to her son and heir, Albert Edward, rather than to Prince Albert, her late husband.

VIDAL, Gore
US novelist (1925–)

1   *On being invited to be a godparent by Kenneth Tynan:*
Always a godfather, never a God.
Remark, 1967
Has also been ascribed to Alexander Woollcott.

2   *When asked whether the first person he had experienced sex with was male or female:*
I was far too polite to ask.
Remark in interview, *c*1971

3   Whenever a friend succeeds, a little something in me dies.
Quoted in the *Sunday Times magazine*, 16 September 1973

4   It is not enough to succeed. Others must fail.
Quoted in G. Irvine, *Antipanegyric for Tom Driberg*, 8 December 1976

5   Never miss a chance to have sex or be on television.
Attrib

6   *On Ronald Reagan:*
A triumph of the embalmer's art.
Quoted in the *Observer*, 26 April 1981

7   *On William F. Buckley Jnr:*
Looks and sounds not unlike Hitler, but without the charm.
ibid

8   *Of Edward F. Kennedy:*
Every country should have at least one King Farouk.
ibid

VONNEGUT, Kurt, Jr
US author (1922–)

9   What passes for culture in my head is really a bunch of commercials.
Attrib

VON STERNBERG, Joseph
Austrian-born film director (1894–1969)

10   *On Hollywood:*
You can seduce a man's wife there, attack his daughter and wipe your hands on his canary, but if you don't like his movie, you're dead.
Attrib

VON ZELL, Harry
US broadcaster and actor (1906–81)

1   *Introducing radio broadcast by President Herbert Hoover:*
Ladies and gentlemen—the President of the United States,
Hoobert Herver.

Quoted in *Current Biography* (1944)

VREELAND, Diana
US fashion journalist (*c*1903–89)

2   *Speaking in 1965:*
I love London. It is the most swinging city in the world at the
moment.

Quoted in B. Hillier, *The Style of the Century 1900–1980*. As a result of
this remark, the *Weekend Telegraph* ran an article on 30 April 1965
which probably put together the words 'Swinging London' for the first
time.

3   [The] beautiful people.

Coinage attrib in *Current Biography* (1978)

WALKER, James J.
US politician and Mayor of New York (1881–1946)

1 A reformer is a guy who rides through a sewer in a glass-bottomed boat.

Speech, New York, 1928

WALL STREET
US film, 1987. With Michael Douglas as Gordon Gekko.

2 *Gekko:* Greed, for want of a better word, is good.

Soundtrack
Compare **BOESKY 42:3.**

3 *Gekko:* If you want a friend, get a dog.

Soundtrack

4 *Gekko:* Lunch is for wimps.

Soundtrack

WALLACE, George
US Democratic politician (1919–)

5 Segregation now, segregation tomorrow and segregation forever.

Inaugural speech as Governor of Alabama, January 1963

6 Pointy-headed intellectuals who can't park their bicycles straight.

Customary jibe
Sometimes it was 'pointed-headed professors'.

7 Send them a message.

Slogan when campaigning for the Presidency (1972)
An invitation to vote symbolically when a candidate has little chance of winning.

WALLACE, Henry
US Democratic Vice President (1888–1965)

8 The century on which we are entering—the century which will come out of this war—can be and must be the century of the common man.

Speech, 8 May 1942

WARHOL, Andy
US artist (1928–87)

9 In the future everyone will be world-famous for fifteen minutes.

Exhibition catalogue, Stockholm (1968)

WARING, Eddie
British broadcaster (1909–86)

1   Up and under!

Stock phrase
A Rugby League football term, used by him in TV commentaries.

2   (He's taking) an early bath.

Stock phrase
Of player sent off the field.

WARNER, Jack
British actor and entertainer (1895–1981)

3   Mind my bike!

Catchphrase, *Garrison Theatre*, BBC radio, 1940s

4   Evenin' all.

Stock phrase
As 'PC George Dixon' in BBC TV series *Dixon of Dock Green* (1955–76).

WATERGATE TRANSCRIPTS

5   Expletive deleted.

Stock phrase
Used when deleting an obscenity from transcripts of conversations between President Nixon and his aides, published as *The White House Transcripts* (1974), but an old Americanism.

WATERHOUSE, Keith
British journalist and novelist (1929–)

6   I cannot bring myself to vote for a woman [Margaret Thatcher] who has been voice-trained to speak to me as though my dog has just died.

Attrib, 1979
See also **THAT WAS THE WEEK THAT WAS 322:8.**

WATKINS, Alan
British journalist (1933–)

7   Politics, as I have remarked from time to time, is a rough old trade.

In the *Observer*, 9 June 1991

WAUGH, Evelyn
British novelist (1903–66)

8   Feather-footed through the plashy fen passes the questing vole.

Scoop (1938)

1   Mr Salter's side of the conversation was limited to expressions of assent. When Lord Copper was right he said, 'Definitely, Lord Copper'; when he was wrong, 'Up to a point.'

ibid

2   [Corker:] News is what a chap who doesn't care much about anything wants to read. And it's only news until he's read it. After that it's dead.

ibid

3   *Author's Note:*
I am not I: thou art not he or she: they are not they.

Brideshead Revisited (1945)

4   'I have been here before,' I said; I had been there before; first with Sebastian more than twenty years ago on a cloudless day in June, when the ditches were creamy with meadowsweet and the air heavy with all the scents of summer.

ibid

5   *On Winston Churchill:*
Simply a radio personality who outlived his prime.

Quoted in C. Sykes, *Evelyn Waugh*

6   *When Randolph Churchill went into hospital to have a lung removed and the trouble was not malignant:*
A typical triumph of modern science to find the only part of Randolph that was not malignant and remove it.

Diaries (entry for March 1964)

WEBB, Jim
US songwriter (1946–)

7   Someone left the cake out in the rain.
I don't think that I can take it
'Cos it took so long to bake it
And I'll never have that recipe again. Oh no.

Song, 'MacArthur Park' (1968)

8   Up, Up and Away.

Title of song (1967)

WEBB, Sidney (later Lord Passfield)
British socialist writer (1859–1947)

1 The inevitability of gradualness.

Speech to Labour Party Conference, 26 June 1923
Meaning that, for Labour, electoral success would come gradually but
certainly, by evolution not revolution.

2 *On the Labour Government's failure to deal with a financial crisis by
coming off the Gold Standard, 1931:*
Nobody told us we could do this.

Remark
The new National Government did.

WEBER, Max
German sociologist (1864–1920)

3 The Protestant Ethic and the Spirit of Capitalism.

Title of book (translation) (1904)
As a phrase, also known as 'the Protestant work ethic'.

WEIGHELL, Sidney
British trade union leader (1922–)

4 If you want it to go out . . . that you now believe in the philosophy
of the pig trough—those with the biggest snouts get the largest
share—I reject it.

Speech at Labour Party Conference, Blackpool, 6 October 1978

5 I don't see how we can talk with Mrs Thatcher . . . I will say to the
lads, come on, get your snouts in the trough.

Remark, London, 10 April 1979

WEINER, Herb
US songwriter

6 Nobody knows where my Johnny has gone.

Song, 'It's My Party' (1963)
Written with John Gluck Jr and Wally Gold.

7 It's my party and I'll cry if I want to.

ibid

WELLES, Orson
US film director and actor (1915–85)

1 *On learning how to use a Hollywood studio, prior to filming **Citizen Kane**, in c 1939:*
This is the biggest electric train set a boy ever had.
Quoted in F. Brady, *Citizen Welles*
See also **CITIZEN KANE 79:2–6** *and* **THE THIRD MAN 323:2.**

WELLS, H. G.
British novelist and writer (1866–1946)

2 □ The war to end wars.
The actual title of Wells's book was *The War That Will End War* (1914).

3 □ In the country of the blind the one-eyed man is king.
Wells wrote a story with the title *The Country of the Blind* (1904) but the saying dates back to the 16th century at least.

4 The Shape of Things to Come.
Title of book (1933)

WESKER, Arnold
British playwright (1932–)

5 Chips with Everything.
Title of play (1962)
Popularized the expression.

WEST, Mae
US film actress (1892–1980)

6 *Replying to exclamation, 'Goodness, what beautiful diamonds!':*
Goodness had nothing to do with it, dearie.
Night After Night (1932)
Film script by Vincent Laurence, from novel by Louis Bromfield.

7 □ Come up and see me some time.
In the film *She Done Him Wrong* (1933), based on her play *Diamond Lil*, what she said was: 'Why don't you come up some time and see me?' In later films, she used the catchphrase in the easier-to-say form.

8 Tall, dark and handsome.
Also used in *She Done Him Wrong* but not original to her.

9 Beulah, peel me a grape.
I'm No Angel (film 1933)

10 It's not the men in my life that counts, it's the life in my men.
ibid

1   I always say, keep a diary and some day it'll keep you.
     Everyday's a Holiday (film 1937)

2   Marriage is a great institution, but I'm not ready for an institution
     yet.
     Attrib

3   Is that a gun in your pocket or are you just pleased to see me?
     Attrib
     Also remembered in connection with her play *Catherine Was Great*
     (1944) in the form: 'Lieutenant, is that your sword, or are you just glad
     to see me.'

WEST, Rebecca (later Dame Rebecca)
British writer (1892–1983)

4   *On H. G. Wells:*
     The Old Maid among novelists; even the sex obsession that lay
     clotted on *Ann Veronica* and *The New Machiavelli* like cold white
     sauce was merely Old Maid's mania.
     In *Freewoman*, 19 September 1912

5   She said she was attracted [to H. G. Wells] because he smelt of
     walnuts.
     Reference in *The Guardian*, 16 March 1983

6   *Of Michael Arlen:*
     Every other inch a gentleman.
     Attrib
     Also ascribed to Alexander Woollcott.

7   *At 1962 Edinburgh Festival Writers' Conference:*
     It would be no loss to the world if most of the writers now writing
     had been strangled at birth.
     Quoted in S. Spender, *Journals*

WESTMINSTER GAZETTE
London newspaper

8   *Correct challenge to win a newspaper cash prize:*
     You are Mr Lobby Lud—I claim the *Westminster Gazette* prize.
     First used 1 August 1927
     Later adopted and adapted by other papers.

WHAT'S MY LINE?

US TV panel game, from 1950 onwards.

1   *Host:* Would the next challenger sign in, please?

     Stock phrase

2   *Steve Allen (panellist):* Is it bigger than a breadbox?

     Stock question

WHEELER, Jimmy

British comedian (1910–73)

3   Aye, aye, that's yer lot!

     Catchphrase

WHEELER, Sir Mortimer

British archaeologist (1890–1976)

4   The archaeologist is digging up not *things*, but people.

     Archaeology from the Earth (1954)

WHELDON, Sir Huw

British broadcaster and TV executive (1916–86)

5   *Advice to TV producers:*
     The crime is not to avoid failure. The crime is not to give triumph a chance.

     Attrib
     Often encapsulated as 'The Right to Fail'.

6   The job of the producer is to pursue excellence—to take his subject and tell it as a tale.

     Attrib

WHITE, E. B.

US humorist (1899–1985)

7   *A mother at table says, 'It's broccoli, dear,' and her child replies:*
     I say it's spinach, and I say the hell with it.

     The *New Yorker*, 8 December 1928
     Caption for cartoon by Carl Rose.

8   Across the Street and Into the Grill.

     Title of pastiche of Ernest Hemingway.
     See **HEMINGWAY 160:4.**

WHITE HEAT

US film 1949. Script by various. With James Cagney as Cody Jarrett.

1   *Cody:* Made it Ma, [to the] top of the world.

Last words of character, shooting it out from the top of an oil tank.

WHITEHORN, Katharine

British journalist (1928–)

2   *On making rude noises:*
If there is nothing you can do by constriction of throat or rectum to head them off, try to move away from the group you are with ('I must find an ashtray' or 'I *say* look at that squirrel!') and create diversionary noises—snap a handbag, scrape a foot. Tummy rumbles are for some reason more OK—laugh if you can.

Whitehorn's Social Survival (1968)

3   Outside every thin girl there is a fat man trying to get in.

Revived by her on *Quote . . . Unquote*, BBC Radio, 27 July 1985

WHITELAW, William (later Viscount Whitelaw)

British Conservative politician (1918–)

4   *Of Harold Wilson:*
He is going round the country stirring up apathy.

Attrib remark during 1970 General Election

5   *Of Irish politics, on becoming Secretary of State for Northern Ireland:*
One must be careful not to prejudge the past.

Attrib remark, 25 March 1972

6   *On kissing Mrs Thatcher (when they were both candidates for the Conservative leadership):*
I have over a period of time, when I have met her—as indeed one does—I have kissed her often before. We have not done it on a pavement outside a hotel in Eastbourne before. But we have done it in various rooms in one way and another at various functions—it is perfectly genuine and normal—and normal and right—so to do.

Reported in the *Observer*, 9 February 1975

7   □ A short, sharp, shock.

Speech, Conservative Party Conference, 10 October 1979
Referring to method of hard treatment for young offenders. This expression had been used by Home Secretaries before him and is a quotation from W.S. Gilbert, *The Mikado* (1885).

WHITLAM, Gough
Australian Labour Prime Minister (1916–)

1   *After the Governor-General's secretary had read a proclamation dissolving Parliament, effectively dismissing Whitlam as Prime Minister:*
Well may we say 'God Save the Queen', because nothing will save the Governor-General . . . Maintain your rage and your enthusiasm through the campaign for the election now to be held and until polling day.
Speech, Canberra, 11 November 1975

WILDER, Billy
US film director (1906–)

2   *On actor, Cliff Osmond:*
He has Van Gogh's ear for music.
Attrib

3   *On working with Marilyn Monroe:*
It was like going to the dentist making a picture with her. It was hell at the time, but after it was all over, it was wonderful.
Quoted in E. Wilson, *The Show Business Nobody Knows*

4   *In cabled response to a relative's complaint that his accommodation in France did not have a shower:*
SUGGEST HANDSTAND IN BIDET.
Attrib
See also **THE APARTMENT** *and* **SOME LIKE IT HOT.**

WILHELM II, Kaiser
German Emperor (1859–1941)

5   We have fought for our place in the sun and won it. Our future is on the water.
Speech at Elbe, 18 June 1901
The phrase 'place in the sun', referring to German colonial ambitions, had been coined by Count von Bülow in 1897.

6   *When an English visitor told him that Edward VII was at Windsor Castle:*
Ah, I thought he was boating with his grocer [Sir Thomas Lipton].
Quoted in W. Churchill, *Great Contemporaries*
An example of his contempt for the English monarch.

1   □ It is my Royal and Imperial command that you concentrate your
     energies for the immediate present upon one single purpose, and
     that is that you address all your skill and all the valour of my
     soldiers to exterminate first, the treacherous English [and] walk
     over General French's contemptible little army . . .

     Quoted in BEF Routine Orders, 24 September 1914
     Giving rise to the BEF nickname 'The Old Contemptibles', this order
     appears never to have been given by the Kaiser—indeed, he later
     denied doing so—and it is now accepted that it was a propaganda ploy
     devised at the War Office by Sir Frederick Maurice.

WILLANS, Geoffrey
British writer (1911–58)

2   This is me e.g. nigel molesworth the curse of st custard's which is
     the skool i am at. It is uterly wet and weedy . . .
         The only good things about skool are the BOYS wizz who are
     noble brave fearless etc. although you hav various swots, bulies,
     cissies, milksops, greedy guts and oiks which whom i am forced to
     mingle hem-hem.
         In fact any skool is a bit of a shambles
         AS YOU WILL SEE.

     Down With Skool! (with Ronald Searle) (1953)

3   There is no better xsample of a goody-goody than fotherington-
     tomas in the world in space. You kno he is the one who sa Hullo
     Clouds Hullo Sky and skip about like a girly.

     How To Be Topp (1954)

WILLIAM, Capt. Lloyd S.
US soldier

4   *When advised by the French to retreat, shortly after his arrival at the Western
     Front in the First World War:*
     Retreat? Hell, no! We just got here!

     Attrib
     Or referring to retreat from Belloar, 5 June 1918.

WILLIAMS, Kenneth
British actor and entertainer (1926–88)

5   Stop messin' abaht!

     Catchphrase, from 1950s
     First heard on HANCOCK'S HALF-HOUR (q.v.).
     See also **BEYOND OUR KEN 40:3–5; ROUND THE HORNE 280:1.**

WILLIAMS, Tennessee
US playwright (1911–83)

1   A Streetcar Named Desire.

Play title (1947)

2   *Blanche:* I have always depended on the kindness of strangers.

A Streetcar Named Desire (1947)
Her last words in the play.
See also **PLAY TITLES 255:2.**

WILSON, Charles E.
US Republican politician (1890–1961)

3   □ What's good for General Motors is good for the country.

Senate Committee on Armed Services, 15 January 1953
In fact what the former President of General Motors said when asked
whether there might be a conflict of interest if he became Secretary of
Defense, 'I cannot conceive of one because for years I thought what
was good for our country was good for General Motors, and vice versa.
The difference did not exist.'

4   *Of the new type of H-bomb tested at Bikini (1954):*
[It gives] a bigger bang for a buck.

Quoted in W. Safire, *Political Dictionary*

WILSON, Earl
US journalist (1907–87)

5   If you look like your passport photo, in all probability you need the
holiday.

Attrib

WILSON, Harold (later Lord Wilson of Rievaulx)
British Labour Prime Minister (1916–)

6   The school I went to in the north was a school where more than
half the children in my class never had any boots or shoes to their
feet. They wore clogs, because they lasted longer than shoes of
comparable price.

Speech, Birmingham, 28 July 1948
Abbreviated reports led to the suggestion that Wilson's schoolmates
had gone barefoot.
See also **BULMER-THOMAS 52:4.**

7   All these financiers, all the little gnomes in Zurich and the other
financial centres.

Speech, House of Commons, 12 November 1956
The term 'Gnomes of Zurich', used to describe tight-fisted speculators
in the Swiss financial capital who questioned Britain's creditworthiness,
became popular again after 1964.

1   Every time Mr Macmillan comes back from abroad, Mr Butler goes to the airport and grips him warmly by the throat.
    Attrib

2   *Of Harold Macmillan's Britain:*
    The candyfloss society.
    Remark, 1960–1

3   I have always deprecated . . . in crisis after crisis, appeals to the Dunkirk spirit as an answer to our problems.
    Speech, House of Commons, 26 July 1961
    Compare **350:3** *below.*

4   This party is a moral crusade, or it is nothing.
    Speech, Labour Party Conference, 1 October 1962

5   □ We are redefining and we are restating our socialism in terms of the scientific revolution . . . the Britain that is going to be forged in the white heat of this revolution will be no place for restrictive practices or outdated methods on either side of industry.
    Speech, Labour Party Conference, 1 October 1963
    Phrase usually remembered as 'the white heat of the technological revolution.'

6   *On the Earl of Home's appointment as Prime Minister:*
    After half a century of democratic advance, the whole process has ground to a halt with a fourteenth earl.
    Speech, Belle Vue, Manchester, 19 October 1963
    See also **DOUGLAS-HOME 102:3.**

7   [We have] a chance to sweep away the *grouse-moor* conception of Tory leadership and refit Britain with a new image.
    Speech, Birmingham, January 1964
    Referring to Harold Macmillan and Sir Alec Douglas-Home, past and present Conservative leaders.

8   What I think we are going to need is something like what President Kennedy had when he came in after years of stagnation in the United States. He had a programme of a hundred days—a hundred days of of dynamic action.
    Labour Party Political Broadcast, 15 July 1964
    In fact, Kennedy had specifically ruled out a 'hundred days', saying in his Inaugural Address that his programmes could not be carried out in a thousand days.
    See **KENNEDY 183:7.**

1   *On an MP who had run an allegedly racist campaign:*
Smethwick Conservatives can have the satisfaction of having topped
the poll, of having sent a member who, until another election
returns him to oblivion, will serve his time here as a parliamentary
leper.

Speech, House of Commons, 4 November 1964

2   A week is a long time in politics.

To parliamentary lobby correspondents, Autumn 1964
Because meetings of the lobby are 'off the record', no one appears
quite certain when or why this celebrated aphorism was first uttered,
but see the author's *Sayings of the Century* (1984).

3   I believe that the spirit of Dunkirk will once again carry us through
to success.

Speech, Labour Party Conference, 12 December 1964
Compare **349:3** *above.*

4   The cumulative effect of the economic and financial sanctions
[against Rhodesia] might well bring the rebellion to an end within
a matter of weeks rather than months.

Final communiqué of the Commonwealth Prime Ministers' Conference
at Lagos, 12 January 1966
Employing a phrase used by Wilson earlier that day.

5   Now one encouraging gesture from the French Government—
which I welcome—and the Conservative leader rolls on his back
like a spaniel.

Speech, Bristol, 18 March 1966

6   *On Communist influence in a national seamen's strike:*
It is difficult for us to appreciate the pressures which are put on
men I know to be realistic and responsible, not only in their
executive capacity but in the highly organized strike committees in
the ports, by this tightly knit group of politically motivated men.

Speech, House of Commons, 22 June 1966

7   Every dog is allowed one bite, but a different view is taken of a dog
that goes on biting all the time. He may not get his licence
returned when it falls due.

Speech to Parliamentary Labour Party, 2 March 1967

1   *After a devaluation of the pound:*
    ☐ The pound in your pocket.

    Broadcast address, 19 November 1967
    In fact what he said was: 'From now on the pound abroad is worth
    14 per cent or so less in terms of other currencies. That doesn't mean,
    of course, that the pound here in Britain, in your pocket or purse or in
    your bank, has been devalued.'

2   Cohorts of distinguished journalists have been combing obscure
    parts of the country with a mandate to find anything, true or
    fabricated, to use against the Labour Party.

    Attrib, September 1974

3   I'm an optimist, but I'm an optimist who takes his raincoat.

    Quoted in the *Observer*, 18 January 1976

4   *To journalists at press conference marking his retirement:*
    I forgive you all.

    Quoted in the *Observer*, 21 March 1976

WILSON, Mary (later Lady Wilson)
Wife of above (1916–)

5   If Harold has a fault it is that he will drown everything with HP
    sauce.

    Interviewed by the *Sunday Times*, 1962

WILSON, Woodrow
US Democratic President (1856–1924)

6   *On the film* **The Birth of a Nation** *(1915):*
    It is like writing history with lightning. And it's all true.

    Quoted in D. Boorstin, *The Image*

7   *Asking for a declaration of war:*
    The world must be safe for democracy. Its peace must be planted
    upon trusted foundations of political liberty.

    Speech to Congress, 2 April 1917
    Usually remembered as 'The world must be *made* safe for democracy.'

8   Never murder a man who is committing suicide.

    Attrib

WILTON, Robb
British comedian (1881–1957)

9   The day war broke out . . .

    Catchphrase, from 1940s onwards

WINCHELL, Walter
US journalist and broadcaster (1897–1972)

1 Good evening, Mr and Mrs North America, and all the ships at sea. Let's go to press!

Standard start to radio newscasts, from 1932 onwards

WINDSOR, Duchess of (formerly Mrs Wallis Simpson)
American-born wife of the Duke of Windsor (1896–1986)

2 I married the Duke for better or worse but not for lunch.

Quoted in J. Bryan III & J.V. Murphy, *The Windsor Story*
But an original saying.

3 You can never be too rich or too thin.

Attrib

WINSOR, Kathleen
US novelist (1919–   )

4 Forever Amber.

Title of book (1944)

WISE, Ernie *see* MORECAMBE, Eric and WISE, Ernie

WODEHOUSE, P. G. (later Sir Pelham)
British novelist and lyricist (1881–1975)

5 Proceed, old gargoyle . . . you have our ear.

The Inimitable Jeeves (1923)

6 Jeeves coughed one soft, low, gentle cough like a sheep with a blade of grass in its throat.

ibid

7 I turned to Aunt Agatha, whose demeanour was now rather like that of one who, picking daisies on the railway, has just caught the down express in the small of the back.

ibid

8 'What ho!' I said, 'What ho!' said Motty. 'What ho! What ho!' 'What ho! What ho! What ho!' After that it seemed rather difficult to go on with the conversation.

'Jeeves and the Unbidden Guest', *Carry On Jeeves* (1925)

9 'Do you know, Jeeves, you're—well, you absolutely stand alone!' 'I endeavour to give satisfaction, sir,' said Jeeves.

ibid

1   He spoke with a certain what-is-it in his voice, and I could see that, if not actually disgruntled, he was far from being gruntled.

The Code of the Woosters (1938)

WOLFE, Humbert

British poet and critic (1885–1940)

2   You cannot hope
      to bribe or twist,
thank God! the
      British journalist.

But, seeing what
      the man will do
unbribed, there's
      no occasion to.

'Over the Fire', *The Uncelestial City* (1930)

WOLFE, Tom

US writer (1931–)

3   Radical Chic and Mau-Mauing the Flak Catchers.

Title of book (1970)
Hence the term 'radical chic' for the fashionable adoption of left-wing ideas, dress, etc.

4   The Right Stuff.

Title of book (1979)
Referring to the qualities needed by early members of the US space programme. The phrase had earlier been used as the title of a novel by Ian Hay (1908).

WOODHOUSE, Barbara

British animal trainer (1910–88)

5   *When training dogs:*
Walkies! . . . Sit!

Stock phrases, TV shows, from 1980.

WOODROOFFE, Tommy

British broadcaster (1899–1978)

6   *Describing the illumination of the Fleet on the night of the Coronation Naval Review at Spithead:*
At the present moment, the whole Fleet's lit up. When I say 'lit up', I mean lit up by fairy lamps.

BBC radio broadcast, 20 May 1937
Woodrooffe always denied that he had been 'lit up', too.

WOOLF, Virginia
British novelist (1882–1941)

1 *Of James Joyce's **Ulysses:***
Merely the scratching of pimples on the body of the bootboy at Claridges.
Letter, 24 April 1922

2 So that is marriage, Lily thought, a man and a woman looking at a girl throwing a ball.
To the Lighthouse (1927)

3 A Room of One's Own.
Title of book (1929)

WOOLLCOTT, Alexander
US writer and critic (1887–1943)

4 All the things I really like to do are either illegal, immoral, or fattening.
The Knock at the Stage Door (1933)

5 [Michael] Arlen for all his reputation, is not a bounder. He is every other inch a gentleman.
Quoted in R. E. Drennan, *Wit's End*
See also **WEST 343:6.**

6 There is absolutely nothing wrong with Oscar Levant that a miracle cannot fix.
Quoted in M. C. Harriman, *The Vicious Circle*

7 Germany was the cause of Hitler just as much as Chicago is responsible for the *Chicago Tribune.*
Radio broadcast, 1943
Last words before the microphone. He died after the broadcast.
See also **BENCHLEY 32:1.**

WORDSWORTH, Christopher
British journalist and critic

8 *On the sports journalist Clifford Makins (1924–90):*
A legend in his own lunchtime.
Remark, by 1976

9 *Travels* by Edward Heath is a reminder that *Morning Cloud's* skipper is no stranger to platitude and longitude.
Book review in the *Observer*, 18 December 1977

YEATMAN, R. J. see **SELLAR, W. C.** and **YEATMAN, R. J.**

YEATS, W. B.
Irish poet (1865–1939)

1   *On Rupert Brooke:*
He is the handsomest man in England, and he wears the most beautiful shirts.
Attrib, January 1913

2   Romantic Ireland's dead and gone,
It's with O'Leary in the grave.
'September 1913', *Responsibilities* (1914)

3   Things fall apart; the centre cannot hold;
Mere anarchy is loosed upon the world . . .
The best lack all conviction, while the worst
Are full of passionate intensity.
'The Second Coming' (1921)

4   A terrible beauty is born.
'Easter 1916' (1921)

5   Cast a cold eye
On life, on death.
Horseman, pass by!
'Under Ben Bulben' (1936–9)
Later carved on his gravestone.

YELLEN, Jack
US lyricist (1892–1991)

6   The Last of the Red-Hot Mamas.
Title of song (1928)
This became the nickname of Sophie Tucker (*c*1884–1966), who recorded the number.

7   Happy Days Are Here Again.
Title of song (1930)
Composed by Milton Ager.

YOUNG, Jimmy
British singer and broadcaster (1923–)

8   Orft we jolly well go.
Stock phrase at start of show, BBC Radio, 1960s

9   Sur le continong . . . sur le telephoneo.
Stock phrases, 1960s

1   B.F.N.—'bye for now.
Catchphrase

'YORK, Peter'
British journalist (1947–)

2   □ The Sloane Rangers, usually known by other regiments as the
Headscarf Brigade or the Knightsbridge Knotteds, after what they
wear on their heads . . . are the nicest British girl.
Article in *Harpers & Queen*, October 1975
The appellation 'Sloane Ranger' was actually coined by Martina
Margetts, a sub-editor on the magazine.

YOUNG, Michael (later Lord Young)
British sociologist (1915–)

3   The Rise of the Meritocracy.
Title of book (1958)

4   *Describing poor standards in British public services:*
The chipped white cups of Dover mentality.
Attrib

ZANUCK, Darryl F.

US film producer (1902–79)

1   Don't say yes until I finish talking!

Characteristic remark

ZAPPA, Frank

US rock musician (1940–)

2   Rock journalism is people who can't write interviewing people who can't talk for people who can't read.

Quoted in L. Botts, *Loose Talk* (1980)
Originally in *Rolling Stone* magazine, 1970.

ZIEGLER, Ron

US White House Press Spokesman (1939–)

3   *Euphemism for lie, at time of Watergate:*
This is the operative statement. The others are inoperative.

Press conference, Washington, 17 April 1973

INDEX

In the index, quotations are represented in capsule form under one or two key word headings or under theme/subject words or names. The key words chosen are the main or most significant words in the original but they appear in the index as they should be written (i.e. ''ole'' under Hole, 'viskey' as Whiskey). See the dictionary for the full and correct text.

America (*continued*)
  like dog, 329:7
  Mr and Mrs North A., 352:1
  Only In A., 318:10
American boys away from home, 177:3
  truth justice and A. way, 63:3
  you die, 10:5
Americans as blind as you, 291:2
  have best of nothing, 182:2
Ammunition, pass the a., 308:2
Amphibious, I feel a., 42:6
Amuse, talent to a., 88:2
Ancestors, follow in spirit of a., 51:2
Anger, telegrams and a., 127:1
Angry Young Man, 251:3
Anguish, howls of a., 157:2
Animal husbandry, 199:8
Animals, all a. equal, 245:7
  never work with a., 9:3
Animated meringue, 219:6
Annihilation, no a., 329:6
Another Country, 255:1
  never be a., 227:5
Answer is blowing in the wind, 105:3
  is in plural, 209:2
  lies in the soil, 40:3
  what is the a., 312:7
Anyone for tennis, 42:4
Anything Goes, 256:10
Apathy, stirring up a., 345:4
Ape, Naked A., 233:3
Aphrodisiac, fame is a., 145:1
Aphrodisiac, power is ultimate a., 190:5
  say he's a writer is a., 31:9
Apollo, young A. golden-haired, 85:7
Apologize, never a., 121:11
Apology for relations, 188:6
Apostles, six not twelve a., 143:1
Appalling frankness, 22:5
Appeal, Last A. to Reason, 164:1
Appeasement, political a., 207:7
Appendix, take out man's a., 157:7
Apple, eat a. through tennis racquet,
  89:6
Apple in the house, 200:5
April, bright cold day in A., 245:9
  is cruellest month, 110:10
Archaeologist best husband, 71:1
  digs up people, 344:4
Argentina, Don't Cry for Me A., 274:4
Arlen, Michael, gentleman, 343:6, 354:5
Arm drops off, 226:5
Armed, we are in a. conflict, 107:3
Armful, pint nearly an a., 152:6
Army, contemptible little a., 347:1
  works like this, 227:8
Aroma, faint a. of seals, 155:4

Arrest most of people, 188:1
  one does not a. Voltaire, 98:4
Arrive where we started and know, 112:1
Arrived, I've a. and to prove it, 55:4
Arse, kick him up the a., 77:4
  politician is an a., 91:4
  stuff child up horse's a., 89:10
Arsenal of democracy, 278:2
Art for A.'s Sake, 100:6
  only interested in a., 291:5
  politics is a. of possible, 54:5
  remarkable example of modern a., 78:6
Arthur, big-hearted A., 15:3
  speak for England A., 5:3
Artist has won through fantasy, 128:4
Asian boys do for themselves, 177:3
Ask not what country can do, 184:2
  Were Afraid To A., 273:2
  when they a. us, 256:5
Asked, I only a., 48:3
Asphalt Jungle, 52:6
Aspirates, try taking a., 305:2
Asquith, H. H., modesty, 16:1
Assassinates, until a. him, 181:5
Assassination is extreme form, 290:3
Assassination, tempered by a., 272:5
Assumed, under a. name, 181:10
Astonish me, 100:3
Astor, Lady, if you were my wife, 72:1
Asylum, inmates in charge of a., 311:5
Asylum, lunatics taken over a., 280:4
Atheist no visible means of support, 52:2
  still thank God, 52:5
Atlantic, cheaper to lower A., 143:3
Attack, no reason to a. monkey, 39:2
  I shall a., 124:7
Attendant, am an a. lord, 110:5
Attlee, Clement, dead fish, 245:4
  empty taxi, 76:2
  mouse away, 76:3
  sheep, 76:1
Auden, W. H., fancied God, 13:1
Audience came out whistling set, 11:4
Audiences don't like plays, 292:3
August for the people, 17:6
Aunt Edna, 268:3
Aussie, come on A., 297:2
Australia, in A. inter alia, 258:6
Author, steal from one a., 230:5
Authors easy to get on with a., 179:1
Autograph as souvenir, 163:7
Award, golden sanitary towel a., 246:9
Away we go, 138:5
Awful place, 286:7
  wedded wife, 323:7
  you are a., 113:9
Axis, not diaphragm but a., 236:10

Camera cannot lie, 263:1
  I am a c., 171:3
Camp near Dover, 51:6
Campbell-Bannerman, H., remembered, 35:4
Canada, don't know what street C. is on, 57:9
  drink C. dry, 30:9
Canary called Onan, 249:12
Cancer close to Presidency, 97:1
Candle in great turnip gone out, 77:7
  light of one small c., 3:1
Candy is dandy, 238:3
Candyfloss society, 349:2
Cannes is where you lie, 271:4
Capitalism exploitation of man, 13:2
  unacceptable face of c., 159:3
Car, buy used c. from this man, 11:5
  told you to wait in c., 23:5
Carborundum, 299:5
Carbuncle, monstrous c., 67:6
Cards, never play c. with man, 3:3
Care, taken better c. of myself, 41:4
  tender loving c., 124:3
Cared, as if I c., 171:5
Careless talk costs lives, 296:15
Carling Black Label, 299:2
Carnation milk is best in land, 10:10
Carry on London, 170:6
  on smoking, 24:2
Cars, fit for selling c., 89:11
Carter, Jimmy, effrontery, 112:7
  my name is Jimmy C., 59:2
Cartland, Barbara, meringue, 219:6
Casbah, come with me to C., 3:2
Cash, all others pay c., 292:5
Cast cold eye on death, 355:5
Casualty, first c., 176:5
Cat on Hot Tin Roof, 255:2
  that walked by self, 189:6
  that walks alone, 28:2
Catch-22, 158:6
Cattle, actors are c., 163:2
Cause of cheering us all up, 34:4
Causes, no good brave c., 246:6
Cavell, Edith, statue, 264:1
Cazaly, up there C., 64:5
Cecil, after you C., 171:4
Celebrity, definition of, 260:1
Cells, little gray c., 70:8
Cemetery, help me down C. Road, 194:7
Censorship, extreme form of c., 290:3
Centre cannot hold, 355:3
  of universe, 138:2
Century, didn't live in this c., 266:2
  of common man, 338:8
Cesspit, swirling around in c., 6:4

Chaff is printed, 166:9
Chains, sang in my c., 323:4
Challenger, next c. sign in, 344:1
Chamber, naked into conference c., 39:3
Chamberlain, Neville, good mayor, 135:6
  speech by, 38:6
Champions, Breakfast of C., 43:3
Chance, game of c., 119:3
  why take c., 270:7
Change, keep c., 115:1
  necessary for everything to c., 193:2
  wind of c., 214:9
Changed a world, 270:8
Changes, she never c., 30:6
Changing gear, 204:5
Changing, Times They Are, A-C., 105:4
Charcoal, till c. sprouts, 122:1
Charge, I'm in c., 127:5
  in c. of White House, 149:1
Charles, Prince, to marry Astrid, 93:6
Charlie, Chase me C., 88:8
  come to C., 68:9
Charm, Hitler but without c., 336:7
Chase me Charlie, 88:8
Chassis, world in state of c., 243:2
Chatham, because you're in C., 12:1
Chatterley, end of C. ban, 195:3
  Lady C., sacred, 276:1
  Lady C., trial, 193:5
  like Lady C. above the waist, 83:1
Cheap, potent c. music is, 87:6
  sell it c., 81:4
Cheaper to lower Atlantic, 143:3
Checkers, going to keep C., 240:4
Cheerful, being so c., 172:6
Cheering, cause of c. us all up, 34:4
Cheese, milk immortal in, 259:7
  246 different kinds of c., 98:1
Chekhov, Anton, comment on, 329:3
Chemistry, sexual c., 129:5
Cheque, have you brought c. book, 54:6
Cherries, bowl of c., 307:9
Chewing, does c. gum lose flavour, 278:8
  gum for the eyes, 51:4
Chic, Radical C., 353:3
Chicago is responsible, 354:7
  on to C., 185:8
Chicken, some c. some neck, 74:5
Chienlit, la c. non, 98:8
Child for eight years, 201:3
  I seem to hear a c. weeping, 106:1
Children boiled or fried, 119:2
  frightened of me, 134:2
  goodbye c., 212:1
  if fond of c., 179:1
  I love c., 230:1
  man who hates c., 118:7